CW01475896

The Black Baron

The Strange Life of
GILLES DE RAIS

By

TENNILLE DIX

Read & Co.

Copyright © 2020 Read & Co. History

This edition is published by Read & Co. History,
an imprint of Read & Co.

This book is copyright and may not be reproduced or copied in any
way without the express permission of the publisher in writing.

British Library Cataloguing-in-Publication Data
A catalogue record for this book is available
from the British Library.

Read & Co. is part of Read Books Ltd.
For more information visit
www.readandcobooks.co.uk

To

WILLIAM FREDERICK DIX

In Appreciation

Gilles de Rais, Marshal of France

ILLUSTRATIONS

GILLES DE RAIS (OR RETZ)

1404 – 1440

Marshal of France and the central figure of a 15th-century cause célébre, whose name is associated with the story of Bluebeard, was the son of Guy de Montmorency-Laval, the adopted son and heir of Jeanne de Rais and of Marie de Craon.

He was born at Macbecoul in September or October 1404, and, being early left an orphan, was educated by his maternal grandfather, lean de Craon. Chief among his great possessions was the barony of Rais (erected in the 16th century into the peerage-duchy of Retz), south of the Loire, on the marches of Brittany.

He joined the party of the Montforts, supporting Jean V. of Brittany against the rival house of Penthiévre. He helped to release Duke John from Olivier de Blois, count of Penthiévre, who had taken him prisoner by craft, and was rewarded by extensive grants of land, which were subsequently commuted by the Breton parliament for money payments.

In 1420, after other projects of marriage had fallen through, in two cases by the death of the bride, he married Katherine of Thouars, a great heiress in Brittany, La Vendée and Poitou. In 1426 he raised seven companies of men-at-arms, and began active warfare against the English under Artus de Richemont, the newly made constable of France.

He had already built up a military reputation when he was chosen to accompany joan of Arc to Orleans. He continued to be her special protector, fighting by her side at Orleans, and afterwards at Targeau and Patay. He had advocated further measures against the English on the Loire before carrying out the coronation of Charles VII. at Reims. On the 17th of July he was made marshal of France at Reims, and after the assault on Paris he was granted the right to bear the arms of France as a border to his shield, a privilege that was, however, never ratihed. In the winter he was in Normandy, at Louviers, whether with a view to the release of Joan, then a prisoner at Rouen, cannot be stated. Meanwhile his fortune was disappearing, although he had been one of the richest men in France. He had expended great sums in the king's service, and he maintained a court of knights, squires, heralds and priests, more suited to royal than baronial rank.

He kept open house, was a munificent patron of literature and of music, and his library contained many valuable works, he himself being a skilled illuminator and binder. He also indulged a passion for the stage. At the chief festivals he gave performances of mysteries and moralities, and it has been asserted that the *Mystére de la Passion*, acted at Angers in 1420, was staged by him in honour of his own marriage. The original draft of the *Mystery of Orleans* was probably written under his direction, and contains much detail which may be well accounted for by his intimate acquaintance with the Maid. In his financial difficulties he began to alienate his lands, selling his estates for small sums. These proceedings provided his heirs with material for lawsuits for many years. Among those who profited by his prodigality were the duke of Brittany, and his chancellor, Jean de Malestroit, bishop of Nantes, but in 1436 his kinsfolk appealed to Charles VII., who proclaimed further sales to be illegal.

Jean V. refused to acknowledge the king's right to promulgate a decree of this kind in Brittany, and replied by making Gilles de Rais lieutenant of Brittany and by acknowledging him as a brother-in-arms. Gilles hoped to redeem his fortunes by alchemy; he also spent large sums on necromancers, who engaged to raise the devil for his assistance. On the other hand he sought to guarantee himself from evil consequences by extravagant charity and a splendid celebration of the rites of the church. The abominable practices of which he was really guilty seem not to have been suspected by his equals or superiors, though he had many accomplices, and his criminality was suspected by the peasantry. His wife finally left him in 1434-35, and may possibly have become acquainted with his doings, and when his brother René de la Suze seized Champtocé, all traces of his crimes had not been removed, but family considerations no doubt imposed silence. His servants kidnapped children, generally boys, on his behalf, and these he tortured and murdered. The number of his victims was stated in the ecclesiastical trial to have been 140, and larger figures are quoted. The amazing impunity which he enjoyed was brought to an end in 1440, when he was imprudent enough to come into conflict with the church by an act of violence which involved sacrilege and infringement of clerical immunity.

He had sold Saint Étienne de Malemort to the duke of Brittany's treasurer, Geffroi le Ferron. In the course of a quarrel over the delivery of the property to this man's brother, Jean le Ferron, Gilles seized Jean, who was in clerical orders, in church, and imprisoned him. He then proceeded to defy the duke, but was reconciled to him by Richemont. In the autumn, however, he was arrested and cited before the bishop of Nantes on various charges, the chief of which were heresy and murder. With the latter count the ecclesiastical court was incompetent to deal, and on the 8th of October Gilles refused to accept its jurisdiction. Terrified by excommunication, however, he acknowledged the evidence of the witnesses, and by confession he secured absolution. He had been pronounced guilty of apostasy and heresy by the inquisitor, and of vice and sacrilege by the bishop. A detailed confession was extracted by the threat of torture on the 21st of October. A separate and parallel inquiry was made by Pierre de l'H6pital, president of the Breton parliament, by whose sentence he was hanged (not burned alive as is sometimes stated), on the 26th of October 1440, with two of his accomplices. In view of his own repeated confessions it seems impossible to doubt his guilt, but the numerous irregularities of the proceedings, the fact that his necromancer Prelati and other of his chief accomplices went unpunished, taken together with the financial interest of Jean V. in his ruin, have left a certain mystery over a trial, which, with the exception of the process of Joan of Arc, was the most famous in 15th-century France.

His name is connected with the tale of Bluebeard in local tradition at Machecoul, Tiffauges, Pornic and Chéméré, though the similarity between the two histories is at best vague. The records of the trial are preserved in the Bibliothéque Nationale in Paris, at Nantes and elsewhere.

A BIOGRAPHY FROM
1911 *Encyclopædia Britannica, Volume* 22

THE BLACK BARON

THE BLACK BARON

PART ONE

CHAPTER I

§ 1

THE roads of Brittany bore upon their rutted surfaces a great convergence of nobility. From Vannes, the ancient former capital, came the bishops and princes of that city, hastening to join the men of Rennes, of Lamballe and of the other Breton towns. Toward Nantes rode, in polished armor and in velvet cloaks, the country nobles. Alain de Rohan, whose name sparkled with the brilliance of war, descended from the north. From his huge castle of Tiffauges, came old Miles de Thouars, the fabulously rich parent of the heiress Catherine. There came also the proud and haughty Lavals, who were cousins to the reigning dukes.

They rode in companies of different sizes appropriate to their wealth and station. Some traveled with a dozen men-at-arms, trotting with a warlike discipline. Others came leisurely in company with a pageantry of retinue. Here and there across the landscape rolled a creaking, protesting coach whose troubled outriders scanned the road ahead with anxious eyes, alert to detect the presence of one of those bands of free companies which, even in the neutral security of this country, roamed the plains and hills, robbing, murdering and falling upon whomsoever they considered to be weaker, richer or more cowardly than themselves.

Occasionally the travelers passed by ruined villages whose

13

streets and squares were choked with grass and whose stumps
of buildings were already overgrown with creeper, or clattered
through the echoes of a place more recently abandoned, whose
emptiness became a stark reminder of its utter desecration.
Upon a hillside, curls of smoke sometimes rose up her-
alding another convert to the company of dead. From an empty
gateway whose gates swung to and fro, there hung a badge of
sardonic welcome. Swinging in the wind as idly as the broken
portals, the entering cavalcade beheld suspended from the center of the arch the body of a woman newly dead.

In the year one thousand four hundred and twenty, conflict
and desolation reigned. War had dwelt in France for a full century, and its rigors were increasing. Armed bands of soldiers
paraded up and down, burning villages and scattering the flocks.
Private nobles held the roads, seizing at will whoever passed
their castles. A famine of alarming proportions threatened star-
vation, while in the cities plagues and pestilences raged. In
the country, entire districts were depopulated, deserted by the
starved and frightened peasants who had thrown away their tools
and, leaving fields untilled and villages in smoking ruins, had
fled to the woods and lived there like wolves.

Nor were the cities better off. Men and women followed the
dog-catcher on his rounds, falling upon his prey and devouring
raw and warm the slaughtered animals. By the roadways children, dropping on account of weakness from the company of
their wild and forsaken fellows, died of hunger, unattended.
Wolves, hungry as the peasants, invaded the walled towns and
dug ravenously in the graveyards. Extra charnel-houses were
built to relieve the congestion of the crowded cemeteries. From
the walls of Paris starving burghers fled, leaving their homes to
the swarms of beggars which paraded up and down the city.
Levels of the graveyards rose in height, and upon the buried
corpses maddened people danced in frenzy a dance of death.

As a symbol of confusion, three popes, each doubly excommu-
nicate, fought almost unheeded for the Throne of Rome by
means of interdict and proclamation.

Upon the throne of France, a figurehead before his nation, appeared sporadically King Charles VI, weary and haggard as he emerged at intervals from madness to rest there, ruling in a brief and terrified authority. Suddenly he would close his eyes and shudder in the known anticipation. And down again, inevitably as even he had known it should descend, would come once more the pall of terror carrying him off in its embrace of madness, filth and squalor.

From England, Henry V, the invader, had swept across the duchy of Normandy and, cementing the conquests of his predecessors, had had himself proclaimed by the Parliament of Paris and by Queen Ysabeau of France to be the regent for the mad King Charles.

This, then, was the political complexion of the year that has been mentioned. France, that small central island about the city of Paris and surrounded by the encirclement of powerful and almost independent duchies, was ruled in the name of its King by Henry, of England. To the north and east lay the vast extent of Burgundy whose complacency allowed the Englishman to keep his hold. North were the duchies of Champagne, Lorraine and Bar, disputed territories. Eastward lay Savoy, independent, neutral and Italianate; while across the south, from the Alps to the Pyrenees, stretched the proudly independent kingdom of Languedoc, ruled by the Counts of Foix, the half-Spanish kingdom of Navarre and the English province of Guyenne. To the westward was the English duchy of Normandy and the Breton duchy of the Montfort Dukes who watched the situation with careful apprehensive eyes.

One more factor must be observed to complete the view. Below the River Loire, in the cities of Poitiers, Bourges and Tours, and in the castles and fortresses of Touraine and Anjou, young Charles, the rebel son of Charles the Mad, was striving with quaking fear to set up a rival southern kingdom. Virtually he was in exile, declared by Henry, by Ysabeau, his mother, and by the Parliament of Paris to be an outlaw, a murderer and a bastard. Yet a portion of the country supported him while he reached out with misdirected zeal the hesitating tentacles of diplomacy.

It was one of these that caused the concourse of nobles and councilors of the duchy of Brittany who rode now, serene and bold upon their horses, called forth from their homes and castles by proclamation and by private invitation, to attend a solemn States-General. Awaiting them, the outraged Duchess, angry and determined, sat between her two children within her husband's castle in the city of Nantes, ready to discuss with them their actions upon an affair of dishonor.

There lived upon his large estates at this time a young man, heir to the family of Penthièvres, who possessed a sort of claim upon the Breton duchy. In the past this family had several times pressed their claims and had been aided by the throne of France.

In an attempt to gain adherents to his cause, young Charles the Dauphin, upon the strong urgence of his minister, Tanneguy du Chastel, now addressed himself to this heir, promising him in return for future support, that he should be abetted in an attempt to supersede the Montfort duke.

Olivier de Penthièvres agreed, and following the tactics laid down by Du Chastel, he paid in state a visit to Duke Jean at Nantes. While there, he begged the Duke for the honor of a return visit to his own castle of Chantoceau. In all innocence Duke Jean accepted the invitation, and set out for the Penthièvres estates, preceded by harbingers and followed by a splendid retinue.

As they approached the castle, they saw the Court and retainers of Olivier riding out in state to meet them. A small wooden bridge over the Tuberbe Brook lay between the Duke and the straight tree-lined avenue which led to the castle gates. Across this the Duke rode, accompanied by his brother, Richard, and by a handful of knights and esquires, while the attendants and men of low estate remained behind, drawing rein with discreet effaciveness.

In the front of the welcoming officers of Olivier pranced the castle fool in scarlet starfish cap, and decked in the jingling bells of his profession. The course of his antics led him to the bridge where, upon an inspiration of drollest humor, he began, with the simulation of frantic rage, to throw its planks viciously into the water. The visitors turned in their saddles convulsed with mirth. Surely this was a capital jester, for the idea of throwing away a bridge was exquisitely ludicrous.

In an instant, however, their laughter died away. Out of a clump of thick bushes there burst a company of forty knights, headed by Olivier's brother, Charles d'Avangour, a warrior from the Court of Bourges. In astonishment Duke Jean exclaimed, "Fair cousin, what is the meaning of this? Who are these people?"

Olivier smiled complacently. "My Lord," he replied, "these are my people, and I arrest you in the name of the Dauphin!"

In this underhand and utterly unchivalrous kidnaping, the Breton nobles saw an insult and an indignity to which they could not submit. Whatever sympathies they might have held in the past outcroppings of this feud, they were now thoroughly united against the barefaced interference by young Charles, the exiled, the discredited and the heir to France.

Under the presidency of the Duchess and her children, pride and vigor, wealth and power were assembling. Through the different gateways in the walls they streamed, threading their ways through the narrow alleys watched by the vulgar burghers from their sagging doorways.

Among these nobles who entered the city from a hundred different directions drawn by a common impulse, there came from his Anjou castle of Champtocé, young Gilles, Baron de Rais, a youth of sixteen years, untried in war but of a great and valiant ancestry. From France he had ridden across the intervening country bringing with his train of servants, a great ambition for deeds of war, and the command of wealth and power almost unequaled in the realm of France.

Into the overhanging streets of Nantes he clattered, followed and accompanied by his cousin, confidant and personal lieu-

tenant, Roger de Bricqueville, and by his liveried retinue. No
one met him at the massive gateway save a crowd of curious
idlers such as hung about the public places in the hope of spectacle and of largesse, for Gilles de Rais was yet unproved and,
except by the rumor of his wealth, unknown. Through the narrow cobbled streets he made his way, splashing through the
mire and refuse that clogged the pavement, turning sharp corners between the heavy balconies of beams and plaster that
projected above the lower stories into the street (almost meeting in some narrower alleys) to the partial and sometimes complete exclusion of the sunlight. From the darkness of a stink-
ing alley, the troop of horsemen emerged into the sunlight of a
handsome square and, crossing it, descended a tunneled archway and halted in the courtyard of a dwelling house.

This building was the Hôtel de la Suze, built of stone and
half timber, famous for the excellence of its appointments and
for the magnificence of its blazoned ceilings and its exterior
carvings.

Within, there waited Jean de Craon, to whom this house belonged. Stern and violent, De Rais' grandfather was closely
connected with the ducal family and, besides being rich, was a
powerful personage in Brittany. Just now, he was replete with
the talk and gossip of the city and eager to impart to his young
relative the plans and projects of the assembled nobles. These
things De Rais must be well acquainted with, for he, as well as
De Craon, was by virtue of his rank a councilor of the duchy.

Duly instructed and advised, therefore, Gilles de Rais entered the huge audience chamber of the ducal castle on the
following day, fully ready to take his place behind the Duchess
among the bishops and the other councilors.

Along the walls stood men-at-arms, their upright lances lin-
ing the room with a fringe of dragon's teeth. Heralds, square
doublets of white silk worn over their coats of mail, guarded
the far entrance, blowing, upon the arrival of each newcomer,
loud blasts upon their silver trumpets. Beneath the black
beams of the ceiling, spread out below the fluttering array of

flags and banners, sat the great and lesser nobles of the duchy, filling the room with an odor of magnificence and listening with polite attention to the speeches in churchly Latin which were read with elegant, though somewhat unfamiliar, diction by the various dignitaries.

From behind the seated Duchess came, now, Jean de Malestroit, Bishop of Nantes, gorgeous in his robes of office. In the hush of expectant silence, he bowed his head and entered solemnly upon a long and rambling prayer. He ceased at last, and amid a burst of "Amens," he bowed again before his Duchess and seated himself in his episcopal chair.

A speech by some official person, filled with Latin rhetoric and involuted precepts, introduced the Duchess. Black-gowned and slightly angry, she rose and read a long paper concocted by some clerks in the service of the Bishop. The work was well prepared and dealt, one could suppose, with the cowardly abduction of her noble husband. At any rate, it was a splendid, if scarcely understandable, report. With a gesture that included both her children, the lady achieved a rounded climax, sat down amid a thundering of cheers, and the meeting began in earnest.

Nobles spoke briefly in every-day and somewhat profane terms, pledging their support. Suggestions were offered and accepted. Others were declined with howls of derision. Jean de Craon made his speech. A vote was taken. More discussion had its place and, in a hush, Gilles de Rais, prodded by his grandfather, rose to add his voice to the assembly.

For a moment he remained silent, tongue-tied before the crowd of nobles, while they observed him. Under heavy lashes, his blue-black eyes appeared to be fixed before him as though they rested before blazing into passion. There was a thin nose, straight now, yet indicative of a future and increasing aquilinity; a nose that widened at the nostrils surprisingly, and the nostrils too were thin. So was his mouth, thin and straight, yet curved proudly. Over the countenance was laid a softness of contour which robbed it of any sharpness and might well be a lingering of milky youth or, on the other hand, a hint of latent sensuality. In all, he was a dark handsome youth, slender, well-matured and strongly muscled.

Holding himself with proud elegance and with an almost impressive dignity, he spoke briefly of what his grandfather had instructed him. Then of his own, he volunteered a private pledge spoken in clear and ringing tones.

"Of my estates and property," he promised, "of my courage and of my life, I wish to offer freely for the rescue of my Lord. Let it not be said that a De Rais was ever lacking in his feudal duty." He ceased and sat down again with over-careful dignity.

The roar of applause that followed shook him. For a moment he forgot the vast estates, the boundless wealth, the multitudes of peasants under his command that caused the outburst. Flushed with pleasure, he listened in a delighted trance, his nostrils distended, drinking in with an intense avidity this joy of a new and startling recognition.

The audience chamber of the castle of Nantes had marked his entry.

§ 2

To the south of the River Loire, bounded on the east by the banks of the Lake of Grand Lieu, southward by the frontiers of the duchies of Poitou and of Anjou, and extending westward to the gray rocks of the seacoast, lay the vast, monotonous and fecund plain that made up the famous barony of Rais.

It was an ancient property whose capital, the castle and medieval village of Machecoul, marked the site of the Roman town of Rezé, from which the barons had obtained their name.

The family of Rais had lapsed with the childlessness of Jeanne the Wise and the estates had descended to adopted heirs. Between the two choices of the wise Jeanne—Guy de Laval, her first selection, and Marie de Machecoul, her second—there had ensued a suit-at-law which ended in the marriage of the Laval heir, Guy, to Marie de Craon, granddaughter of Marie de Machecoul and daughter of the soldier, Jean de Craon.

The marriage took place early in the year 1404, and in that autumn a son was born. This boy, held over the baptismal font by his grandfather, Jean de Craon, received the name of Gilles and was given, by the terms of the agreement betwen his parents, the surname of De Rais.

To this infant descended a vast inheritance. Of lands he became the richest and most powerful man in Brittany, a very dean of the Breton nobility. From the ancient house of Rais, at the death of Jeanne the Wise, came the rank and title of Baron, with the great fortress of Machecoul and the lesser estates of Pornic, Princay, Vuë, St. Etienne de la Mer Morte, and the island-fortress of Bouin. From his father and the house of Montmorency-Laval, descended the seignories of Blaison, Grattecuisse, Fontain Milon and Chemillé in Anjou; together with the estates in Maine of Ambrières and St. Aubin de Fosse-Louvain. While from his mother and grandfather he had already inherited or was heir to the Craon estates of Sénéché, Voulte, Loroux-Batereau, Benate, Bourgneuf-en-Rais, and the two strategic fortresses, Ingrandes, and Champtocé on the road to France, both of these within the duchy of Anjou. From these Craons, also, Gilles de Rais was heir to the sumptuous Hôtel de la Suze in the city of Nantes, whose walls were covered with the finest of Flemish tapestries, and the luxury of whose appointments was famous throughout the whole extent of Brittany.

To these estates could be added another and colossal fortune in gems and tapestries, gold and silver plate, vestments, horses, emblazoned coaches and objects of virtu. It is impossible to estimate the value of such a property, but it laid in his hands a tremendous yearly income.

It was through this territory that Gilles de Rais was now progressing, accompanied by his cousin, Roger de Bricqueville. With a real enthusiasm he hurried through his lands, commandeering retainers from his castles, collecting from his overseers his unremitted rents and supervising the arming and equipment of the rapidly recruited private army which he had promised to supply upon the occasion of the meeting that had recently been held at Nantes.

Throughout the tour, Gilles de Rais conducted himself with a continued burst of energy. No pains were spared, no expenses shied at. All was new and glittering. The lances were new—so were the pikes. A corps of gunners armed with gigantic harquebusses was formed of the more experienced. Even a number of culverins, half cannon and half fowling pieces, were mounted on light carts and given to the command of the personal Angevin guard which had come from the castle of Champtocé.

And at length, at the head of this array of troops and of the caravan of provision wagons, Gilles de Rais returned to Nantes, his force well-disciplined and even exceeding in size and armament his promised quota.

Nantes was teeming. Men-at-arms, newly conscripted, thronged the square and market-place, strutting boldly in the sunshine, filled with boasts of future glory for the benefit of one another and of the girls of the city. Assemblies of the nobles were held in the castle, in the archepiscopal palace and in the great hall of the Hôtel de la Suze. Since the earlier meeting of the States-General, several lords had chilled in their ardor, but the majority had returned, bringing the troops and treasure they had promised.

At last, the details were finished, and under the great De Rohan, the army of fifty thousand men set forth from the southeast gate to invade and conquer the territory of the Clissons, and to effect the rescue of the captured Duke. In new and gorgeously mounted armor, over which he wore a cloak of silk embroidered with the arms of Rais, the young Baron rode at the head of his united baronies, chatting with solemn excitement to De Rohan, commander-in-chief of the expedition.

"If we turn just beyond the next village," he suggested eagerly, "there is a path which I know direct through the forest that will lead us quickly to Chantoceau wherein the Clissons have secured our Duke."

De Rohan smiled indulgently. "I have thought it better," he

said, "to be more roundabout. By taking the lesser fortresses on the way, the greater may be more easily reduced. Besides the men are largely untrained and practise will do them no harm."

"But while we delay My Lord The Duke will be waiting. Let us go at once to his rescue."

"Are you so impatient then?"

"I burn to rescue him from the hands of his enemies."

"A little waiting reposes the soul," said De Rohan calmly, "even the dungeons of Chantoceau are conclusive to helpful meditation."

Gilles de Rais rode in silence glaring at the bobbing ears of his horse. De Rohan saw the disappointment written on the figure of his companion, and his teasing mood departed.

"It is my plan," he said brusquely, "to root them out once and for all. They have plagued our duchy long enough. Once the Duke is rescued, there will be a truce; and before that, I wish that all their fortresses be taken."

Gilles de Rais was mollified. De Rohan, he saw, meant no treachery, and he apologized. "It is most wise," he said, "to finish their rebellion and to teach a lesson to the King of Bourges."

They camped that night in a flat plain. Tents were pitched for the commanders, while about the camp-fires men-at-arms, wrapped in their blankets, slept upon the ground. Leaving the council tent, Gilles de Rais explored the field, visiting the men from his estates and counting them with a pleasant satisfaction. Late at night he returned to his tent and, wearied from the fatigue of the road and the excitement of his first day of war, fell easily to sleep.

In all, it was a fine gay war as the forces of De Rohan moved with scarcely a check across the lands and villages of the Clisson property. Occasionally they met resistance, but in the beginning all was opened before them. It was a war of dashing steel-clad charges upon some ill-protected gateway; of awe-inspired villagers scurrying to cover as the cavalcade of knights galloped furiously across a littered market-place, sparks flying from their horses' hoofs; of long rides in pleasant company across the roads and fields of Brittany, while in the rear there wound the dusty train of soldiery; and best of all, of the deep slumber in a comfortable tent after a full day in the open. Perhaps there was a scarcity of the more delicate luxuries of the castle or city, but when one's soldiers were also one's servants, and there yet remained delicacies in the market-places and pretty wenches in the fields, the hardships of campaign were not intolerably burdensome.

One by one the towns and villages fell into the hands of the advancing troop until they arrived at last before Lamballe. This was a town well fortified by heavy walls and towers, and manned by a considerable force of defenders. Moreover, the garrison was determined to resist. The army of De Rohan spread itself in a great circle below the walls and established a camp. Culverins and cannon were set up at convenient and strategic points from which they rained down stones and bullets upon the defenses. Attacks were organized, and groups of soldiers threw themselves against the heavy gates, while those not so engaged cheered them on from behind the moat, waiting their turn at the effort. Some, wounded by a heavy stone dropped from the ramparts, would withdraw from the struggle or fall upon the ground beside the walls. From the bank a rescue party crossed the pile of fagots that filled the moat, seizing their comrade and bearing him to the tent of the wounded.

Attempts were made with tall scaling ladders to take the place by storm. Sometimes two attacks would take place simultaneously at opposite sides of the city. Occasionally a sortie was made from within, only to be met with joyous clash of steel, whereby the defenders were driven back in exciting haste to their citadel.

For fifteen days the city held out despite the tricks and stratagems of De Rohan and of Gilles de Rais. The latter, for all his youth, already showed a taste for, and a grasp of, the principles of war that surprised and delighted the older commanders.

He had a sort of rash courage that they admired, and his activity was tremendous. Of all the nobles, he alone took the business seriously, chafing at the delay that kept them from Chantoceau and the imprisoned Duke. At one moment he was with the miners digging their way beneath the walls, only to find that the fortifications extended deeper than they had thought. From there he crossed the moat and was at work among the ladders or directing the attack upon the stout oak doors of the double-towered gateway.

At last Lamballe fell. The great doors, battered by two weeks of intermittent hammering, weakened, sagged and gave way, falling inward with a heavy crash. From the camp, the men-at-arms swarmed across the fagot-filled moat and fell upon the bristling pikes of the defenders, thrusting them from their path by weight of numbers.

§ 3

On their route through the Clisson-Penthièvres estates, the other towns and fortresses fell easily. Guingamp, Jugon, Châteaulin, Brune, Château Andreu followed in varying degrees the fate of Lamballe until at length the army of victory encamped itself beneath the walls of the great Clisson stronghold, Chantoceau, itself, wherein Countess Margaret de Clisson, daughter of the constable, and her son Jean were well defended by their able strategist and soldier, Captain de Bressières.

The war, for all that their objective lay before them, now became exceedingly tedious. No longer were there pleasant rides and marches with easy victories ahead. No longer the novelty of changing country and the pride of subjugated villages. Chantoceau resisted their attack; resisted too with a stubborn skilfulness that defeated all attempts at storm or stratagem. For three months the knights and men-at-arms sat stupidly without, vainly attempting assault after assault to utter weariness. Nobles longed for their homes and their hunting parties, while the valiant soldiery longed for their farms.

While waiting beneath the walls of Chantoceau, a young man

appeared at De Rais' tent with letters of introduction from Jean de Craon. The old noble, foreseeing such an event as a protracted siege, had sent this young man, fresh from the University of Nantes to be a tutor to his grandson. Gilles de Sillé was a distant relative of De Rais and, being of no estate, had planned to enter the Church. He expected to take orders that autumn and commence then his religious career. In the meantime, he was only too willing to act as tutor, companion and playmate to his wealthy cousin.

Bored with the monotony of the siege, the two young men became quick friends. De Sillé's church-trained mind was amazingly quick and nimble; too agile for the conventional bounds of safety. His studies of righteousness and orthodoxy had already acquainted him with the pitfalls of heresy and sin, and he loved to discuss them with his younger cousin.

Heresy especially appealed to him; without ever subscribing to its teachings he knew the basic point where this error departed from the truer faith and knew as well the weakness in the Catholic argument that allowed this departure. This weakness was the aspect of sin, from which another argument progressed.

Gilles de Rais was more downright. His belief in God was as absolute and unthinking as his belief in chivalry. He knew, to be sure, of evils and abuses in the Church; of corrupt monks and of priests who were robbers and thieves. Who, indeed, did not? He knew of bishops who had never said a mass. Of prelates robbing corpses they were paid to bury. Of monks snoring in filthy drunkenness upon the floors of taverns. These were common and familiar figures. Like many other good and pious Christians, he too had laughed at the satirical margin decorations of the fine, expensive Flemish manuscripts. Yet all these servants of the Lord, pious, prating, honest or scoundrelly, were armed with commissions from their Master. And being lackeys at the Divine Portals, one of them would serve as well as another. God Himself (or a specially designated saint) heard one's prayers. God Himself converted the Host into the Sacred Body and the wine into the Sacred Blood. The relationship was a simple thing. One prayed, attended mass; one confessed and one received the sacrament; and as long as the officiating priests were not actually heretical, one's prayers were heard and one's grace insured; their character mattered little.

Like most of his generation, Gilles de Rais shared the nearly universal hatred of heresy. It was, of course, no less than treason. To claim the grace and livery of God while in a state of excommunication was treachery of the deepest sinfulness. Cheats and frauds, these folk, false servants and spies of the evil one. In their hands the prayers of the unwary were deflected to the services of hell. Unburdened by a thousand trials and sworn confessions, these heretics stood convicted of a list of treacherous and abominable practises that made one gasp in horror.

One of these discussions had taken place on a warm afternoon in early August. The two young men had ridden across the country a considerable distance from the camp below the defiant walls. They had halted at an inn for supper, and returning, their path led them through a flat and vacant plain. In the cool evening they had forgotten faith and heresies, and the talk had become tinged with the supernatural. The dusk of the evening, the flat low-lying country and a backwash of the earlier talk had conduced the mood. A light mist hung about the occasional clumps of scrubby trees and, emanating from these copses, crawled along the earth in ghostly filaments. Gilles de Sillé was leading the conversation. His erudition led him into a maze of Breton stories, legends of the dark forests and of the cold rain-swept plains. To which De Rais replied with peasant stories of enchantment and of ghostly people which he had heard from some nurse or vassal.

As though in warning, De Sillé laid his hand suddenly upon De Rais' arm and in silence they drew rein. In the course of the story, they had entered a sort of copse and stood motionless among the trees just before the edge of a small clearing. From within this open space came sounds of festivity, cries and shouts as of drunken peasants and the weird howling of bagpipes. Without speaking the two young men dismounted, secured their horses and approached the clearing, hiding themselves cautiously behind a clump of brush. From there they commanded a good view of the enclosure surrounded at the sides by the wall of trees and partly roofed by overhanging branches.

To the left stood two men in black clothes, their faces hidden, playing upon one of those two-man bagpipes not uncommon in the duchy; the one puffing and squeezing the bellows, the second attending to the pipe itself from which issued shrill and inharmonious notes. The music was of an old and wailing Breton chant, transformed by the players into panting rhythmic beats. Strange music, to which a weird dance was in progress. About the center of the space, a ring of dancers moved slowly, circling about a central object. Back to back, arms interlinked, the couples revolved counter-clockwise, writhing and leaping, stumbling and scrambling; and from their lips rose up an obscene chant whose blasphemies caused a chill of horror to freeze the hidden spectators. Faster played the pipes, and faster the dancers moved in their irregular prancings. One felt the tension rise with the quickened beat to lull again into a slower and more sensuous rhythm.

Under the shade of great oaks, a rough table littered with the refuse of a meal stood deserted and forgotten. A young goat tied beneath its legs bleated faintly, ignored by the dancing throng. Bodies swayed with the heavy beating of the music, caught and held by the oppressive emphasis of the measured rhythm. A premeditated and enforced languor fell heavily upon them; a languor too ominous to be comfortably borne. The chant fell to an intense and articulated murmur. Passion subdued below the level of endurance. The chanting died heavily and was replaced by the breathing of the dancers, drawn and expelled in labored gusts. From the slow revolving mass figures fell away like soggy leaves and lay where they had fallen, singly and in pairs, writhing upon the ground in time to the renewed moaning of the bagpipes.

Again the music quickened. Some of the dancers broke ranks, wrenching themselves suddenly free of their partners, shrieking and prancing about the circle of moving figures, bursting into yet more extravagant and abandoned capers, leaping high into the air, whirling about or seizing some new partner with shouts of unholy merriment. In the confusion, figures bumping, jostling, kicking, would suddenly trip over an obstruction and, falling heavily to the ground, would roll hurriedly out of the path of the bounding feet and lie still for a moment of rest before springing up to resume their places.

They formed now a sort of strange processional, and the pipers varied their music. The dance became a stately march in parody. As they receded from the center of the ring, they revealed a form seated upon a wooden stool or throne, an uncouth black figure, goat-horned, yet bearing the figure of a man. A torch blazed at the end of the littered table and as they passed, they caught up candles from a pile and ignited them in its flame. Long black candles, these were, flaring as though made of pitch, and armed with these, they approached the seated figure.

In the light they could be more clearly discerned as men and women clad for the most part in long black gowns, but many a peasant's rags appeared below the hem, and here and there a glint of fine brocade was visible. Over their faces were masks —strange, horrible, bestial disguises which hid from the watchers and one another their features. One by one they approached the goatlike figure, motionless upon his central throne. One by one they did obeisance, bowing backward and raising their left legs high in the air. Then passing behind him, they paused in a second reverence.

A pile of fagots before the central throne blazed brightly, illuminating the seated figure. Like the others he was masked, but with a mask of leather that fitted tightly about his head. His body and legs were hidden in a great circular cloak that fell about him from his shoulders. He watched them motionless as they performed their homage. One could not tell whether he was, in truth, a statue, a man or a god.

Two figures brought the true goat from its place beneath the table. They both were women. By their movements one could be judged a hag, while the light step and quick deft motions of the other betokened a girl scarcely mature. Between them they held the beast before the fire. It had ceased to bleat. About the three clustered the remaining participants, crouching forward, intent upon the impending sacrifice; in their hands flamed and smoked the long black candles.

Above them the cloaked, goatlike figure of the master of ceremonies stood suddenly upright. In his hands was a bowl from which he sprinkled them, as a priest sprinkles with holy water. The rest of the contents he emptied upon the ground; and as it fell, the light of the fire showed it to be red, like blood or wine.

The true goat, before the fire, was struggling for its life. The two strong hands of its younger attendant were buried in its throat, choking out its life. For a moment it fought viciously, tugging and kicking in a last effort to escape. A massive cleaver was raised in the hands of the older woman; for a moment it rested aloft, bright in the firelight; then with a vicious arc, it descended and the sacrifice fell limply before the fire, bespattering its worshipers with its blood.

The bagpipe, aloof by the table, commenced its slow measure. About the fallen carcass of the beast, and about the seated figure of the beastlike god, the dance recommenced, slowly and easily as if in wearied relief.

A candle had fallen beneath the table, sputtering in the wet moss. By its darting light a second object was revealed. Beside the place where the young goat had been tied, a bundle of clothes lay carelessly hidden. Through the already quickening music of the dance this second sacrifice gave forth its cry of death. No bleating of a soulless brute this time but a wail too unmistakable to doubt: the feeble crying of a human infant.

Gilles de Sillé clutched his cousin's arm with icy fingers. "For Jesus' sake," he was chattering, "let us go quickly!"

He turned to the boy who had been beside him, but De Rais had fainted. De Sillé dragged him to where their horses were tethered and mounted the inert boy before him on his saddle. Abandoning the other horse, Gilles de Sillé galloped in headlong terror for the camp of Chantoceau.

CHAPTER II

§ 1

THE siege of Chantoceau was tiresome. For the moment there appeared but slight prospect of immediate success. In the heat of the summer the nobles moped in their tents, breaking the monotony with heating wines and long vigils at cards or dice. In the camp the men grumbled and sweated, while one by one they drifted off without leave for their homes.

But one morning, with a great blowing of trumpets, a messenger, armed with a giant flag of truce, emerged, with a handful of attendants, from the castle gates. Through the crowd of inquisitive soldiers he made his way to the tent of De Rohan and delivered to him a copy of a treaty signed by the imprisoned Duke and by his captors. By this paper Duke Jean was granted freedom upon the promise that the Penthièvres and all connected with the affair should be forgiven their sins and granted perpetual immunity from molestation by the ducal forces.

Two days later the Duke himself emerged from the castle, well fed and exceedingly cheerful; and the siege was raised. The army, except for a sufficient number to provide for an impressive show, was at last disbanded; and in triumph the knights and barons returned to the elaborate welcome of Nantes.

As they entered the flag-draped Breton capital, Gilles de Rais, an embroidered coat suspended from his shoulders, rode at the side of the Duke. While De Rohan had commanded the expedition, the young noble was undoubtedly the more popular figure. He had shown a real aptitude for the art of war, and before him had run tales of his brilliance and his courage. To the folk of Nantes he was already a hero. Youth and gracious

31

good-looks had already charmed them, while his immense
wealth made him a being of fabulous and romantic interest. He
had left as a sort of courageous and gilded mascot, a son of the
duchy whom they would some day be proud of. He returned a
brilliant and successful man of war. The Duke himself commended him publicly and bestowed upon him a portion of the
Clisson lands. (For in their counter-attacks the Penthièvres had
ravaged a portion of the barony of Rais.) To the welcoming
crowds of feudal Bretons he appeared almost godlike. And
they were not reticent in their praise.

For several days the welcome continued, and the city lived
in a state of extended holiday. Processions of thanksgiving
emerged from the churches, crossed and recrossed the city under a tumult of flags and banners. Free food and drink were
dispensed in the public squares. Banquets were given by the
nobles and prelates of the city, and the veterans were entertained everywhere.

Through the milling, cheering streets Gilles de Rais rode
upon his great horse, attended by an increased body-guard, scattering largesse to the admiring crowd. In the midst of this triumph he moved as in some glorious and incredible dream. To
be admired was a new wine of astonishing headiness. A wine,
moreover, of which he had always felt the need, but of which
until this day he had failed to taste.

Jean de Craon was a man of abrupt disparaging remarks. He
was not given to songs of praise in honor of his handsome
grandson, especially within the latter's hearing. Some flattery
had come from Roger de Bricqueville, cousin and majordomo;
certain tutors had admired his learning, but he knew as well as
they did the dependence of their position.

By this unprecedented outburst of adulation De Rais' head
was completely turned. He lived now openly in the public eye.
His retinue was increased and wrapped in yet more gorgeous
liveries. His dignity and impressiveness became colossal, and
to the churches of Nantes he bestowed astonishing and lavish
gifts. Piety and munificence were added to his virtues.

Small trace, if any, of his new conceit appeared in his dealings with the corps of nobles. He had not grown suddenly conscious of his virtues. Their existence he had always known. It was their sudden recognition by the crowd that came near upsetting him with joy. The crowd was his audience, cheering and shouting at his approach. The nobles were his friends and equals appreciating him perhaps, but for the most part recognizably older and wiser than he. His grandfather assisted this point of view.

§ 2

With the close of the Penthièvres war Gilles de Rais journeyed south to his handsome castle of Champtocé. Save for his well-armed guard of honor, he rode alone. His grandfather preferred to remain within the doors of the Hôtel de la Suze, while Gilles de Sillé, his cousin and tutor, had departed for St. Malo to take up the commencement of a clerical career.

The castle of Champtocé was his haven of privacy. It was in a way his very own, and although he was not as yet, either by the process of attaining his majority or by an emancipating marriage, completely freed from the guardianship of his grandfather, he was allowed without interference to manage both the castle itself and his own life there in whatever way suited him. Being already a grown man and a soldier, tutors were of course no longer necessary, while all the routine complications of management were attended to by Roger de Bricqueville. Untrammeled by responsibility or family restrictions, and aided by a handsome income to which no strings were tied, young De Rais could give free rein to whatever fancy possessed him.

He began to take an interest in the fittings of his castle. The kitchens were renovated to permit of a more elaborate cuisine. New chefs were obtained from Angers or from Nantes and instructed that only the most delicate of viands should issue from their spits. Merchants were summoned to discuss the merits of the most exquisite vintages. Old hangings were torn from the walls to be replaced by masterpieces from the tapestry weavers of Angers and of Flanders.

With his natural vigor, he entered into the transformation of Champtocé from a somewhat bleak, though comfortable, medieval fortress to a palace whose luxury equaled if not surpassed any in the land of France and made the Loire châteaux of the impoverished Dauphin resemble, by contrast, large though ill-attended outhouses.

He assembled a library of choice bindings and beautifully written and illuminated books. In an excess of zeal he even obtained a set of colors and tried his hand at this delicate art. Book collecting was a fashion of the day. It denoted in the collector a depth of culture that set him above and apart from the herd of rough untutored warriors who, though able perhaps to write a good enough signature, or to read the easier passages of a treaty, must look in awe upon those gifted scholars who could read with ease, and did so for their own pleasure.

At Mehun-sur-Yèvre, now in the possession of the Dauphin Charles, the Duke of Berry had assembled a rare library, the treasure of which was a book of hours by a celebrated Fleming. René of Anjou, son of Queen Yolande, delighted in the illumination of the fashionable Bergundian and Flemish miniaturists. The father of Viscount Miles de Thouars, having been refused a certain missal of prodigious beauty by the monks with whom he was negotiating, promptly had besieged the abbey until the miscreants had come to terms and accepted for the precious volume (being forced to do so) a sum so large that with it they tore down their old and somewhat uncomfortable quarters and erected on its site an entirely new and resplendent monastery.

Besides Breton and French, Gilles de Rais was also at home in the Latin tongue. The works of Valerius Maximus and the annals of Tacitus lay upon his shelves. He had given a high price for an Ovid *Metamorphoses* done on parchment and bound in gilded leather, with copper clasps and locks of silver gilt, upon whose back cover reposed a crucifix beautifully wrought in silver.

There were books in French and Latin; books of legends and theology; religious works and the newer editions of the Roman writers. Among them too were books of the theater: mystery plays, miracles, sotties and farces, in which he took a great delight. Along with his illumination, he had attempted as well to imitate these dramatists; and in his library, he composed certain short pieces that he caused to be performed for the benefit of his associates and companions.

But of all his books there were two in which he found especial pleasure. The first was Saint Augustine's *City of God,* which threw him into a state of emotional exaltation and aroused in his breast a sense of supernatural piety. Emotionally religious, this book appealed to his intelligence, justifying and supplementing to him the more purely emotional experience of the mass. It enabled him to comprehend the mystery of communion, and to know, with a tremor of awe, the true nature of the sacrifice of which he partook.

Once as he knelt before the gorgeous altar of his chapel, he allowed the consecrated wine to remain for a moment beneath his tongue, savoring it with a sensuous delight in the recognition of what it was. Stricken with remorse, he confessed his sin and prayed earnestly, with deepest piety, for his forgiveness.

The second book, a curious contrast to the first, was a copy of Suetonius, ornamented with pictures and very well designed, in which were portrayed the lives and glories of the pagan emperors. A comparatively harmless book, perhaps, but to De Rais, to whom, like most persons of his age, books were more real than life, a terrible and fascinating pleasure. He read of the power absolute, unlimited and uncontrolled, of these rulers; of their freedom from accounting to guardians, duke or king—their very freedom, in fact, from God—with an excitement that almost overwhelmed him.

He read therein the history of their luxuries and their obscenities with a vast excitement, touched perhaps with a trace of pious horror. In the ancient writings he lived, in all details, the feasts and orgies of Caligula. To him they were no more remote than the recent entertainments of Nantes. With thrilling envy he pursued the accounts, visualizing them as though they appeared in actuality before his eyes.

The shameless and unnecessary cruelties of the emperors burst upon him with appalling force, and he experienced a strange emotion. In a fever he read how Caligula and the other Cæsars sported with children and took a singular pleasure in their martyrdom. Closing the book with feverish haste, he left his library to pace the ramparts in an effort to cool his emotion.

§ 3

Of all the estates to which he was an heir, Champtocé was the one that Gilles de Rais considered his home. It was for one thing the most comfortable of his castles, and here he had lived, with the exception of certain irregular visits to the urban pomp of the Hôtel de la Suze or to the melancholy castle of Machecoul, for the greater part of his sixteen years.

Though not of great extent, the palace was a veritable fortress, a warlike and forbidding structure, effectively guarding the road to France and blocking, if need be, the very Loire itself. Raised above the river upon a rocky platform, the granite walls followed the curves of the rock upon which it was built.

Stories of battles and sieges, of sudden descents upon the highway were easy to imagine for a boy brought up in this place. One had but to walk along the covered ramparts and half shut one's eyes in order to see quite clearly a hostile army encamped upon the green fields beyond the moat. As a child, De Rais had delighted in the tales of war, and listened with eager interest to the stories concerning Du Guesclin and John Chandos; and had played at being a soldier.

There was a pond against the walls and a drawbridge over the moat that could be raised and lowered. At one corner of the massive defenses stood an audacious, cone-capped donjon in whose base he had once, as a child, discovered a series of ancient prisons, and a maze of subterranean galleries. He had spent an entire day there, while frightened tutors searched the castle for him. Exploring the dark recesses and passageways in an ecstasy of fear and excitement, he had come upon a deep shaft, a forgotten well, the bottom of which was lost in darkness. Unfrequented stairs worn by mailed feet descended into the damp earth to new and deeper and more terrifying dungeons. Once he thought he had found a gruesome clue to a distant tragedy, and held before him the gnawed soup-bone which some castle cur had tried to bury in the packed earth. It gave him for a moment a thrill of delightful horror. Old rusty implements lay about the floor of a large chamber. He searched among them for the sinister accouterments of the torture chamber. A broken helm, a sword rusted through and bits of broken armor were all that rewarded him, save for an obvious and prosaic butcher's cleaver. A curiously formed belt of metal and leather, of clamps and a great lock puzzled him. It did not belong to any suit of armor that he knew and he was very sure it could not be used with mail, nor did the peasants in the fields wear such things. He decided to ask his tutor and left it behind. Coming out of this room he climbed a dark stone spiral of steps that ascended, turn after turn. The exploring fit was over and he felt unpleasantly lost. Climbing up wearily, a shaft of daylight suddenly rewarded him, and he came out into the afternoon sunlight through a narrow doorway at an angle of the battlements not far from where he had begun his journey.

His life at Champtocé was in the main uneventful, and he was thrown much upon his own resources. René, his brother, was of course too young to be a companion, while in his heart De Rais despised his tutors, who were men of low estate and gifted with but mediocre intelligence. He spent his time in hunting, in riding about the countryside on his favorite horse accompanied by a few men-at-arms, in sports and contests with his cousin, Roger de Bricqueville, in the castle yard and, as he grew older, in reading and in continuing certain studies which amused him and in which he already surpassed his teachers.

He grew up into a tall, graceful young man, handsome beyond doubt, with the dark hair and eyes and clear olive skin that is not uncommon in Celtic lands. At sixteen years he was fully grown, possessing a mature and developed mind of an unstable brilliancy of which he was thoroughly aware.

Guy de Laval, his father, died in October, 1415, when Gilles de Rais was eleven years old, after having made a will giving the tutelage of his sons (Gilles and his brother René who was ten years younger), to a cousin, Jean de Tournemine who it was expected would attend in a satisfactory manner to their proper upbringing.

But Jean de Tournemine seemed a poor sort of guardian to old Jean de Craon, who had no idea of letting the management of his two grandsons, to say nothing of their valuable property, pass into the control of any outsider. He ignored De Tournemine in menacing silence and brought the two boys to his own fortress of Champtocé in Anjou. Shortly after the death of Guy, his widow, De Craon's daughter, remarried. It was unsafe to remain in the state of widowhood long. Too many castles were equipped with dungeons eager to receive such unprotected ladies of fortune and to entertain them in darkness and somber odors until their minds were changed and joyful weddings took place in the shabby halls above ground; weddings whereby the bridegroom received settlements well repaying his efforts of courtship. For a husband, Marie de Craon chose Charles Desouville, Lord of Villebon, and left her two children to the care of her father. She had never cared for them greatly.

They were brought up mostly at Champtocé, whose eleven towers could be seen profiled against the horizon of the Loire. Craon, himself, now that he was assured of their control, left them well alone. He had many interests to busy him, while the managing of so vast an estate left him little time to play nursemaid to his two grandsons.

§ 4

Shortly after Gilles de Rais' return from the festivities of

Nantes, his grandfather, leaving the Hôtel de la Suze, arrived at Champtocé to pay him a visit. Something about the young man's activities troubled him. With a grandparental touch of condescension he admired the new hangings and tapestries, and commended the young man upon the taste and elegance of his chapel.

They dined alone in the privacy of a small apartment, contiguous to the handsome banquet hall. The meal was sumptuous, though not extensive, depending more upon the spicing of its pastries than the more robust appeal of well-cooked roasts. On the whole, Jean de Craon thought the dinner precious, more of a meal for women than a soldierly repast, though even he could not dispute its excellence. Of the older generation, he rather distrusted this luxury that was coming into fashion. At the conclusion of the meal they sat in comfort before the half-cleared table, goblets of wine before them from which they drank at intervals.

"What of your life, Gilles?" began the grandfather. "I confess that since your great success at Nantes I have given your future more than several moments of thought. You will, of course, be in time quite a considerable personage in Brittany; and it is not too early to give it thought."

"I have," said De Rais.

"A good beginning. I am glad you are not merely idling, as all this evidence of luxury might have led me to believe. A serious purpose is a valuable, if not essential, thing to have, and all possible careers are open to one in your position."

"I have decided," De Rais announced, "upon a career of war. What I have already seen of this business has greatly pleased me, and I feel that no other career is so admirably fitted for a gentleman."

Jean de Craon was vastly pleased. "Excellent," he said, "and very clearly put. Activity is the proper existence of youth; and where can activity and honor, to say nothing of rich reward, better be found than amid the campaigns and battles of the field?"

"I had not thought of rewards so much as glory; and the glory of a victorious general is greater than any triumph of a peaceful statesman or prelate. Greater, often, than that of a king."

"Before you embark upon this fine career," said his grandfather, "what do you think of the plan of marrying?"

"I have not considered it at all since our last misfortune."

De Craon ignored this remark. "There are many advantages. In the first place," he enumerated, "I am still your guardian, and even though I strive not to interfere in your affairs, I am sure that the very fact of my nominal control must, at times, seem irksome; such is only natural to any high-spirited youth."

"It does. Not the fact itself; you have been most lenient, but the idea that I am not completely responsible is galling."

"Marrying would end my guardianship. Until that moment I am legally held accountable for you. Secondly, for such a person as yourself, a wife would bring rich dower rights: châteaux, lands, income and valuable or powerful connections."

"I hardly need them, you know."

"Still no one ever frowned upon additional wealth. As far as I can see there is no objection."

"Except the bride herself."

"Nonsense, Gilles, I have the very girl for you."

"I had already suspected that."

"Suppose you do not like her," De Craon went on with defensive earnestness. "Because you are married, does that mean that you must live with her continually? For a while, yes. You ought to have an heir. But if she displeases you, it is easy enough to pack her off to another castle, or imprison her on the excuse of her having a lover, or merely forbid her your presence. That is nothing to worry about."

De Rais grinned. "Is she as ugly as all that?" he asked.

"Suppose I tell you she is most attractive, what objection have you then?"

"Oh, I have none. I am merely curious about my bride."

De Craon laughed with relief and took a great gulp of his wine. "Good boy," he chuckled, "I knew you would listen to reason."

This was not the first time that the question of marriage had been discussed between them. Before Gilles de Rais was thirteen, his grandfather had arranged a wedding for him. The idea of marrying off the boy occurred to De Craon whenever he felt that he was growing old, or that De Rais needed younger company or a stabilizing influence. It became action only when he had located a bride rich enough or powerful enough to match against the estates of Laval, Craon and Rais.

The first betrothal took place on January 14, 1417, some months before his thirteenth birthday. The bride selected was young Jeanne, the daughter of Foulques Peynel, Lord of Briquebec and Hambuic.

This maiden had, at the time of her engagement, achieved the ripe and pleasant age of four and was rich in her own right, being an orphan. In order to insure the performance of the marriage, after the necessary intervening years had elapsed, old Jean de Craon had promised, with a lordly gesture, to pay her grandfather's debts (which were considerable) once the ceremony was performed. Young Jeanne, however, possessed a guardian who was blessed with other plans. He himself had a son of seven years for whom he intended the heiress. A petition was dispatched to the Parliament of Paris, and her marriage to Gilles de Rais was formally forbidden.

With his next attack of match-making, a second engagement was arranged. The lady, who it was hoped would share the huge estates of Gilles de Rais, was chosen in the person of Beatrix, daughter of Alain IX, Viscount de Rohan and Count de Porhoet who two years later was selected by the Breton Assembly to lead the armies of the duchy, including those of his once considered son-in-law against the rebellious Clisson fortress.

The second nuptials were held in the ancient capital of Vannes, to which city came a great concourse of the Breton nobility.

De Craon and Gilles de Rais entered the town attended by a veritable army of heralds and men-at-arms, witnesses and lackeys in gorgeous equipage, while Alain de Rohan, slightly less magnificent but quite as imposing, welcomed them in prodigious state.

This affair satisfactorily concluded, the bride-to-be most inconveniently fell sick, and died before the wedding could be performed.

§ 5

There existed in the land at that time a certain noble, Miles de Thouars, who lived in a vast estate not far from the Craon-Laval properties. This knight, besides being enormously wealthy, was possessed of ill-health and of a daughter who was heir to his lands. And on these lands, old Jean de Craon now cast a covetous eye. They consisted, firstly, of the vast and rambling castle of Tiffauges, lying about fifty miles to the south of Nantes in a harsh sterile valley where little grew except brushwood. Through this valley flowed the River Sèvre, and at the juncture of this river and the Crume rivulet was constructed the irregular trapezoidal fortress. It had been built, for the most part, during the twelfth century, in that heavy-handed, medieval fashion that rendered it almost impregnable. It was a valuable, though melancholy place, and a worthy mate for the great fortress of Machecoul. But besides Tiffauges, old Miles de Thouars possessed the important and valuable lands of Pouzauges, Chabanais, Confolens, Château-Morant, Savenay, Lombert and Grez-sur-Maine, an inheritance for Catherine that overshadowed the fortunes of Jeanne Peynel and Beatrix de Rohan, Gilles' former fiancées, so greatly that even had these fortunes been added together, Jean de Craon could well curse his stupidity for ever having considered them.

De Craon had seen the daughter, and in view of her lands she had appeared to him a most attractive young lady. She was of marriageable age, sixteen in fact, which was an excellent age for a bride. She was, in addition, not blind, lame or otherwise deformed, nor was she cross-eyed. One could, indeed, regard her with equanimity if not with pleasure. If she did not appear over-intelligent, so much the better; she would in consequence be more docile, and as every one knew a brilliant wife was a constant source of trouble.

Accordingly, Gilles de Rais, accompanied by his grandfather and a considerable force of men-at-arms, set out on a crisp morning in late November for the castle of Pouzauges, where Miles de Thouars, his daughter Catherine and the remainder of his family were living. It was a pleasant day to ride, and at the head of his troup, De Rais was filled with a happy sense of adventure. They passed a number of villages whose inhabitants eyed them in wondering awe, not unmixed with apprehension. Had another cruel war commenced?

The small estate of Pouzauges was loosely guarded. A single lookout, wrapped in a heavy cloak, dozed upon the roof of the donjon. It was a time of peace, and as the days of inter-castle war were supposedly at an end, there was little need of vigilance. Miles de Thouars lay upon his bed, a fire blazing in the hearth and all the shutters closed. He was not sick, he said to himself, but his gout pained him and the light hurt his eyes. Presently he would get up.

Catherine was tired of the castle. A stolid child, she was nevertheless bored by the stupidity of the household. Her father was in bed pretending to be sick, and her mother was busy. No one else was about. There were no guests. She emerged from a door of the main wing and crossed the courtyard to the stables. Here she found her horse, a somewhat placid mare looking sadly in need of exercise.

At her command the mare was saddled, and she set out for a ride along the valley. The country around Pouzauges was singularly free from danger, and for a considerable distance she would be under the supposedly watchful eye of the lookout. She had ridden thus a thousand times in perfect safety.

When Catherine, therefore, on her white mare rode quietly

up the Valley of the Sèvre with but a few of her women and guarded by an ancient forester and his two stalwart sons, she was considerably surprised to find her way barred by a handsome and most determined young man about her own age, blocking her path upon his tall black horse. She recognized him at once as the hero of the late war, Gilles, Baron de Rais, who had so lately ridden beside the Duke on the occasion of the triumphal return to Nantes. He bowed to her respectfully and motioned her to approach him.

Her attendants drew rein and waited anxiously close together in the center of the road, while Catherine walked her horse slowly toward the motionless horseman and said:

"My Lord de Rais, have you wish to speak to me?"

De Rais bowed. He turned his horse so that he was beside her and his hand grasped her bridle. "Mademoiselle Catherine," he said with great formality, "I regret my rudeness in so interrupting your pleasure, but I have decided to make you my bride. As it is conceivable that objections might be raised by various of your relations, I believe it necessary to avoid any such consultation. In reality, the matter is an affair which concerns only ourselves, which fact you can easily appreciate; and as I detest family bickerings, I have come, in company with my grandfather and a few men-at-arms, to escort you to my home where, without further ado, we may be comfortably married."

Catherine was startled and quite suddenly frightened.

"Would you carry me off, sir?" She pulled at the reins with frantic terror. "Leave go, sir! I demand that you loose my horse. What right have you to hold me here? Let me go!"

De Rais allowed a slow smile. "My dear child," he said, "don't be fractious. We are about to commence our wedding-journey. Come," he said sternly. His spurs dug at the white mare, which sprang forward startled by so heavy a blow, while the tall horse at her side sprang at the same instant.

A scream from Catherine echoed down the valley. "Bertrand! Michel! Eonet! Help me!"

Out of the woods, on the left, sprang Jean de Craon on his gray stallion. Charging sharply into the roadway, he brought his animal beside the white mare. Shoulder against shoulder the three horses galloped furiously up the long avenue, their flanks touching, while behind them the men-at-arms swung in a great arc out into the road, two abreast, closing in the rear, their axes free and their hands tight on their reins, ready to turn at any moment upon any possible pursuers.

But old Bertrand, the forester, Eonet, his son, and Michel, struck with astonishment, stayed where they had been standing. What use for three men on ancient mounts to chase half a hundred well-armed and desperate soldiers? They stared blankly after the cloud of dust from the flashing hoofs, then turning about, returned sadly to the château of Pouzauges.

At Champtocé, Catherine was given quarters in a wing somewhat isolated from the parts of the castle occupied by the male members of the household. Women and serving maids were obtained and attached to the person of the bride-to-be, while she was allowed whatsoever freedom did not risk the chance of rescue by her parents.

Protests and demands came regularly from Pouzauges; but as no heed was paid to them, they mattered little. As for a more strenuous rescue, Champtocé was a powerful fort and very well armed, while in the Penthièvres war De Rais and Jean de Craon had shown a most creditable force of well-armed soldiers. Futile to attack. Miles de Thouars besides had by the course of time grown old and feeble and greatly disinclined for wars. He even seriously recalled the strict law of the duchy forbidding private war among the nobles. So in' the end he contented himself with protests and demands, in the hope that an offer of compromise would be forthcoming.

It was not, however, De Craon's aim to treat with Miles de Thouars. Catherine was his sole heir, and considering the ill-health of her father, any compromising would be absurd.

Instead, on the thirtieth of November, 1420, Catherine and Gilles stood at the altar of the private chapel at Champtocé in the presence of Jean de Craon, Roger de Bricqueville, Gilles de Sillé (who was as well a cousin to Catherine, and had made a special journey from St. Malo for the purpose of sponsoring her), and of Gilles' brother, the six-year-old René de la Suze. While the chorus of the beautifully selected choir sang like young nightingales one of De Rais' newest compositions, a hireling monk attached to the castle performed the ceremony, and in faulty, though elegant Latin read a long benediction. Side by side the couple knelt, and the choir burst forth again into a triumphant hymn.

There followed a feast in the beamed dining hall. Roasts and fowls, smothered in heavily flavored sauces were brought in silver platters from the spits and copper kettles of the kitchens. Salads of tenderest leaves sprinkled with seasonings relieved the monotony of the meats. There were pastries and puddings and curious little sweets from the confectioners of Paris, and before each diner was found an array of goblets from which he might choose of beer or mulberry juice or the exquisite wines that De Rais had obtained from the merchants of Poitou and Touraine.

Catherine ate little. The wedding had been no triumph for her. All of that had been arranged and planned by the bridegroom even to the selection of her costume. It appeared that she had attended in a capacity less important than that of the smallest of the rosy-cheeked choir-boys in whom De Rais took so great an interest. Save for the necessity of a bride being present, she would hardly have been missed from the ceremony. De Rais himself had scarcely looked at her.

She rose and slipped away from the table, and no one noticed her departure. The men were leaning together talking loudly, tremendously interested in their own conversations. De Sillé was already drunk and was declaiming with a multitude of misquotations after the habit of all exhilarated scholars. De Craon was boasting. Once from the stone walls of Champtocé, he had swept down upon the highway, and at the points of his lances had robbed of her rings and jewels Yolande of Aragon, the Duchess of Anjou (the very duchy wherein Champtocé it-

January: From an Old Calendar of Occupations and Pleasures of Each Month

self was located). And not only that, De Craon went on with a great laugh, but of her horses as well, leaving the coach helpless in the mud, its shafts digging uselessly in the roadway. Who, he demanded proudly, even the Duchess herself, would dare lay finger upon a De Craon or (with faint condescension) upon a Laval.

De Rais, almost bursting with the wine and intoxicated with a heady pride in his own achievement, rose to his feet; he was trembling as though with passion, his face curiously flushed. "God can deny nothing to a Laval!" he shouted. "Nothing. And should he ever deny, there is always the Devil."

De Sillé started uncomfortably as, amid a burst of cheering, the young Baron resumed his seat. The feast roared on. An orchestra at the end of the room was almost drowned by the shouting at the table. A dancer performed unwatched, lost in the hubbub of the feasters. And now at a vacant chair at one end of the long table, a huge man appeared armed with a heavy triangular lute of outlandish pattern. On this he strummed for a while in dull heavy chords, then raising his head, he burst into a deep-throated version of a well-known hunting air, a fine, rich, rollicking song, filled with opportunities for amateur accompaniment. The talk of the diners fell, and one by one they joined in the music.

The music ceased, and De Craon threw a purse to the singer. He bowed, grinned in pleasure and withdrew. The orchestra at the far end of the hall recommenced. De Craon rose.

"Come, Gilles," he said heartily, "the day of the bridegroom is ended, but the bridal night has yet to commence."

De Rais rose, slim, elegant, straight as a lance, insisting with a desperate steely grip that he was yet in command of his faculties. He brushed back the lock of his black hair that had fallen over his eyes, and bowed with proper ceremony to the company. Head high, his face frighteningly white, he marched in an arrow-like line through the great length of the hall, and passed through the round arch at the far end on the way to his bride.

§ 6

As a matter of routine, the wedding was duly reported to Hardouin de Bueil, the Bishop of Angers, in whose diocese it had been performed. This worthy prelate, considering the matter carefully, did not by any means approve. Whether he had lent his ear to the protests of the bride's father, or whether his own scruples had intervened, is difficult to say. At any rate, after not a great deal of diligence he discovered that the bride and bridegroom were too closely related to receive his official sanction. In other words, they were found to be relatives of the fourth degree, a condition in which marriage by the laws of the church was strictly forbidden.

Hardouin de Bueil thereupon disapproved the marriage and declared it void. Gilles de Rais, in the security of his castle, ignored the Bishop and retained his rich wife.

From a romantic point of view, the marriage itself could scarcely be called successful. On closer inspection of his bride, the young Baron found her sullen and dull. She lacked wit and the sympathetic quality that is essential in a wife. Her very docility was heavy and unwilling. She wept at the wrong moments and, to his way of thinking, required entirely too much wooing. Already he had begun to dislike her.

Even in bed she was distasteful. Being not without passion, he was profoundly disturbed by his feelings. Even at the most intimate moments he was aware of his disgust and wished furiously to beat her.

One night she asked him to stay away, but he had drunk much wine and the desire to annoy her overcame him. It ended their honeymoon. De Rais consigned her to separate apartments, a corner tower being given over to her use, and refused definitely to co-habit with her.

Providentially another States-General was called at this time in the city of Nantes, and Gilles de Rais welcomed the opportunity to escape for a while from his domestic situation. The purpose of this convocation was to consider the advisability of sending an embassy to England to negotiate the ransom of Arthur, Count de Richemont, brother of the Duke who had been held there as an honored captive ever since the great disaster of Agincourt, eight years before.

In these intervening years De Richemont had waited patiently, and without hardship, for, except for the fact that he was forbidden to leave the island, his life had been pleasant enough. His mother, at the death of her first husband, had taken as a second, Henry IV of England, so that being by his death again a widow, she was well able to provide adequate entertainment for her prisoner son. Nevertheless, De Richemont was restless, and being a soldier of large reputation, it was thought that he could be made of use in Brittany or in France. The States-General thus decided, voted, collected and dispatched to England the ransom demanded by his captors, and under an oath that he would not oppose the English King, De Richemont was released.

A second war was brewing within the duchy, a war of even less importance and less danger than the first. Its conduct was given to De Richemont, and into this affair Gilles de Rais threw himself with all his force and energy. In its course, he again distinguished himself and came under the notice and friendship of this great general.

Save for an interval while he was busy raising troops at home (in celebration of which occasion Catherine emerged for a day from her tower), he was away for the greater part of a year, leaving the management of his properties to the abilities of his cousin, Roger de Bricqueville, who to all outward appearances performed his duties with the greatest skill and integrity.

The war at last concluded, De Rais returned to Champtocé, where Catherine in her private tower showed most distressing signs of approaching motherhood. De Rais, remembering the ban of the Bishop of Angers, and not desiring his son to be born illegitimate, hastily sent a petition setting forth his cause to Pope Martin V in Rome. Martin was prompt and obliging as became his somewhat precarious position, and on April 24,

1422, Hardouin de Bueil, Bishop of Angers, pronounced a separation and absolved the couple from their past sins. Two months later he gave them a solemn nuptial benediction in the church of St. Maurille de Chalonnes in the presence of many lords and vassals.

About this time old Miles de Thouars, Catherine's father, died while on a visit to the town of Meaux, leaving his widow in possession of his estates. To the widow, Catherine's mother, De Rais now offered the castle of Tiffauges, which he had seized as dowery, the estate of Beaurepaire and an income of one hundred livres on condition that she remarry.

The lady agreed and, espousing one Jacques Meschin of poor estate, claimed her promised property. The actual giving over of such valuable lands had never entered De Rais' head, nor the head of his grandfather for that matter. Instead, they swooped down upon the unfortunate lady and placed her securely under lock and key. Her new husband, seeing both his bride and his newly acquired (or promised) lands no nearer him than ever, sent a solemn embassy to Tiffauges, where De Rais and De Craon were making themselves at home, demanding his wife. To grandfather and grandson there seemed only one logical reply. The embassy was seized and thrown into one of the family prisons. And so the matter rested.

A period of dulness now settled over the life at Champtocé. For two years there had been a succession of exciting events, one tumbling upon the heels of that which had gone before; two wars, one wedding (two if one counted the ceremony in the private chapel), imprisonments, defiance to royal and episcopal authority, plunderings, triumphs and spectacles; a busy existence for a youth between the ages of sixteen and eighteen. Suddenly it had all come to an end, and looking about him, Gilles de Rais saw himself peacefully married without a cloud upon his horizon.

A single event remained. At the appointed time, Catherine took to her bed and delivered herself of an heir. To their great disappointment the child turned out to be a daughter, fat and ugly and squalling prodigiously. The proud father had the child brought to him and regarded it curiously. It was said to bear a strong resemblance to Catherine, except for a crop of soft black hair rather like his own. One glance sufficed him. It was, undoubtedly, Catherine's child and he took no further interest.

Instead, he puttered about the castle leaving the maternal tower strictly alone. He was utterly through with the pair of them. If Catherine the bride displeased him, Catherine the mother almost made him ill. Even the prospect of a male heir, he decided, could not induce him to go near them.

He buried himself restlessly in his music, his collections and his chapel, buying new ornaments and hangings from the richest merchants of the country, whom he summoned to his castle for the purpose, and perfecting the elegance of his religious service. His theatrical efforts also occupied him and under his direction became yet more elaborate and more ambitious.

But the inaction distressed him, and he passed rapidly from one interest to the next with but little zest. Life had grown suddenly stale, and he longed for war and grew morbid. But a tedium of peace afflicted the duchy. The Breton wars were over.

CHAPTER III

§ 1

TOWARD the middle of June, 1423, there arrived at the Court of young Charles (which was at that moment situated at the city of Bourges) a cavalcade bearing Yolande of Aragon, Queen of Sicily and Jerusalem, and Duchess of Anjou, who was as well mother-in-law to this unfortunate Prince. Braving the discomforts of the journey, this lady had traveled from Provence to attend the birth of her grandchild.

In honor of this semi-royal visit (for Yolande was a queen by courtesy only) a ball of welcome was given in the royal castle of Bourges. The long hall had been cleared of benches and tables, swept out and garnished with hangings and banners, many of which were borrowed for the occasion. At one side a thin, reedy orchestra piped its pale music from a carved gallery.

The large chamber was but half filled with guests, while the boxes scattered along the walls were for the most part empty. Somewhere near the center, the dancing was taking place in a half-hearted and desultory fashion. About the dancers other guests were scattered, standing in little groups or promenading aimlessly. Voices seemed to burst suddenly forth out of a semi-silence and interrupt the whining of the musicians. There was no steady hum of crowded conversation. One seemed to walk great distances between the isolated groups and to feel conspicuous in the process. In the echoing emptiness there could be no easy mingling, no turning casually about to find a companion of a former war or bed suddenly at one's elbow. The atmosphere was stiff and self-conscious; too polite to permit gaiety, too uncertain to be boisterous.

The keynote, as at all royal functions, was set by the King, who sat rather stiffly beside his handsome mother-in-law in the royal box opposite the musicians. Charles, as usual, was ill at ease and bored by the festivities. He disliked the formality of so large a gathering and recognizing the responsibilities that rested upon him, he felt it his duty to remain sober.

The music was miserably poor, yet what could one do when the wretched fellows demanded payment in advance? He wondered how the couples managed to dance at all and was glad for a moment that Marie, his wife, was kept to her bed. She danced so badly, always tripping and making him uncomfortable. Nevertheless, he missed her presence beside him; for he was truly fond of her. A month, at least, he supposed, must elapse before she would be again presentable.

He wondered whether the child that was coming would be a son or daughter. For himself, he should prefer a girl, but the kingdom, he knew, required a male issue. At the thought of his kingdom he smiled wryly to himself. Since his exile, Charles had done little toward extending his possessions. At Poitiers he had tried to gather together what of the country was yet loyal and had achieved the allegiance of the six Loire provinces to which was added the duchy of Berry, to the east. A few of the nobles had answered his call and sworn fealty, and while the provincial estates had given him their support, his Parliament of Poitiers, which was intended to rival and outshine the one of Paris, remained in rags, unpaid and largely unconsidered. The south was generally loyalist and supported him feebly, but northward his province stopped at the Loire.

How long, he wondered, would his realm continue, and how soon would come the day when he should be forced to flee from Bourges, as not so long ago he had been forced to flee, rescued by the valiant Tanneguy du Chastel, from the walls of Paris? Already he had been advised to retreat and set up about the city of Grenoble a new and safer kingdom. Perhaps he should not be allowed a second escape, and in time it would be he and not his friend, Count Armagnac, who should be dragged at a horse's tail, naked through the streets.

From the seclusion of his box, Charles regarded the sparse throng of revelers. Almost all of them he knew by name and many of them were more than intimate acquaintances. My Lord Regnault de Chartres, Archbishop of Reims, banished from his See by the English party, was conversing in hushed and prophetic tones to a gentleman whose face and figure were hidden from the King. Regnault de Chartres was a considerable personage at Court, a vain bullying person with a vast belief in his own diplomacy. He was not, as yet, of the front rank; but after the great ones, Louvet, Pierre, Frotier and Tanneguy du Chastel who between them controlled and ran the country, the Archbishop of Reims came next.

For some reason the Archbishop did not seem to be showing off, and Charles wondered to whom it was that he was talking. An intervening courtier moved from the line of vision, and Charles beheld an enormous expanse of back. So huge and bloated a figure could belong only to one person, namely—to Georges de la Trémoille, the former companion of Louis of France, Charles' elder brother who had died of mastoid some years before. La Trémoille was neither rich nor possessed of very noble lineage, yet he was, one felt, a powerful personage. It must have been his size and a certain gross vitality that made Charles fear him. For clever as he probably was, this human mountain had achieved as a reputation only that of a tremendous appetite and an unlimited gusto for food and drink and for the pretty ladies of the Court. So far this hogshead of a man, almost as fat as Queen Ysabeau, Charles' Bavarian mother, who by her size was prevented from passing through certain doors in the palace of the Louvre, had kept himself aloof from active participation in the affairs of state; but Charles dreaded the day when those sharp, cold eyes should fall with envy upon the royal treasury or on France itself.

From the bulk of La Trémoille, Charles turned his attention elsewhere; to Pierre Frotier, the insolent, unscrupulous man of war, the military genius of the administration, boasting in the center of the room of his valor to Charles of Anjou and to Guillaume d'Avangour lately returned from taking part in the fiasco in Brittany; to old Raoul de Gaucourt, the honest and practical Governor of Orléans; and to Jean of Blois, the defeated son of Margaret de Clisson, wandering sullenly alone across the floor. Among the dancers he saw the Lord of Giac watching with cruel jealous eyes his young wife, with hawklike vigilance.

The ball was not a success. Already little groups were coming up to the royal box to take their leave on the plea of urgent excuses. And out of the corner of his eye, Charles saw others from time to time pass from the room and escape, almost unobserved. The music whined on, and Charles wished he could afford a better orchestra.

Queen Yolande touched his arm. "I am tired," she said, "and I think I shall go to bed. Besides, I want to call on Marie and see that she is being properly taken care of. As for you, I advise you to try dancing. Certainly it can be no more fatiguing than sitting here on these hard chairs and talking to stupid people. Perhaps it would improve your state of mind. I notice that you are becoming much too solemn."

The music opposite gave forth a feeble blast. It was more of a bleat than a proper blare, but at its signal the Queen of Sicily, preceded and followed by a group of courtiers, swept across the room and retired amid respectful bowings and curtsyings.

Suddenly deserted, King Charles looked about him aimlessly and then, descending from his box, walked slowly across the floor to where the lady whose hair was concealed in two huge gilded cones was smilingly awaiting him.

To the smiling lady, the King could hardly have presented a handsome figure as he ambled toward her. His rather long body mounted upon unsteady, crooked legs, was encased in a tight-belted tunic of green plush, already wearing out its second set of sleeves. Nor did the somewhat worn edgings of brown fur about the neck and skirt add to his elegance. The costume was unbecoming and made him look shorter than he was, while its grassy color caused his sharp gray eyes to appear too green for beauty. Nor was his face imposing. Beneath a large forehead, his aquiline nose was too long and too sharp, while the effect of a heavy jaw was destroyed by his thick lower lip, which had a tendency to sag uncertainly.

Almost anywhere among the well-dressed courtiers or bold-faced knights about her, the lady could have chosen better. But Charles, despite his lack of beauty, was a king, and though she knew her husband would not be pleased, she awaited him complacently. Any king was worth an effort (on account of their rarity alone) and a royal conquest could always be of value.

Across the path of royalty strode the brusque figure of the Royal Maître d'Hôtel. Forging his way through the crowd like a wedge of Flemish troops through a fleeing company of conscript farm-boys, Tanneguy du Chastel implanted himself solidly before the approaching Charles. Muttering a few sententious phrases, he led his unwilling victim away from the gold coiffed beauty to the seclusion of a corner, where he could press his demands for a fresh subsidy intended for the upkeep of the army; of which grant sufficient could be deflected for the purchase of a golden platter set with rubies and lapis lazuli that he had been shown by Abraham, the traveling Jew; a bauble that Tanneguy du Chastel sorely coveted.

The lady watched this intrusion with concealed disgust. Leaning quickly toward the young man at her side, she whispered to him delicately behind her fan. He was, as it happened, an exceedingly handsome gallant, and Charles would not spoil in the waiting.

§ 2

Queen Yolande had found on her arrival that the Court at Bourges was even more distracted than she had anticipated. Hopelessness and despair had settled upon it. Even the ministers, busily engaged in acquiring wealth and fortunes for themselves, seemed downcast.

Charles, himself, had changed little. It occurred to her that during her absence he had lost rather than gained in self-assurance. He was now a little over twenty, a pious, humble soul, gentle in appearance and speaking in low embarrassed tones. Naturally trusting and free with his confidence, his successive debacles—from the ill-advised plundering of his mother's fortune (which naturally alienated the sympathy of that bitter lady), to his presence at the murder of a Duke of Burgundy upon the Bridge of Montereau—had almost destroyed his illusion of himself.

During her stay at Bourges, Queen Yolande grew exceedingly fond of her royal children. The look in Charles' eyes troubled her, and she wished to do something for him to rearrange his life. She had gone to infinite trouble about Marie's maternity, but for that she was already well rewarded. A wealth of grandmotherly compassion enveloped the tiny, wizened baby that yelled so loudly for his dinner. He was not a pretty child, and as far as could be told at so early an age, he was in figure destined to take after his father. It was a misfortune, no doubt, but Yolande thought, or pretended to think, that she saw in young Louis (later to be called the Eleventh) a gleam of intelligence that could only have descended from her.

Since the dangerous fiasco of the Penthièvres attempt against the Duke of Brittany, little effort toward improving its position had been made by the party of Charles; while in the north, the English, with the aid of Burgundy, were busy consolidating their possessions and taking at their leisure whatever loyal cities remained above the Loire.

In 1423, when Yolande returned from Provence, the impatience which had once suffused the followers of Charles had settled into a state of chronic quiescence. While they were no worse off than they had been in 1419, still they assuredly were no better.

On the other hand, the year before had brought three events into the life of the Dauphin that had raised his status considerably above that of an outlawed pretender and should, if properly handled, have given a new impetus to the cause of which he was an apathetic, if not actually an unwilling chieftain.

In the summer of that year Henry V of England, regent by his own appointment for the mad King of France, had decided to end once and for all the controversy. With a large army he set out from Paris with the avowed purpose of subduing the south. He got no farther, however, than Melun where he was seized with the cramps of dysentery. Turning about, he was brought back in haste to Vincennes, just without the gates of Paris, whence, after a short illness, he died on August thirty-first, leaving the kingdoms of France and England (in so far as he was able to bestow them) to his infant son, the child of Prince Charles' sister, Catherine of France. The late Henry's brothers, the Dukes of Bedford and of Gloucester, became regents for this infant; Bedford taking command in Paris and Gloucester in England.

The second event of importance was Charles' marriage to Marie of Anjou, to whom he had been engaged for nine years. And it was the birth of their child that brought Yolande, her head full of schemes, hurrying across France in the heat of June.

But the most important of the three occurred when Charles had just returned in the autumn to his château at Mehun-sur-Yèvre. On October twenty-fourth a messenger had arrived at Court breathless, riding upon a spent and lathered horse. From Paris he brought the news that Charles VI, the mad King of France, was dead.

Charles received the news and gave the proper commands. Clad in the lavender clothes of mourning, he attended the funeral service for his father held in the chapel of the château, standing with bowed head among his knights while the service was repeated and the funeral chant went up to heaven. At the conclusion, the knights about him gave a great shout and hailed him Charles VII, King of France.

On the thirtieth of October, he formally took the title of king and moved with his retinue to his new capital of Bourges. There on the first of November, he held in the great cathedral the ceremony of a solemn coronation.

But the war, such as it was, dragged on without change or alteration. States-Generals were convoked with the usual regularity, while the majority of the funds thus granted were dissipated or found their way into the pockets of Tanneguy du Chastel, Louvet and Pierre Frotier, Chief Ministers to the King. Yolande hated this war. She knew that it was fruitless and felt that it was continued largely to supply these courtiers with an excuse for looting the purse of her son-in-law.

Yet any alteration of the situation must come, she knew, from without; and by the word "without" was implied either of the great duchies of Burgundy or Brittany. For the present, the hope of detaching the former from the English alliance seemed out of the question. Brittany, however, appeared more promising. Yolande was sure that if she could transform the struggle of King Charles for recognition and for his inheritance from a purely civil conflict to the status of a Franco-British war, this duchy could be enlisted.

The obstacle across the path of friendship between the Courts of Nantes and Bourges was the horrible blunder of the Penthièvres plot which had detained Duke Jean a prisoner for an entire summer in the castle of Chantoceau. More strictly, this obstacle was the presence in the inmost royals councils of Louvet and of Tanneguy du Chastel, its authors. It was in fact the same obstacle which had alienated Philip of Burgundy by causing the murder of his father and which now caused the conduct of the war to drag along in such an inconclusive fashion. Moreover, these ministers had filled the Court with a horde of discredited Armagnacs, Gascons and free captains whom no one cared to trust.

With these folk in the saddle, failure in the final conclusion was inevitable. The enemies they made were far too many.

Nevertheless, Yolande was determined that the squalling Louis should some day have a kingdom to inherit; and a kingdom in its proper meaning rather than a confederation of semi-

hostile duchies and provinces such as Charles, his father, now
enjoyed.

To achieve this, Yolande saw one clear and definite course.
To her service a leader must be attracted whom all would willingly obey. There was needed as supreme commander a man of
reputation and of honor, a man devoid of enemies (unless they
be the English) who could by the dignity of his name command
the respect not only of the Court of Charles, but also those of
Dijon and of Nantes. It was in pursuance of this decision that
Yolande made several visits to the Breton capital and there entertained with lavish hospitality and with her famous Spanish
wines the Duke, his minister, Jean de Malestroit, and various
of the important nobles. A disastrous defeat created a vacancy
in the high command of Charles' armies; for in the battle of
Verneuil, the Earl of Buchan, Constable of France, had fallen.
And with this vacancy the Queen of Sicily planned an important
move.

§ 3

To her castle in Angers, she invited Jean de Craon upon a
visit, adding a hint in her request for his presence, that more
than entertainment was promised. Jean de Craon came, of
course, and was lavishly feasted. The culmination was a small,
though elaborate dinner at which De Craon was seated as guest
of honor on the right of his hostess. At his side, Yolande was
able to maneuver him into a state of mellowed complacency.
Times, she intimated, were dull, and a deplorable languor
seemed to have fallen over the land. What were the younger
generation doing? In comparison to the gay lives their elders
had lived, she felt that they lacked spirit.

This opening was sufficient to start De Craon upon his long
career of warfare and highway robbing and, encouraged by the
Queen, he pursued it with unflagging delight, bragging shamelessly of his past feats of strategy and daring. Yolande laughed,
admired him and broke in with short episodes of her own that

served only to prod his memory for fresh anecdotes. And all the while she watched with quick glances that his glass was never allowed to be quite empty.

At length the other guests departed, and Yolande settled herself beside the elderly warrior in a confidential mood.

"Tell me about your grandson," she began. "Now that we old people are somewhat retired from the world we must look with interest upon the doings of our children. In their activities lies our only hope of reliving our youth. From your story of his marriage he appears to be a descendant worthy of your own heart."

"So he is," said De Craon, "a bold spirited youth. In that he takes after the Craons. But just now I am, I confess, a little worried about him. For nearly two years he has remained at home puttering about like a bishop. He spends his time worrying about the colors of his ceilings, and dressing up his servants like lords or mountebanks and causing them to perform in plays as though they were traveling minstrels. Not that the fool things are badly played," he added with pride. "Never in my life have I seen such excellent productions. Why, last time I visited him he had them perform a farce about a knight who, overtaken by a storm, took refuge in a nunnery. I thought my sides would burst with laughter. I laugh now to think of the poor fellow hiding in the clothes press."

"You quite surprise me," said Yolande. "From what you have told me of him I imagined that a career of war would be more suitable to a man of his temperament."

"And so it is," said De Craon. "These theaters, brocade-covered walls, and super-elaborate church services are, no doubt, all very well in their way. I am not one to decry this new craze for luxury, while I can not deny that if it is the fashion, it is certainly fitting that a man of Gilles' position should do well by himself to a certain extent. But, by Saint Michael, the lad is a soldier. It is the career he has himself chosen and yet he sits idly at home fussing with baubles. I confess, your Majesty, that I am worried about him. Money runs out of his fingers like wine out of a fallen cup. Of course, he is very rich, but no one can pour out gold with the skill and abandon of my grandson without endangering his very estates. And it is not as though he were happy about it. He actually mopes."

"But his wife," suggested Yolande, "does she not keep him cheerful?"

De Craon drank from his cup. "She was a mistake," he admitted. "He does not even sleep with her. Why the lad does not take a mistress, I can not imagine. I suggest it regularly."

"I believe," said the Queen, "that he is badly in need of a war. Youth must needs be active. One can not sit at home and maintain one's health."

"Of course he is. Why, in the troubles we had here but recently he performed extraordinary feats. The Duke himself commanded him and rewarded him generously; but now, unfortunately, we in Brittany are at peace."

"There is war in France, you know."

"As a war, it is dull, without battles or glory."

"But there are battles. One took place recently."

"Nevertheless, there is little enough chance for a young and active captain. The English have wrung their country dry and have no money to pay their adherents. Even De Richemont, great soldier that he is, waits idly in Paris, while all the estates that are worth having are already bestowed. And as for Burgundy, young Philip is scarcely a combatant. He contents himself with allowing the English to play his game for him."

"So that there remains, my friend, but the party of Charles, my daughter's husband."

Jean de Craon looked at her sharply. "By our Lady, your Majesty," he burst out, "surely you are not suggesting that we support the cutthroats and kidnapers who abet the King of Bourges?"

"Amedeo of Savoy, the Duke of Bourbon and the Doge of Venice are scarcely cutthroats."

De Craon was impressed by these names. "No," he said uncertainly.

"Nor is the Count of Foix, nor the Duke of Alençon, nor Richard of Brittany."

"Nevertheless, they do not run the Court. It is of the true leaders that I speak."

Yolande leaned toward him, a wise smile on her lips. "But suppose, my friend, that these men, Louvet, Frotier and Du Chastel were removed, replaced by a new and trustworthy leader?"

De Craon sat upright, suddenly interested. "To whom do you refer?" he asked eagerly.

"It is, of course, somewhat of a secret, and before I proceed further, I should like your advice. What do you think of my old friend, De Richemont?"

De Craon sat for a moment in startled silence. Arthur de Richemont, famous soldier, brother of the Duke of Brittany, was in the English service, having been released by them from captivity on a sort of parole. Moreover, the bells of Dijon had scarcely ceased their ringing upon the occasion of his marriage to Marguerite, the sister of the Duke of Burgundy. Yet as he considered, De Craon became more and more convinced that the idea might well be a practical one if Yolande chose to see it through. It was notorious that De Richemont loathed the English, while the death of King Henry had technically ended his parole. Nor were the English over-fond of him. At any time, a break between them was to be expected; and at that moment, the Queen of Sicily had much to offer.

Arriving at his conclusion, De Craon laughed delightedly. "The very man!" he cried. "Your Majesty has planned a master stroke. For many honest men would follow him."

"Will you help me, then?"

"To the last ditch, your Majesty. It is the scheme of the century. But what causes you to think that our noble general will accept?"

"I have no grounds at all. But should he break with the English, I have the Constable's sword to offer."

De Craon was vastly pleased. "I am just the man," he said,

"to carry weight with the Duke. I shall speak to him at once, and I guarantee to win him over."

"Of course, it is as yet merely a hope in a woman's breast."

"But a brilliant one, your Majesty."

"By the way," said Queen Yolande, "you are a vassal of mine, are you not?"

"Yes," said De Craon, "both Champtocé and Ingrandes and also several other of my places are within your duchy."

"It might be," said the Queen, "that in the event we were speaking of just now, I should need a governor for Anjou. I should, of course, be too busy to attend to my property in person, and my son is away so much."

"In all things, your Majesty, I am yours to command."

"I hope to leave for St. Malo within a few days to escape the heat at the seashore. I heard by chance that the Duke is to be there also. If I have the opportunity, I shall speak to him again concerning his brother. But a word or two before his departure might prepare his mind."

De Craon arose. "I understand, your Majesty, and shall speak a discreet word. I shall also have a talk with my grandson."

"I doubt if much persuasion will be needed there," remarked Yolande.

§ 4

Finally the matter was arranged. The expected break between De Richemont and the English took place, and the former was once more at liberty. The Constable's sword was offered, and was accepted with the concurrence of Duke Jean who held the hope that by strengthening the French party and prolonging the struggle, the independence of his duchy would be furthered. Even Philip of Burgundy found no objection to De Richemont's new position, as he himself had just had a minor quarrel with his English allies.

On October nineteenth, Charles VII entered Angers in state,

upon an official visit to his mother-in-law. On the twentieth Arthur de Richemont arrived at the head of an imposing array of men-at-arms and met the King in formal conversation in the beautiful gardens of Yolande's château.

The following day they came to terms. The Constable's sword was definitely offered and as definitely accepted, while Jean of Brittany, reenforced by the findings of a Breton States-General, formally approved. With this, the conference came to an end. No specific mention of the proposed retirement of Louvet, Frotier and Du Chastel had actually been made, but the matter was completely understood. As an evidence of good faith, De Richemont was given the command of Lusignan, Chinon and Loches, the chief fortresses of Charles' northern border.

With the conclusion of this meeting, the various parties rode away: Duke Jean to Brittany well content with his strategy; De Richemont in the direction of Burgundy for a final conference with Philip, and Queen Yolande toward the Court of Bourges.

In her mind there raced a dozen schemes for settling the life of Charles, and for setting him once more upon a solid throne. Yet in the accomplishment of this, more than Yolande's skill was needed: for into her scheming was destined to be drawn a horde of folk, rougher, stronger and more dangerous than she had ever dreamed. And long before the fate of Charles was finally secure, there would appear an almost endless caravan of knights and rogues; of wealth and desolation; of treachery and of death. Sieges and battles traveled in this train, while at the head marched diplomats and princes arm in arm with murderers and thieves. In their midst, surrounded by a company of monks, would ride a saint in white armor upon a stolen horse. These were to be the companions of Yolande's scheming; but in the end the affairs of Charles were ultimately to be arranged.

Leaving the conferences of Angers, Charles VII, accompanied by Jean de Craon, set out for the castle of Champtocé where he was to spend a few days with his vassal, Gilles de Rais, who, by the efforts of his grandfather, had recently been enlisted in the French cause.

It had been Charles' plan to return, once the tiring councils of Angers had ended, to the pleasant city of Tours. But the last moment suggestion of his mother-in-law, that he pass a few days with a young noble amid the luxury of the handsomest castle in Anjou, had pleased his fancy. He turned from the straight course and took the road which descended to the Loire. He was in no hurry to return to his Court, and the pleasant excuse of resting for a short while in the home of one of the richest of his vassals appealed to his wearied spirit. Rest was needed before facing again the bullying of his councilor-jailers. He needed time also in which to gain courage for the task of dismissing these men whom he knew to be so much stronger than himself.

Gloomily he rode beside the elderly man who boasted and joked at his side. Relaxation he craved, with luxury and wine to take his mind from himself, and relaxation was promised. He was, too, somewhat curious about his host of whom his companion bragged so tiresomely.

He had expected a palace of far more imposing proportions than Champtocé presented to his vision. Yet its bold outlines pleased him as he rode up the gentle slope to the castle gates. Before he was allowed to reach them, he was met by a company of heralds, emerging from within. While the men-at-arms, their lances upright, formed with military precision a lane of steel, creating on either side a shining picket of their spears, the heralds advanced four abreast and raised the trumpets in silver greeting. A special dignitary now appeared as the heralds drew back to either side of the pathway and read brief but grandiose welcome in throaty Latin. He, too, drew back, and from the heavy gateway a dozen knights in brilliant armor galloped full tilt from beneath the portcullis. In a cloud of dust they pulled up their steeds, barely short of the escort of the King. From their midst a figure rode out alone in greeting. Charles recognized him at once, by his bearing and by certain descriptions he had already heard, as Gilles de Rais, his host.

Flinging himself from his horse, the Baron knelt in the roadway by his sovereign's stirrup. At once Charles signaled him to rise, and he, too, dismounted. For a moment they stood in formal converse, repeating the proper phrases of politeness and regarding each other critically. Then remounting, the combined company rode up the avenue of lances and entered the castle.

Charles had been struck with the handsome appearance of his host even more than by the dramatic welcome he had received. The Baron de Rais was indeed a remarkable person. There was in his eyes a gleam of one born to live intensely, of one who could burn with a tremendous passion. Charles guessed that his career was misdirected, and that the passion lacked an outlet.

Emerging from his suite, Charles was led by his host about the rooms and gardens of the castle. Had he been disappointed in the exterior of Champtocé, his misgivings had vanished with the appearance of the heralds, who were clad in the finest of heavy scarlet silks, while the tassels of their trumpets were of gold. These were but heralds, also, of what lay within, and Charles was astonished by the lavishness of the fittings. In every bedroom, he was told (and there was no reason for disbelief) there was to be found a ewer of solid gold, whose sides were embossed with delicate designs and which was kept constantly filled with warm water scented with melissa or roses. He beheld entire walls covered with cloth-of-gold and he trod upon floors tiled in alternate squares of white marble and of jade. The library itself was of priceless value. There were books of the latest manufacture, adorned by the most expensive of the Flemish miniaturists. In one of them he had seen pictured a complete and marvelous city raised upon a hill, while below it in a fabulous valley a clear blue river wound its way, and upon the river he saw microscopic boatmen loading goods upon microscopic boats. It was a marvel of craftsmanship, and the whole could be covered by the palm of a hand.

"It is a present," De Rais remarked, "from My Lord Philip of Burgundy, painted by his new Court painter."

They passed through doorways sculptured with exquisite skill from polished bog oak, under ceilings painted with heraldic designs in blue and gold. Elaborate fireplaces were carved and sculptured out of stone. They found tall windows of red and blue stained glass admirably traced, galleries, courtyards and gardens all in perfect and beautiful taste. Surely this was the most magnificent castle on the Loire. A sad contrast, Charles thought, to the bare châteaux in which he was forced to live.

More than the castle itself, the banquet was a triumph of De Rais' greatest efforts. To entertain royalty, he had surpassed even himself. They sat in the long-beamed dining hall where the King could look up at intervals from the food before him to the high tapestry-covered walls and the sumptuous ceiling painted by the hand of an Italian artist.

At the royal table sat the King in the place of honor, between De Rais and the silent Catherine, who was permitted to emerge from her tower to grace so august an occasion. Farther down, Jean de Craon and his new, though elderly wife, flanked them while the rest of the royal party was made up of Roger de Bricqueville and a few of the important Breton nobles.

Descending a few steps, one discovered the tables for the lesser members of the household; the librarian, the priests of the chapel, a few youths of noble birth who were in the castle service as squires and secretaries, the captain and officers of the private army (the body-guard, as it was usually called), and a few monks more or less permanently attached to the household, among which latter group was found the one who had performed the ceremony of De Rais' private wedding.

Yet farther from the platform on which the royal board was raised, stood other tables filled with the common folk. Here sat the balance of the ecclesiastical staff, the organists, the lesser clerics, the choristers and the like. Among this group were seated the other minor officials and certain prosperous vassals from the villages of his domains, and among them an occasional merchant or traveler who had claimed hospitality for the night.

It was all quite old-fashioned and medieval, but it made an effective spectacle.

A superb orchestra played pleasant music which was varied by the occasional introduction of solos and choruses from the finest voices of the chapel, while about the diners, servants in the livery of the house of De Rais moved quietly and deftly throughout the room. There seemed to be whole companies of them, bearing trays and goblets, dispensing yet more wine and an endless succession of meats.

Before the King, dishes were offered in amazing profusion. A nod, and they were placed before him; a shake of the head, and they were whisked away and others substituted. Pasties of beef, rich with fragrant herbs, young pork stewed in milk and wine, pies made of the breasts of small birds, and well-hung venison. There were, as well, delicacies unknown to the vulgar table: cranes and seagulls whose native flavor was well disguised; peacocks' meat chopped in small pieces and, best of all, the glory of roast stork. About King Charles' plate were little dishes of jellies and sweetmeats to rest his palate, and before him a parade of goblets filled with wines such as he had never tasted, together with delectable and curious cordials, while before him stood a mug of beer with which to quench his thirst.

His host was in high spirits over the success of his feast. Truly it was a masterpiece of design. He ate and drank well, talked without cease and applauded his musicians vigorously.

"A magnificent voice," he said to Charles, as a boy in white velvet descended from the orchestral gallery. "It is a flute of silver, enriched with chasings of gold. He is a discovery of my own, for I heard him first singing for pennies at a fair in Dieppe."

The ladies rose and left the table, and the meal was at an end. Stewards appeared with cordials and the talk became more intimate. As usual Jean de Craon brought the conversation around to the subject of war, yet moving more warily than was his wont. For once, Charles was not bored. Instead he took up the topic and turned it more and more to the campaign in France, yet fol-

lowing in a general way De Craon's theme of the glories of a
military career. In the back of his mind he wished to attract his
gallant host to his cause. At least, he hoped, there would then
be a friend and a pleasant companion at his Court. He led De
Rais along in this train of thought, carefully nursing his growing enthusiasm, until the King too began to feel a spirit of excitement.

De Rais was well aware of what had taken place at Angers;
and the importance of the event excited him beyond the bounds
of generalities. "By Saint Michael, your Majesty," he shouted,
"I crave a valiant war again. I am sick to death of this quiet life
and of these everlasting trumperies."

For once in his life, Charles rose to the occasion. He sprang
to his feet before the assembled company.

"Then the war is at hand," he declared boldly. "This day we
have decided to pursue our destiny to the utmost of our forces
and to the last extent of our endurance. In this campaign the
great De Richemont has consented to be our leader and will
wear the Constable's sword. But De Richemont alone is not
enough. I shall need the services of brave and able men, of
money and of courage, without limit. For I intend to make once
more, of this torn and bleeding land, a reunited France. I call
upon you, Gilles de Rais, and you gentlemen of the duchy of
Brittany, to join me in my enterprise."

Charles stopped and sat down quickly. His unexpected ardor had suddenly embarrassed him. He had no thought of
speaking so emphatically and he half wished to retract his
speech, but Gilles de Rais had already risen.

"Your Majesty," he began in a loud clear voice, "I have already served with Arthur de Richemont. To my mind and conviction there is no greater soldier in the land of France. Under
his leadership I could ask no greater opportunity than to be allowed to follow the cause that he now represents to the very ends
of the earth and to uphold it with the whole of my resources and
my honor. Solemnly, before this gathering, I offer my services
to your Majesty."

A short applause greeted this speech, and Gilles de Rais sat down.

Again King Charles was standing before the crowded hall. "I accept," he said, with a curious earnestness, "in the name of my heritage, your generous offer. With deepest gratitude and animated by a renewed hope, I thank you for your loyalty."

§ 5

At Court there began at once a sifting and rearrangement. De Richemont took over the conduct of the military forces (although not without considerable struggle with the remnants of the Louvet factions), drawing to him new commanders and nobles, granting them honors and commands subject only to himself. An imposing and splendid list of names appeared overnight at the head of the royal forces: the Duke of Bourbon and his young and elegant son, the Count of Clermont; the Duke of Alençon; Alain de Rohan; the Counts of Harcourt, Vendôme and Foix; the Marshal de Boussac; Raoul de Gaucourt, Governor of Orléans; and the great professional captains, Ambroise de Loré, Beaumanoir and, most renowned of all, Etienne Vignolles, called by the world, La Hire.

The diplomacy was placed in the hands of Yolande, and she strengthened the loyalty of her allies with handsome gifts, while by more gifts she attracted fresh adherents. She arranged a meeting with Jean of Brittany at Saumür, whereat, amid great pomp, the Breton Duke did formal homage as loyal vassal to Charles VII, King of France. A tremendous step this was from the cautious alliance of the year before. Brittany, by this act, seceded from their alliance with the English.

But while the new order made this fine beginning, all did not run smoothly. In reply to the Breton defection, the English descended upon that duchy in force and took as a reprisal the city of St. James de Beuvron.

To its walls De Richemont hurried accompanied by Gilles de Rais and other commanders, leaving behind him as chief of government administration the Lord of Giac, who had served under the astute Louvet. This was an error, for although money had been granted for his campaign, De Richemont received none of it and his troops were restive in consequence.

After an unsuccessful attack the French were driven off and while they rested in their midnight camp, the tents unaccountably took fire, precipitating such a rush of terrified panic that the Constable was overwhelmed, swept from his horse by the impact of the stampeded troops and left to spend a painful night in a ditch, his shoulder having been dislocated in his fall from the saddle.

Being returned the following day to his army, the Constable was filled with rage and, acting upon some private information, swooped down upon an ancient enemy whom he accused of treason. This enemy was none other than Jean de Malestroit, Bishop of Nantes. And him, despite his episcopal protestations, De Richemont dragged to Chinon and its dungeons.

Descending upon the Court the faithless Giac was snatched from his bed, hurried in his nightshirt across the country to Dun-le-Rois, where, after a mock trial, he was sewn neatly into a sack which, properly weighted, was dropped into the Auron River.

CHAPTER IV

§ 1

IN SEARCHING for a successor to take the place recently vacated by the ill-starred Giac, the choice of De Richemont and of Queen Yolande fell upon a certain Louis de Chalençon, who was appointed to this position. But this person, by the very pliancy that had recommended him, proved to be totally inefficient. So pliant was he in fact, that the actual control of the state machinery passed easily through his hands and became grasped by a courtier who was named Camus le Vernet, but was called for some reason Camus de Beaulieu. Now this Camus enjoyed a financial scrupulousness that was perhaps even less rigid than that of Giac, while his purse-lining skill was consummate.

It was a misfortune that neither the Constable nor the Queen of Sicily knew how to administer. And for this reason also, they forebore to replace him.

From the troublous Court, Gilles de Rais traveled south in great state, men-at-arms, servants and esquires in his train. He had received a polite though insistent invitation from his cousin, Georges de la Trémoille, to visit him at his castle of Sully, an invitation that had obviously more than friendly hospitality as its basis.

Nevertheless, the hospitality of Sully was magnificent. Hunting parties across the vineyards and fields of surrounding grain had been organized. Banquets and feasts, where wine and hypocras flowed with astonishing prodigality, were daily affairs, and pretty women seemed to sprout upon the very staircases. A week of luxuriant and unbridled revelry took place and though,

73

at its conclusion, the guests were beginning to show signs of wear, the fat host remained unimpaired and unperturbed, as though he were amused and slightly scornful of his own entertainment and thoroughly unimpressed by the characters and appetites of his guests.

To De Rais he had spoken no word of explanation as to his urgent invitation; and to the young Baron a week's acquaintance, in wine or on horseback, had brought the Gargantua no closer than he had been when, at the welcoming, he had ridden out clumsily astride his powerful charger.

But this Georges de la Trémoille, now about forty years of age, was an adept at revelry, and it was scarcely to be expected that in its course he should ever be incautious enough to give himself away. With a wealth of experience, he carried his greed, his gluttony and his lusts as easily as he carried his weight of sensual flesh. For always his cold eye saw clearly the course he wished to pursue and fixed itself tenaciously upon the approaching object of his desire long before his clumsy body had wallowed its way past the object at hand. This saved him.

The death of Guy, the father of this notorious Georges, had left the family fortune in bad condition. The estate consisted largely of a handsome collection of debts and of little ready money. To add to this misfortune, the son was captured—a sort of skunk-cabbage among the flower of French nobility—at the disastrous defeat of Agincourt. But poor or not, George de la Trémoille had quickly paid his ransom, and returned to France an exceedingly impoverished nobleman.

To recoup, he at once married a lady of fortune, Jeanne, Countess of Auvergne, who happened to be, unfortunately, a little beyond the first flush of youth. For this reason, as well as any other, he promptly shut her up in a draughty castle in Auvergne and waited idly for her to die of natural causes.

The seizure of her lands well occupied him for a considerable period; Montereau and the Penthièvres affair taking place almost without his knowledge. While his looting soldiers pillaged Auvergne on a commission basis and for policy shouted, "Long live Burgundy," La Trémoille watched the affairs of France and remained neutral.

Now, he had decided, was the time to intervene; and being well allied to each of the three parties, he chose the one of Charles as offering greater rewards and more frequent opportunities. Yet, so far, he had not committed himself. Instead he remained at Sully observing the world and entertaining with tactful skill a host of possible adherents.

Toward the end of the week in question, he came upon his guest, Gilles de Rais, seated comfortably upon a window-seat regarding through the open casement the doings in the stone-flagged courtyard below. Almost for the first time since the week of restless gaiety began, De Rais was alone save for a young and personable lady who shared his seat and tried with vain but pretty efforts to interest him in her charms and person.

Below him in the courtyard a circle of men-at-arms knelt or squatted on the flagging, watching, with a wealth of cries and gestures, two game-cocks giving mortal combat in the center of the ring. Watching the scuffling birds while evading the girl with proper and sufficient gallantry, so engaged De Rais that he did not hear the entrance of his host, and only turned slightly startled at the soft sound of the fat man's voice. At the approach of her master, the girl rose hastily, and modestly slipped away.

"Did I interrupt some pleasant dalliance, my boy?" purred La Trémoille.

"I was watching the cock fight," De Rais replied. "I was not interesting myself in the lady."

"Perhaps you were missing the greater pleasure."

De Rais was silent.

"You do not seem to care greatly for my little wards?"

"I find them, like all your possessions, my Lord, amazingly well selected and beautiful."

"But not stimulating, eh? You must allow me to apologize. In my almost senile state, I grow careless and forget that I am

apt to be unique. I should, of course, have inquired in advance
as to your tastes. In my youth, I knew a courtier who could
abide nothing but negresses—a most expensive taste, I assure
you. As for myself, I am easily pleased. Too easily, I sometimes fear. To be so is the death of all ambition."

"I wonder if you have the ambition after all?"

"Yes, my boy," the fat man assured him, "I have. But I
play my game slowly. Men are difficult toys to move about the
board. Despite their mean fiber and wretched surface, they
make excellent pawns. I enjoy playing with them, but for this
game my set is not as yet complete. Some of the pieces are
missing."

"Which ones?"

"Oh, the gaps are scattered; but before I make my initial
move, all must be on hand. Knights, castles, bishops and
pawns, even the two key pieces of the game. For I intend to
win."

"Who," asked De Rais, "will be your opponent?"

"The chair is empty at present, but doubtless some one will
occupy it. I shall place a large stake upon the table." La Trémoille regarded his cousin through puffy lids. "I am looking
for partners, not opponents," he said, "let us drop the analogy.
It is particularly inept."

"And hence, my cousin, the invitation."

"Exactly. I need a link. And I have selected you. You are
intelligent and honest. More than that, you have energy and,
I am given to understand, courage. As to your skill in war, I
know nothing beyond your pretty reputation gained in a nurs-
ery pageant, but I mean to find out."

"De Richemont will testify as to my ability," said De Rais
haughtily.

"Then you are interested?"

"Naturally."

"I will then put my case. I intend to place King Charles
upon the throne of France. I intend to drive out the English,
and I intend to grow rich in the process."

De Rais nodded. "The last sounds the most plausible," he announced. "As for me, I have thrown myself with Charles, and him I intend to serve loyally and to the utmost of capacity though in so doing I die in poverty. I have no other motive."

"Nor other loyalty?"

"In this matter, none."

"Then," said La Trémoille, "we can be friends. You are a man, and in this great struggle that lies before us, we shall be sadly in need of men. We face a war, my boy, that is vaster than any we have ever seen; for the nation of France shall be pitted against the nation of England, while Burgundy looks on from the side-lines, listening to the drooling mouths of minstrels. We shall see a fight to the death, and shall watch men drop again and again from the struggle. For, in my career, I shall be pitiless. Count your loyalty to France, and to me; for I alone shall rule. I shall be France."

De Rais listened to the voice of his cousin with astonishment. The ringing sincerity seemed absurdly out of place issuing from this obese, luxurious schemer. Yet the authority of his expression was without question.

"You amaze me, cousin," he said, "yet I believe that you mean what you say. I look forward to aiding you."

The fat man's eyes bored into his. "I shall hold you to your word," he said, "and I shall demand sacrifices. Not of gold or privileges, but of other loyalties, and my demands will be exacting. In return, a great place shall be yours. Gilles de Rais," he murmured, "Marshal of France. Who knows?"

§ 2

Under De Richemont's management, the war with the English was again progressing, despite the usual monetary embarrassments. And with the war, progressed also the career of Gilles de Rais. For a while he held a relatively unimportant command over a section of country lying between Maine and Anjou, for whose defense he had supplied a considerable portion of the defenders, raised in person from his various estates and secure in their allegiance, as he paid them from his own pocket not wishing dependence from the uncertain royal treasury.

Relieved from this command, he joined forces successively and collectively with the great professional captains, serving again with Beaumanoir and Loré, making the acquaintance of De Boussac and of LaFayette and even joining, for a time, the famous La Hire before the city of Montargis.

In the capture of La Lude, De Rais became a hero. In company of Beaumanoir he had stormed and bombarded this Anjou fortress until the walls were almost crumbling. Despite the strength of the attack, it still held out. Blackburn, the English commander, was stubborn or expected aid from up the Loire.

At last, however, it was taken. Against a weakened stretch of rampart, the troops of De Rais made a sudden and determined attack. With a rush and a cry of victory, they carried their ladders to the city and pressed them against the defenses. In the face of a flight of stones and arrows, De Rais himself sprang upon the rungs of the first ladder and ran furiously toward the top. Above the ramparts, the redoubtable Blackburn appeared, ready to strike down the first of the besiegers. But at the top, De Rais ducked and leaped clear, on to the wall. His drawn sword caught the Englishman a slashing blow, and he fell quickly, his head nearly severed, into the ditch below. His companions drew back in startled horror, and in that instant the followers of De Rais were upon the walls and the city was taken.

At Court, La Trémoille had completed his chessmen and had begun his game. Camus de Beaulieu, Grand Chamberlain to the King, became, at last, unsufferable, and by joint action of Yolande, De Richemont and La Trémoille was gently deposed. So gently that no one save his friend, the King, was in the least upset by his passing. It was admirably managed.

The wary Camus was, on one fine afternoon, riding his mule

along the river barely out of sight of the castle itself. Suddenly and quite without warning, he was set upon by a half-dozen masked riders. Screaming and fighting he was dragged from his mule and utterly destroyed. So complete, in fact, was his demolition that his mortal remains, unable longer to ride the mule even after the fashion of a sack of meal, had to be scooped up by his servants and brought home in a closely woven basket. So much for Camus.

With his demise, the administration of the kingdom was given as had been expected to La Trémoille.

"I warn you against him," Charles said to De Richemont. "He is more dangerous than you think."

Once in power, La Trémoille well justified Charles'.premonitions. At once he assumed complete control, ordering about the generals, influencing the diplomacy and running the Court to suit himself. Somehow he enlisted the King, and assumed a complete supremacy over the royal mind. Above all, he played upon Charles' distrust of the Constable; for in that one point they both agreed. La Trémoille disliked the military; but where Charles was terrified, his minister was completely contemptuous and was, to Charles, magnificent in his courage. De Richemont himself held no terrors for La Trémoille who, without turning a hair, practically banished him from the royal presence.

In August, 1427, while De Rais and La Hire were busy raising the siege of Montargis, the Constable found it necessary to form a league consisting of himself, the Count of Clermont and Bernard d'Armagnac to oppose La Trémoille. With their army, they approached the King at Lusignan. Arriving before Chatellrault, they found, to their amazement, the gates shut against them, while from the walls the captain of the city read a royal proclamation, commanding them to depart for Normandy and remain a considerable distance from the royal presence.

De Richemont was furious, and half inclined to march to Lusignan, take it and destroy, in person, this creature that he had himself installed. But the thought of rebellion was distasteful, and he could not bring himself to war against his King. Instead he withdrew and signed later a truce with La Trémoille. But by his loyalty he lost a great position; for during the war to come he remained unpaid and ignored, completely in the background; while other men—men of La Trémoille's choosing—fought, commanded and reaped the glory. In this short space of time, the light of De Richemont, risen amid a burst of rockets, had burned ignominiously low, spluttered and practically gone out.

§ 3

The town of Rainfort was resisting the efforts of De Rais' forces. Under the tutelage of the professional soldiers, the young Baron was making excellent headway in the art of war. Occasionally they had met with defeat as in an expedition into the enemy's country, whereat they had been driven out again across the Loire. But in the main, they had been remarkably successful—more remarkable in that the other branches of the royal armies could barely hold their own. The reason lay, perhaps, in the experienced wisdom of Loré and of the professionals themselves. But De Rais also fought with a dash and a serious courage that contributed much. From the point of view of morale, he was most valuable, and his reputation was on the increase. His name had already begun to mean success. Ambrières, Château Malicorne, Montargis, La Lude (which was his great triumph) and the rest had become heralded as his personal victories. There was, therefore, a necessity that Rainfort fall.

This city was well defended by the English garrison, while the French within the town were most averse to surrender. With the English, too, served a company of French mercenaries, and these cared even less for the thought of a victory achieved by their besieging compatriots. Professionals in victory were never gentle with the capture that was given them to loot, but more

than that these mercenaries feared certain utterances of De
Rais concerning renegades, utterances which they were inclined
to take personally.

There had come into the camp in the unobtrusive fashion
that was always typical of his movements, the young priest,
cousin of De Rais, who during the summer campaign against
the Clisson fortress had been his tutor and companion.

In converse with De Rais, Gilles de Sillé showed himself
more priestly or, to be more exact, mystic than ever. He spoke
vaguely of hidden things, referring continually to some fount of
secret authority to which the non-cleric had no access. The
"we" with which he denoted the clergy seemed to bespeak a
powerful fraternal order enveloped in masks and in obscure
machinery, while in his discourse he spoke often of a vague
opposite designated by the word "they."

"They," De Rais gathered, were an enemy, hated and feared,
yet by no means despised, even perhaps to be flattered and encouraged. Sometimes they were dignified—De Sillé referring
to them as the "Other Faith." Eagerly the Baron listened to
the rambling and incoherent talk of his cousin, understanding
but about one-tenth, yet fascinated by the idea of secret and
opposing forces unknown by the world fighting each other in
darkness.

"We watch them with eternal vigilance," said De Sillé,
"marking their every move lest they circumvent us. For they
are, of course, wily and subversive."

"But, cousin," objected De Rais, "why not attack them
openly? Surely there should be no difficulty in that. Destroy
them once and for all, so that their menace may be removed."

De Sillé shrugged. Such tactics were abhorrent to his tor-
tuous mind. "We can not," he said. "For once warned, they
would withdraw themselves, seeming to disband only to sink
themselves deeper into their obscurity. Who knows by day
who they are?"

"It seems to me that they could be unmasked. Do you remember the night we came upon their revels in the forest by

Chantoceau? A group of peasants dancing by candle-light—
perhaps a score. Three knights could have destroyed the lot."
From memory De Rais spoke contemptuously.

"Do not forget goats, cousin. Goat sacrifice, goat-demon
and, under that wooden trestle, the goat-child doomed for propitiation. They who deal in death fear not men-at-arms. No
one has attacked a Sabbat and lived. There is greater power,
cousin, than the sword."

De Rais shuddered. "Old wives' tales," he muttered.

"None the less, even we who know our enemy are not
ashamed to fear. Men can die by unseen hands, watched by
their closest and dearest. Out of the darkness an unseen arrow
may pierce the heart leaving no visible mark, yet the body
blackens and falls suddenly to dust. Even in battle men have
died thus."

"Let them be burned. In so great a world, it seems needless
for a flock of carrion to live. Surely they can easily be rooted
out. A handful against the power of the Church."

De Sillé extended his arms. "You who live the simple life of
war can not be made to understand their strength. They are
the lords of madness and of death, leaping their shuddering
rhythm upon the mounds of uncut graves. Macabre dancing
with clacking finger-bones, whirling in obscene capers in the
moonlight—corpses living and corpses dead beating their palms
in clacking invitation. Dancers of death they are, flying through
the air, powerful and secret and unafraid."

De Rais stared at his cousin. "I have seen them," he said,
"and fainted at the sight."

His cousin dropped his voice to a whisper. "And I have
danced in their company. They are cold to the touch—cold as
death, yet lustful with the passions of ice."

"Why are you here, Gilles?" asked De Rais suddenly.

De Sillé became suddenly matter-of-fact. "I have been sent,"
he said, "upon my mission. I need say no more, but you
may understand the reason. Now I must go for affairs commence at midnight."

They rose and walked to the door of the tent. There the priest paused. "I dare not make the offer," he whispered, "but I walk slowly and am easily overtaken. A mask and cloak become, in the forest, a passport, while victory as well as death is often brewed within a witch's cauldron."

De Rais glared angrily at the priest. "Beware, Gilles," he said, "that you too do not succumb to Hell. I have not liked your talk. These are things that are unhealthy for men to see. God is above. Serve Him in honor and homage, and leave to Satan his own. Who are you, then, to meddle?"

The priest smiled secretly. "I am Gilles de Sillé," he murmured in answer, "of the diocese of St. Malo."

§ 4

Rainfort seemed to its burghers to be in a hopeless plight. Their appeals for succor remained unanswered, their food and water was running low, while without Beaumanoir, Loré and the terrible De Rais, who with his own hand had slain the Captain Blackburn, stormed the gates and were steadily demolishing the walls. Their fate was inevitable.

Conferences took place in the council chamber of the town hall. The governor and his magistrates held midnight meetings with the captain of the garrison, and in the end they decided to submit. Word was sent to the besiegers, certain provisions were insisted upon respecting life and property of the townsfolk, and Rainfort surrendered on terms.

Slowly the gates were swung open, and the attacking army rode sedately into the town. Before the church they halted filling the square with their bristling members. The chief magistrate read the terms of the surrender, which were accepted in a brief speech by De Rais. Other details were agreed upon, while the English garrison escaped in silence by back alleys and the postern.

Not so the French mercenaries, however. In the agreement they had not been mentioned, it being assumed that they were a part of the garrison. Instead these men were collected, herded together and brought before the commander.

"What do you want with them," Loré asked.

"Wait," De Rais replied. "You shall see."

In a huddled knot the terrified mercenaries waited. The next move they knew was coming from their captors. They had heard tales of the ferocity of this black-haired young commander: of his love of blood, of commands forbidding the taking of prisoners, of his executions sudden and swift of suspected traitors. Were they to be imprisoned, poor men that they were, and held for impossible ransom? Who would pay for them? Would they be flogged or branded for their defection? Yet they were only as other soldiers, fighting for whoever wished to hire them. Would their leaders be hung? And if so, who indeed were leaders? The English had recruited them and one man of their company was no better than another. Apprehensively they watched the figure of their captor, muttering among themselves, and waited.

Gilles de Rais moved his horse forward a step from the places of his colleagues and held up his hand for silence.

"Carrion!" he shouted to the cowering mercenaries. "You are without honor and without bowels. You are traitors to your King and traitors to your race. For you, there is no respect and no hope of pity. Nor will I have compassion. Dogs, serpents, murderers that you are, you shall pay the penalty of your disgrace! Let your names shout warning to your brethren, and let your deaths cry forth to heaven my stamp upon your treachery."

Loré kicked his horse and came up beside the Baron. "What are you doing!" he demanded sharply. "This is no abattoir."

"This is my affair, Loré. Allow me to proceed."

"I protest, De Rais, against this barbarity. There is no excuse for needless cruelty, nor can I, as a soldier of honor and reputation, countenance an action of this sort. Let them go. I add a personal plea for their behalf. I should be ashamed to be connected with the affair."

De Rais turned upon him. "You have nothing to do with this. I take these men upon my own responsibility and upon my faith in God, and I shall do with them as I see fit. They are, in the eyes of God, traitors. And the reward of treachery is death."

In the center of the square the gallows was already half set up; the hangman aided in his task by a score of willing soldiers.

Again De Rais turned toward the crowd.

"Regard these dogs!" he shouted. "Traitors they are and traitors they shall die. I alone, Gilles, Baron de Rais, condemn them."

A hushed murmur waved over the crowded square, and a cry of agonized terror leaped from the huddled prisoners.

"Death," said De Rais, through shut teeth, "let them die their death."

The gallows were up, and through a lane of archers the first of the doomed prisoners was dragged, struggling and crying for mercy, to the foot of the gibbet.

Behind the Baron, Loré spoke to Beaumanoir in a troubled voice. "Something revolts me in this," he said, "though, God witness, I have seen a plenitude of death."

"Needless," Beaumanoir returned, "unnecessarily cruel, but nothing will stop him. Regard his face."

De Rais was sitting facing the execution as man after man was hoisted, kicking and contorted upon the gallows. His face was white and set, terribly rigid, yet his lips were opened in a frozen grin. Curious too those thin nostrils distended outward like the nostrils of a panting race-horse. "Regard the face," whispered the simple Beaumanoir, "how evil it is!"

Loré turned his horse, and the two captains rode off in silence.

But in the square De Rais remained, watching with his fixed staring the rapid succession of deaths.

PART TWO

CHAPTER V

§ 1

THE city of Orléans marched in procession, led by the Bishop of the city, Jean de St. Michel, now holding the office in direct ecclesiastical descent from the blessed Euverte, who with his friend and successor, St. Aignan, were the patrons of the city. Behind the Bishop and behind his train of abbots and canons, who led the multitude of priests, novices, choristers, together with all and sundry who add by their multiform services to the glory of the Church, came the citizens and defenders of the city, marching in slow step to the sacred music of the psalms, chanted for the pleasure of God. So they marched in the hope that such devotion would appease and gratify the heavenly guardians of the city.

Leading the citizens, there marched Raoul de Gaucourt, Governor of the city, a little in advance of the twelve elected magistrates who, under his supervision, ruled and legislated upon municipal affairs. On the heels of these marched, in rich robes and furs, the nobles of the city, proudly secure in their wealth and prestige. Protected by gold against even so great a calamity as possible capture by the enemy (for their ransoms could be paid), they too joined, condescendingly, the rabble of burgesses, for the defense of their home. They were content to march, albeit haughtily, at the head of the ranks of the guilds, and after them came the artizans and mechanics grouped according to their trades: armorers, coopers, boatmen and tavern keepers, carpenters and other villains who in common cause took part in the great pleading for divine protection.

86

There came, also, the paid defenders: Guillaume de Chaumont; Jean and Poton de Xaintrailles, professional captains of great ability; Pierre de Chapelle; the Baron of La Beauce and Don Mathias of Aragon, surrounded by a host of other adventurers assembled in the city for its defense. Out of loyalty they had assembled, enlisted by the promises of gold for their services, of ample food and drink for their bellies and of pleasant entertainment, such as the Orléanais knew well how to give.

They had formed at the southern entrance of the city, at the double-towered gateway from which a stone bridge was thrown across the Loire to terminate in the twin towers that constituted the fort of The Turrets. From here they had wound their way, in a long procession, through narrow twisting streets overhung by dark houses of stone and timber, tramping carelessly upon the filth and mud that lay accumulated upon the broken cobbles. Occasionally an open sewer, coursing its malodorous way, caused them to separate sidewise letting it pass between the ranks. About the doorways and in the windows of the houses crowded a rabble of folk considered both by Church and guilds unworthy of so great a spectacle. Thieves and cutthroats jostled one another in the narrow casements of the houses of ill-fame, while in the roadway beggars and prostitutes pressed themselves against the walls to let the procession pass. Though they did not march, they too—the evil, the pauper, the witchwife and the depraved—sent with the fine procession their desperate hope and their tarnished prayers.

Leaving behind the crooked alleys and the wider streets and smaller squares of the city, the Bishop of Orléans led his train of followers into the large open plaza in the center of the town. This famous market-place for all of Orléanais and even for a part of adjacent Blésois was cleared of its long tables and stalls, emptied and swept clear for the ceremony.

Here before the holy bulk of the cathedral, the procession lost its threadlike character. Pouring from the mouth of a dark roadway, it bellied out, swelling to both sides and filling the square with its body.

While yet it came, distributing itself across the empty space and still issuing in steady stream from the opening at the far end, the Bishop and his suite ascended the steps of the church and stood there waiting and surveying the field of men below him.

They entered and the square was full. At a sign from the Bishop, they knelt upon the hard stone paving side by side, trusting to his guidance and joined with him in humble supplication to their intercessors. From the height of the cathedral porch he surveyed them with benediction, counting their numbers with his eye.

He saw the knights and archers glinting with polished steel; the fishermen, tanned and roughened by their trade; a pale knot of scriveners close by the illuminators of fine books; near them were the gold and silversmiths, whose fingers were stained and cut with tiny scars; there in the center knelt the butchers, brawny men in leathern aprons, while the princes and nobles crowded the steps dressed in velvets and costly furs. Among the crowd were monks of half a dozen orders, weighted by their heavy garb of black or gray or brown. There were nuns, occasionally, guarding little groups of children; there were teamsters and vintners and fellows of the University, whose heads were bowed in scholarly abstraction. And here and there, although the Bishop knew it not, were those who were not Christians: wizards and midwives and those who danced at midnight before the shrines of Hell.

Looking down from his high place, Jean de St. Michel beheld a sea of kneeling suppliants, bowed beneath a forest of banners and crosses, through which stood forth in glory the Cœurs de Lis of the city and Fleurs de Lis of the Orléans dukes.

Upon the steps of the cathedral, as their spokesman, he turned his face to heaven and delivered up their prayer.

§ 2

The cause for the long procession of the Orléanais was that after so many years of delay, the English had at last decided upon a definite and drastic step in the direction of victory. The great fortress of Orléans was the keystone of the Loire. In the hands of Charles VII, as it had so far been, it dominated the river and formed a bulwark against the English. For without it, no advance against the loyalist provinces was possible without running the serious risk of being cut off from the rear. In English possession, it would open the gateway to the south and would form, upon the north bank, a powerful base for operations against the lower towns. If Charles VII, the upstart of the south, was to be crushed at all, Orléans must first be taken.

In the summer of 1428, the Duke of Bedford returned to France with a new army and with large subsidies granted by the English Parliament. Heretofore, he had been oppressed by the continual wasting away of his armies through sickness and desertions, while the controversies at home between his brother, the Duke of Gloucester, and the Cardinal of Winchester had kept him very short of both men and cash. But now these matters were settled, and there was no longer need to remain entirely within his previous French boundaries.

Orléans itself was mightily perturbed. From Janville (to the northward), which the advancing English took on the fifth of September, came the customary heralds demanding surrender. The heralds were received, well entertained (which in time of war was a rather wise precaution) and politely refused submission. The English prepared to approach, and the Orléanais prepared their defenses.

And their defenses were strong. In their hearts, the burghers and citizenry felt little fear as to the outcome of the attack. After all, their fall meant the fall of Charles, and consequently no effort would be spared to relieve them. The city was massively walled and wherever stone parapets were lacking covered ones of wood were already erected. Over a score of small towers, not counting the huge corner donjons nor the massive gateways, were placed at intervals along the wall. Seventy cannon had been set up, including one at the postern tower that could hurl stone cannon-balls, weighing one hundred and twenty

pounds, clear across the river to the fort of The Turrets, which
guarded the stone bridge at its farther end.

It was almost certain that the English would attack from
the south, for otherwise, during the course of a long siege, they
would be constantly open to dangerous sorties from the garrison
within, but the south wall was the strongest of the defenses.

In thickness, the wall itself was about six feet, rising in parts
to a height of thirty-eight feet which was considerably higher
than at any point on the other three sides. It was defended also
by thirteen towers of a size varying from the enormous New
Tower at the eastern corner to a small postern half-way between it and the entrance of the bridge.

Along the river, the wall was equipped with a stone parapet
upon which cannon and mortars were mounted, and along
which archers and men-at-arms could parade, throwing down
scaling-ladders, attacking the besiegers with stones dropped
through convenient holes in the masonry, or shooting at them
with comparative safety through the narrow embrasures.

There was, however, a weak spot in this defense. In the very
middle of the wall there rose a huge double-towered gateway,
named the Porte du Pont, and from here there stretched across
the river a stone bridge lined at each side with a row of houses,
and resting upon nineteen large stone arches. The two towers
of the Porte du Pont were heavily guarded by massive doors
and by holes in the masonry through which boiling oil or heavy
stones could be dropped upon those who worked below. Across
the river, at the end of the double row of houses that crowded
the parapet of the bridge, rose the strong fort of The Turrets—
two towers built as continuations upward of the side buttresses
which supported the bridge below them. These small towers
were connected by a gallery of stone, below which gates and
portcullis also could be dropped, barring the bridge at its very
entrance.

Beyond The Turrets lay the suburb of Le Portereau, where
dwelt the colony of fishermen who plied their trade beneath
the arches of the bridge or tied their boats to the little islands

in the river near the New Tower; and from here issued out the long white road to the south.

Within, the city had become a veritable storehouse of defense; for the siege was by no means unexpected. An entire tower on the northern wall had become an overflowing arsenal stuffed to bursting with powder and cannon-balls, extra cross-bows and unfinished culverins, while in the shops and houses of the citizens were stored great quantities of corn and cattle and wine for the defenders. Vacant lofts became repositories for the accouterments of war, housing darts and arrows for the bowmen, lead for the making of bullets, shields of mortised wood and iron-pointed bolts for the powerful crossbows.

It was claimed that of food and gold and wine, there was already on hand sufficient to maintain an army of two thousand for the space of two entire years.

Accordingly, when messengers arrived at the gates with the news that the English were on their way from Janville, the information was received calmly. At once a company of men were sent across the bridge to pull down the houses, the church and monastery of Le Portereau so that no shelter should remain for the enemy.

The work was but three-quarters completed when, in the distance, the workmen saw the approaching dust cloud that betokened the arrival of the English. Fire was set to the remaining buildings and the company retreated past The Turrets across the long bridge and reentered the city through the massive gateway of Porte du Pont.

From the ramparts and towers, from the higher windows of the houses along the bridge, the inhabitants watched the great caravan move slowly across the flat country toward the ruins of Le Portereau. They came, these victors of Verneuil, with an invincible slowness that was methodically menacing. The great heroes of the Enemy were approaching: Thomas, Lord of Scales, Governor of Pontorson; Salisbury himself; William Glasdale; William Gethyn Baille of Evreux; Thomas Rampston, Bedford's Chamberlain; John Pole and his brother William. Veterans and able commanders were these men, known by name and reputation to all the watchers from the ramparts. With them they brought a host of soldiers and knights and of archers on horseback, while great ox-carts lumbered heavily in their midst, laden down with crossbows and muskets, fowling-pieces and large cannon. There were wagons of arrows and yet more wagons heavy with provisions and engines of war. With them they brought as well master gunners and master miners, cooks, carpenters and laborers and, less conspicuously to the watching Orléanais, a considerable number of women to act as spies and in other capacities. Barred by the fort of The Turrets, they halted and encamped among the ruins of Le Portereau.

On the third day of their visit, they set up their cannon upon a little eminence and began the bombardment of the city. Throughout the day citizens lived in terror; but at sunset when the bombardment ceased (the working day having finished) they counted the damage and found it anything but irreparable. The only casualty was an old woman who lived somewhere near the bridge. Unfortunately, she had been killed. Regarded in this light, the bombardment became a thing of little consequence. An old inhabitant of the northern quarter gently asserted that death was indeed much too mild a punishment for the rabble that lived by the Porte du Pont.

On the twenty-first, the English stormed The Turrets and were driven off to the satisfaction of the defenders. But the master miners were at work aided by their active apprentices, and two days later the attempt again was made. For four hours the defenders worked bravely, while from the city a bucket brigade of housewives carried out along the bridge an endless chain of pots filled with coals or boiling fat to be thrown upon the besiegers. In the evening the work of the miners was complete, and sorrowing, the defenders abandoned their fort and retreated toward the city. Retiring, they built a barricade across the bridge cutting two of the arches, one in front and one behind. The latter they bridged with removable planks.

On the twenty-fourth, a small child playing on the ramparts came upon a culverin whose gunner had deserted it momentarily in search of a glass of beer. With childish curiosity the infant touched the trigger and set off the bolt flying in the direction of The Turrets. It chanced that Salisbury himself, the Chief Commander of the English, was standing in this fort examining the city from a window. The bolt from the culverin struck, dislodging a bit of the window-frame which in turn, striking Salisbury in the eye, killed him.

The same day brought a further cause for rejoicing to the embattled burghers. There arrived toward late afternoon a large company of reenforcements under a brilliant command of officers. There came that day the Lord of Chaumont, the Marshal de Boussac, Jean de Bueil, Theauld de Valpergue, the able and terrible soldier La Hire and greatest of all, Lord Jean, Grand Chamberlain of France, the Bastard of Orléans, half-brother to their own Duke who was yet a prisoner to the English. And with them they brought eight hundred archers and a company of Lombards and Gascons.

Nevertheless, the siege continued. Unable to progress further, the English established a camp and waited. With the approach of winter, the supplies of the besiegers ran low, and leaving a garrison of five hundred men ensconced in The Turrets, the rest retired to Meung and Jargeau to find better shelter and to renew the organization that had been disrupted by the death of their commander. Meanwhile, the garrison within the city busied themselves with the destruction of the remaining suburbs, but curiously enough, they made no attempt to dislodge the five hundred men who were living quietly at the far end of the bridge.

On Christmas Day there was, of course, a truce, and there was sent from the city a troupe of singers to entertain the English who, being far from home, had no musicians of their own.

Five days later the bulk of English returned and commenced the siege in earnest. Yet despite the renewed bombardment and despite the erection at strategic points outside the walls of forts or bastions supposed to encircle the city within their grip, municipal life was not greatly affected. Convoys of food and arms came and went unhindered. In January, seventeen hundred wayward hogs entered through the gates without molestation, while the arrival of cattle, horses, sheep and fodder became an almost daily occurrence. In February, fifteen hundred reenforcements entered the already crowded city. The siege had become the subject of jests.

A monstrous cannon-ball had fallen in the very center of an outdoor dinner party, crashing upon the table and hopelessly destroying the crockery. But no one was hurt, and the roast had yet to be served. Another struck an octogenarian, tearing off the toe of his boot but leaving the ancient otherwise unharmed.

Master Jean, a culverin shooter, stood regularly upon the ramparts shouting defiance at the English until some one incautiously came within range, whereupon Master Jean let fire with deadly accuracy and with a roar of laughter. Sometimes he fell back, clutching at his heart as though he were shot, and thereupon caused himself to be carried off as dead along the ramparts. After a decent interval, he always reappeared, manning his culverin and laughing his loud laugh. Master Jean became a great hero of the taverns, and his joke, for all its thousand repetitions, grew funnier at each enactment.

In February, the farce grew tiresome, and those in command decided to deliver themselves from their feeble enemy. It was known that a convoy of food for the hungry besiegers was on its way from Paris. To intercept this, King Charles dispatched an army of troops from Auvergne under the young and elegant Count of Clermont. At Blois this youth was joined by the troops of John Stuart of Darnley and by the Viscount de Thouars.

From Orléans there went out to join them fifteen hundred veterans under the professional defenders of the city; that is, under William Stuart, Poton de Xaintrailles, Guillaume d'Albret, the Bastard of Orléans, the Marshal de Boussac and La

Hire. They were to meet Clermont's army of Auvergne farm-boys at Rouvray and to march from there upon the English convoy to destroy it. La Hire and the men from Orléans arrived on time, but the Auvergne and Bourbonais troops had not appeared.

It was the convoy instead that they saw approaching. Quickly word was sent to Clermont begging leave to attack and destroy the English, but the young courtier, not wishing to miss his first engagement, instructed them to wait; and the convoy forwarned, entrenched itself.

At this point, William Stuart lost patience and charged upon them with his three hundred men. It was an angry and futile gesture. He was routed and killed while Clermont's men were yet pillaging the cellars of Rouvray. The Bastard of Orléans now gathered what men he could and joined the attack, only to be wounded in the foot. Meanwhile, La Hire and Xaintrailles struggled to reassert order and stay the retreat. But once a flight is started, such a task becomes almost hopeless. La Hire, collecting about him fifty or sixty men, now fell upon a small detachment of English and thoroughly routed them. But his victory was too small to count. The French and Scotch were driven back to Rouvray, where Clermont, beholding at once the rout and the approaching English, gathered what troops he could and set forth in haste for Orléans, followed by the rest of the army in great confusion. Last of all, and carefully guarding the rear, La Hire and Xaintrailles rode in sullen silence with a few of their company, compactly preserving the great army from utter disruption by the pursuing English.

It was another great disaster, for confidence was again destroyed. Once more it had been demonstrated that the English were invincible, and that the power of France was as naught before them.

§ 3

The battle of Rouvray marked, it seemed, the end of all hope for the Orléanais. Of the great army of mighty defenders and

valiant soldiery that had marched from the city gate to subdue
a wagon train of Lenten fish, there had returned a routed rabble in whose midst a few discomforted nobles rode with bowed
heads, filled with recriminations against their companions. Of
the lot, only a few of the mercenaries, men like La Hire and
Xaintrailles, who as every one knew were anything but noble
commanders, could command respect. Even the noble Bastard,
his wounded foot swinging loose by his side, did not cut any
imposing figure.

The story in all its details had fled even faster than the retreating army of the realm of France, and the populace waited
in silence for the defeated heroes. A few cheers, feeble and sympathetic, greeted My Lord The Bastard and the Marshal de
Boussac, but the silence, cold and unforgiving, that greeted the
elegance of the returning Count of Clermont was icily insulting.

No banquets were prepared. No processions wormed their
way through narrow streets. No wine flowed freely and warmly
in the taverns that night. The quiet of the city became the
stillness of bereavement, as the defeated broke ranks and slunk
away to their quarters. From two low taverns down by the
Chesneau postern, there floated toward the square occasional
bursts of drunken revelry, evidences of the private celebrations
of La Hire and Xaintrailles who, though the city held its head
in silence, decided that they at least deserved a welcome and,
in their professional and independent way, took it for themselves.

The morning dawned with the cry of trumpets and the shuffling of marching feet. In the square before the cathedral, the
Count of Clermont, descendant of the Bourbons, was assembling
his army preparatory to his departure. There were no regrets
among the townsfolk, for no one wished to feed an army that
would not fight. In silence they watched as the troops took
order and, banners flying, marched for ever from the city.

But in the afternoon, a howl of protest rose from those same
citizens who had been so glad to see the last of the Auvergne
troops. For in the square more men were forming. La Hire and

the Admiral de Coulant were assembling two thousand men for the purpose of following the Count of Clermont. In answer to the cries of dismay, they assured the citizens that they would soon return and were merely setting forth on a quest for fresh supplies. But to the townsfolk, it seemed that already the rats were leaving.

Of the great commanders, only the Marshal de Boussac and My Lord The Bastard remained, assisted, of course, by a host of lesser men. It now became the turn of De Boussac, who, because of the death of his brother at Rouvray, thought it best to claim the vacated estates before they were snatched by some less worthy person. The excuse was valid and honest. Nor was there a possibility of doubting his promise to return. Nevertheless, the feelings of the Orléanais were not relieved.

The next to leave was Regnault de Chartres, Archbishop of Reims, whose proper place, as every one knew, was in the council of King Charles at Chinon. But with him, went Jean St. Michel, Bishop of the city of Orléans and official mediary with the heavenly powers whose assistance was so urgently needed.

The gloom of betrayal settled upon the city. What value remained of their elaborate preparations, of the powerful culverins along the walls, of the corn and wine and oil so carefully stored in the attics of the burghers? What need now, in their abandonment, of the gold to pay an army of two thousand? In sadness and despair, the people walked the streets, their heads bowed in defeat, rousing themselves only to voice an occasional shout for the wounded Bastard or old Raoul de Gaucourt, Governor of the city.

As a further omen, this brave and grizzled Governor fell from his horse upon a steep cobbled street and broke his arm. Together they rode sometimes, dismally prophetic, the Bastard's foot hanging idly from his stirrup and De Gaucourt nursing the useless arm that was pinned into a sling.

Through the fog of despair, there shot hysterical bolts of panic. Rumors of treachery spread like quick fires, to be extinguished with difficulty. Some one found a breach in the walls,

and the news flew from palace to tavern. The hinge of one of
the lesser gates suddenly rusted through, and imaginary marks
of the file were discovered.

In their depths of discouragement, an embassy was sent to
the Duke of Burgundy, offering a conditional surrender; provided that it was he and not the English who took possession.
The bravery of the early days had vanished, and even the bombardment became more terrible.

The English had become, in the excited imagination of the
citizens, no longer mere invaders of a foreign race, but fearful
and besieging demons—the tailed ones they were called—aided
by sorcery in their adventure.

From the hope of arms, the Orléanais turned toward supernatural speculations. "Repent, ye blasphemers!" cried the
priests. "Repent, ye proud of heart. Repent, ye sinners of the
land of France!"

Prayers were delivered to their patron saints, and the
churches blazed with candles. Religious processions crossed
and recrossed the city, while the priests grew rich with gold.

Among the fervent, praying folk, Gilles de Rais became conspicuous. Under the advice of La Trémoille, he had remained
in Orléans, dispatching continual messages to the fat Minister.
In the religious regeneration, he among others was doing his
part. In the churches his own mass was celebrated by his proper
priests and garnished for the greater honor of his Deity by the
lavish vestments and by the golden voices of his incomparable
choir.

The affair, in its tremendous gravity, had passed beyond the
power of the patrons saints. It was useless to invoke them. God,
Himself, must intervene, and to Him all prayers were offered. In
a way, it was unorthodox to make so direct an appeal, but to the
terrified penitents, the situation justified their rashness.

Yet, in the very darkest moment, a rumor so vague that it
could scarcely be given voice was moving within the city. Somehow an undercurrent of hope was stirring sluggishly beneath
the upper waters of discouragement. Hints of some new and

mysterious turning were carried almost wordlessly from mouth to mouth, spreading a revivifying contagion from priest to soldier, and from garrison to the guilds. God, it seemed, was about to change His mind.

Out of nowhere, unnoticed by the folk of Orléans, Gilles de Sillé, De Rais' priestly cousin, made his appearance, attaching himself unobtrusively, yet with a catlike smile, to one of the minor chapels. Here it was that De Rais discovered him.

"Be not discouraged," said De Sillé softly, "I have news for those who understand."

"For me, cousin?"

"I do not say, for I am not the messenger. My name must remain for ever hidden."

"I shall respect the confidence. What news?"

"The news is true and miraculous as is its verity. A savior is at hand."

"Why are you telling this to me, Cousin Gilles?"

"So that you, in turn, may tell others. Listen, there has been found a boy who is divine. He bleeds on holy days. You understand. On his feet and on his hands are marks of the nails, and in his side a wound opens at high mass."

De Rais gripped his cousin's arm. "By Our Lady," he cried. "It has come! Let us give our thanks to God!"

"Yes," said the priest absently, "it is an omen. But understand another thing. And this is not to be spoken. He comes not by the way of priests and bishops, but by another path."

And while De Rais wondered, De Sillé slipped away into the darkness of the sacristy.

"Another path?" mused De Rais. A similarity of phrase struck him. The "Other Faith"? But no, the boy bled on feast days. It was God, Himself, who had relented. Filled with renewed enthusiasm, De Rais hurried away to his usual conference with De Gaucourt and the Bastard of Orléans.

But despite the bleeding boy, the siege continued unabated. Lying rumors grew without foundation. Burgundy, it seemed, was about to send an overwhelming force to take the place by

storm; while Charles, the story announced, had given up and
had fled at last to Scotland. Other notables, and this was nearly
certain, were preparing to leave the foredoomed city to its fate.

Nevertheless, in the face of all these adverse rumors, convoys
of food continued to arrive, slipping past the English bastions
with consoling regularity, while already troops were returning
and adding strength to the growing garrison.

Upon the dim horizon, other saints appeared, surrounded by
a mass of vague and contradictory detail. There was, it seemed,
a mysterious Breton woman named for Saint Catherine, who
dealt in miracles. Another from the city of La Rochelle had
dreams of prophecy. About them and about the bleeding boy
there grew a maze of legend that was utterly unsubstantiated,
garbled and manifestly absurd. Yet largely it was believed. People solemnly quoted Merlin and the Venerable Bede in words
that they had never spoken.

In the very midst of these uncertain legends, there grew
another that was clear and credible. It did not differ greatly
from the reports of the woman of La Rochelle, nor from the
stories of the prophetic Breton, yet more easily it gained belief.
While Catherine and Pierronne appeared and prophesied, lost
in a jungle of obscurity, this new saint, this Jeanne of Lorraine,
without forecasting, stamped herself upon the minds of her adherents. The story was clear and remarkably insistent, nor did
it ever vary from its original form. While the others ceased
gradually to be novelties, Jeanne became to the Orléanais a
definite hope; and her cult grew.

She was, it was learned, yet in the duchy of Lorraine, deep in
prayer and in daily converse with the saints. How much more
comfortable a thought than the antics of the bleeding boy! In
everything the saints guided her, nor were the heavenly councilors left in anonymity. Saint Margaret, Saint Catherine and
Saint Michael attended her, and the choice seemed wise.

Three things she had promised with divine clarity. There
was in her words, at least a peg on which to hang one's hope. "I
shall deliver Orléans." Important, timely and wise. "I shall
rescue Duke Charles from the English." Noble, chivalrous and

right. "I shall cause the Dauphin to be anointed with the holy oil of St. Remy." Come to think of it, this was indeed needed. A matter-of-fact saint, agreed the Orléanais, understandable.

To Raoul de Gaucourt, Gilles de Rais spoke interestedly. "Is she not right after all to refer to our King as Dauphin? God knows that neither he nor the English boy whom our enemy have crowned as King have yet received divine sanction of the holy oil of Reims. This may well be our trouble—or part of it, at least."

"Consecrated king or feudal lord," replied the Governor, "our duty is the same. Loyalty needs no anointing."

"Nevertheless," put in My Lord The Bastard, "I wish the wench were here. Saint or hypocrite, she might put heart in these frightened burghers. Let the men think they follow a saint, and a saint it is who leads them."

In the cathedral, De Rais came again upon his cousin. The young priest was kneeling before the shrine of Saint Catherine, surrounded by a host of candles. His head was bowed and his body shook with an intensity of prayer. As De Rais passed, De Sillé rose from his devotions and stopped him. De Rais stared in amazement at the change that had come over the little cleric. Gone was the look of shy secretiveness with which he had spoken of the bleeding boy. Gone also was his jauntiness and care-free daring. His face was drawn and tortured, strained by a new fervor, intense and terrified. It was the face of one blinded by the sudden radiance of heaven and shaken to the depths of his soul by the revealment of the vision. Suddenly he had believed.

"Gilles," he said passionately, "believe my words, for I have had a revelation. God's hand has touched the earth and has left behind a saint. Praise God for His wisdom and beg His forgiveness. The day is at hand."

"Which saint, cousin?" asked De Rais. "There are so many."

"There is but one," said De Sillé. "I, too, have been misled. "Jeanne of Vaucoulours is God's anointed. The others are false."

"All others, cousin?"

De Sillé shook with a spasm of terror. "False, false!" he

cried. "All are false save Jeanne. Some are frauds of their own manufacture—some are creatures of the priests. And some are otherwise," he concluded harshly.

"Prophets of Satan?"

"Yes," whispered the priest, "prophets of Satan, endowed with deception and armed with terrible powers. Beware of these, Gilles, for they are dangerous. You and I know whence they come."

"What of the boy who bleeds?" demanded De Rais. Suspicion had already crossed his mind.

De Sillé stared intently at the pavement. "He sinned and must not be believed."

A sharpness came into De Rais' eyes. "Tell me," he demanded, "was he, too, of this company?"

The priest's face was white with fear. "Yes," he whispered. "God forgive me!"

At his lodgings De Rais discovered a messenger standing in the doorway by the head of his muddy and lathered horse.

"A letter, most noble Lord," he said, "from the gracious lord, my master."

The Baron dropped a piece of gold into the expectant palm and, taking the note, entered his lodgings.

As he emerged, the woman to whom the house belonged greeted him. She was a stout pleasant person whose husband was a well-to-do merchant of wines. She bowed reverently.

"Have you heard the news, my Lord?" she asked, fairly bursting with excitement. "The maid of Vaucoulours—she who is a saint, you know—this Jeanne of Lorraine (may her name be blessed) has at last been summoned to our King. Even now she is on her way to Chinon, and the news is all over the market-place. Every one is talking. They say that she has been truly called, and will lead the hosts for the deliverance of Orléans. I pray, my Lord, that it be so."

"I also," De Rais said quietly, "am going to Chinon. I have been sent for by the Court. Perhaps I shall see this maid. Who knows?"

CHAPTER VI

§ 1

WHEN Gilles de Rais entered the audience chamber of the castle of Chinon, he believed that he was prepared for almost any encounter. He was, nevertheless, in prospect of the meeting filled with a vague and unfamiliar nervousness. While no one knew, of course, just what to expect, the Lord of Champtocé had already encountered the saint by hearsay. Neither the mystic hopes of Gilles de Sillé nor again the utter skepticism of Georges de la Trémoille aided him in building a cohesive picture. A saint, a play-actor, a weeping and holy nun, a well-disguised satanist, all of these were possible conceptions, and unable to choose between them, he became uncomfortable and impatient.

The hall was well decorated with banners and hangings. Men-at-arms lined the wall, their palisade of polished lances glittering in the light of fifty flaring torches. In the center promenaded the flower of the realm, knights in Court dress or velvet or brocade touched with lacings of gold or edgings of fur above their tights and pointed shoes. Ecclesiastics, speculating mildly, trailed long robes of scarlet and purple. Ladies paraded mincingly in voluminous sweeping skirts, their bosoms cut low into their tight bodices, and their sleeves flowing. The armor of the soldiers sparkled with inlay of silver or of gold as they moved heavily about the field of blazing color. The ladies' head-dresses, often railed at by sensation-loving priests, were outrageously elaborate. Slanting cones of stiff material supported veils of gossamer fineness. Curious horns and rolls of cloth hid completely the locks of modest hair, leaving the faces prettily revealed. The "crowning glory" was reserved for the intimacy of the boudoir —even the eyebrows being plucked.

Across the chamber that was filled with the confusion of expectant voices, Gilles de Rais walked slowly, threading his way through the maze of gay brocades and sparkling jewels. Moving with deliberate elegance, pausing to bow to some acquaintance or to kiss the tips of perfumed fingers that were extended toward him, he presented a grave and elegant appearance. Dark and handsome, he was clad in magnificent black velvet, edged with sable. At his waist, a silver sword hilt was his only ornament.

At the end of the room, the King stood in the center of the largest and most elaborate group, a group arranged in the form of an uneven crescent. And it was toward this that Gilles de Rais directed his steps. Close to the royal person, he beheld Regnault de Chartres, resplendent in his ecclesiastical vestments. The Archbishop of Reims was talking idly with skeptical, deprecating gestures. By profession he dealt with spiritual things, and as a consequence he distrusted the unorthodoxy of a saint in flesh and blood. Beside him lounged the Count of Clermont, heir to the Duke of Bourbon, in white and almost foppish elegance. Raoul de Gaucourt, Governor of Orléans, waited solidly, self-conscious in the robes and badges of his position as Grand Master of the King's household. Near him, the blond Duke of Alençon conversed with inquisitive eagerness to De Rais' two cousins, Guy and André de Laval, prideful young men, not yet at home in the Court.

A special delegation had arrived from Orléans. My Lord The Bastard of Orléans was talking in low and earnest tones to its two ambassadors, Jamet du Tillay and Archambaud de Villars.

In the background, the bulky figure of Georges de la Trémoille presided with discreet aloofness. He had come to take no part— of this, his attitude was eloquent—but to watch, to observe and, if possible, to profit.

In their midst, Charles himself was extremely doubtful. In this matter he had been over-persuaded by his wife and mother-

Charles VII of France

in-law and thrust unwillingly into the responsibility of making a momentous decision. The saint had written that she could pick him out from among the crowd of courtiers, and to oblige her the King had not ascended his throne.

But upon his throne or off, Charles was hardly difficult to distinguish. His meager appearance was well known throughout the land, while his long nose and uncertain lip were the subjects of as many jests as were his curious unsteady underpinnings. Even to-day, clad in his best doublet (perfect, save for a space about the seams), he was not majestic. And despite his authenticity, he bore little resemblance to the lordly kings so familiar in the pageants and mysteries. His knees were never made for hose.

It was almost a tradition that saints appeared at intervals before the Kings of France, but legends were one thing, while a miracle in the castle hall is yet another; and Charles was nervous. Suppose she were a fraud that had been clever enough to foist herself upon him? Surely in that case she was clever enough to deceive him further. Suddenly the rashness of receiving a strange woman under so august circumstances appalled him. Perhaps she had been sent by the English to destroy him. Surely they were not above such tactics. It occurred to him that Lorraine was not a very loyal province, while Vaucouleurs itself had already surrendered on terms to the enemy even before her departure. It was indeed a diabolic opportunity for treachery; and in this light, it appeared impossible that the English had not seized upon it. The priests, who certified her, might easily be his enemies, for the clergy had always its own ends to serve. The business was, he saw, extremely dangerous. Watching the farther doorway, he unconsciously withdrew a step into the circle of courtiers as though to hide himself. "Let them decide," he said to himself. "I shall reserve decision, and if there is a mistake, for once I shall have the laugh."

Gilles de Rais was also staring at those closed portals and speculating upon the saint. Imagining her a witch, cold shivers attacked him. He shuddered at the power of these creatures;

merely being exposed to their presence one ran the risk of strange and horrible disorders should they not feel pleasantly disposed. Chills and fever were at their command, misfortune of all kinds, mysterious wasting away, the sudden loss of one's virility or a fluent eruption of boils.

An eagerness had attacked the Court, the chattering voices dropped to an expectant whisper while the doorway strained under the weight of their glances. None knew what to expect, all were prophesying. Old knights whispered warnings of sorcery among themselves in the matter of ancient cronies about a fire. Skeptics nudged one another at the credulity of the King. Others gossiped idly—and a few believed.

Four heralds stepped before the guarded portals, raised their silver trumpets and the Court stilled. Through the crowded chamber, the blast of announcement reverberated, and the doors swung open. There issued forth, clad in the regalia of Master of Ceremonies, the Count of Vendôme who, accompanied by a second blast upon the trumpets, introduced to the awaiting Court, the prophetess, Jeanne of Domremy.

In the back of its mind, the assembled Court had awaited a saint, whether real or false: A creature of at least divine appearance. Ethereal, they were sure, and clad in white, with hands delicately folded like the pictures in illuminated books. Not, perhaps, a winged angel stepped to life from an altarpiece, but certainly one of those gentle unsubstantial Flemish figures drooping softly in her swirls of drapery.

They received an odd shock. Behind the Count of Vendôme marched a solid, firmly built young woman who was clad in a man's breeches and jerkin. While by her side walked two knights of no distinction, dazzled by the brilliance of the spectacle. Except for a certain fullness of her figure, the saint might easily have been a handsome peasant lad, fresh from the fields of any one of their estates. Obviously she was real, and obviously she was honest and determined. Startled, the Court strove to readjust its values.

Her companions appeared ill at ease, but Jeanne did not.

Looking straight before her she marched the length of the room between the lines of eager courtiers, beat back by vicious batons of the efficient ushers, and stopped before the King.

Like all about him, Gilles de Rais was staring at her rudely. For a moment she stared back, then turned her eyes from him to the Duke of Alençon. But in that moment, an intimacy had been established. De Rais experienced a sudden and warm enthusiasm, and adopted this sturdy wench as his friend.

Before the King she bowed and stood looking at him with an appraising boldness, magnificently unconscious of the form and ceremony which she was overriding. Then, facing him, she addressed him as man to man.

She took off her cap and said:

"God send you long life, gentle Dauphin."

Charles was startled and asked her name. Her reply was equally direct.

"Fair Prince," she said, "my name is Jeanne, the wench. The King of Heaven speaks to you through me, saying that you shall be anointed and crowned at Reims and shall be Lieutenant to the King of Heaven who is King of France."

A strange greeting for this Jeanne to give the King. Where in her words was the meekness of the saints, or the proper craft of wizardry? Where, more, was the due humility of a well-trained peasant girl? Yet once spoken, it was inconceivable that the speech could have been otherwise.

De Rais studied her carefully as she stood so unabashed before the power of royalty. He felt that she was not ashamed before her King, nor could be ever so before God or man. To him it was a strength new to his experience. No words were needed to support it. Had she appeared naked before the Court, he felt she would not have been embarrassed. To everything she was oblivious, blinded by her purpose in life and by her mission.

Already she was talking of it, promising to raise the siege of Orléans and asking the King for troops to assist her. They had imagined, these fools, that she would deliver the city with prayers. How childish an idea it now appeared! In a world of fact, for the accomplishment of deeds such as this, arms were needed, and men, and above all courage. In the eyes of Jeanne, Gilles de Rais read this courage.

Faced by the girl, the King was hesitating stupidly as though he sought to evade her glance. Incredibly, he seemed in doubt about a self-evident fact. In disgust at his obtuseness, De Rais stepped forward automatically.

"I beg, your Majesty," he said, "most earnestly to heed this girl and to grant her what she requests." The enormity of his presumption startled him, but he was not sorry that he had spoken. In a voice, he was supported by his cousins, Guy and André de Laval and by the blond Duke of Alençon. Others muttered their approval, and suddenly My Lord Bastard added his voice.

"There is character in the wench, your Majesty," he said bluntly; "no harm to hear her."

Somehow Charles and the girl, Jeanne, had withdrawn a little, passing out of the hearing of the awaiting courtiers. No one knew whether or not she had actually taken his arm, but certain it was that they were talking earnestly and alone. Charles was listening with a puzzled look in his eyes, yet one saw that he was impressed. He spoke now as though asking her a momentous and very secret question, and to him she replied bravely, her head up in an assurance of confidence.

A hum of excitement had spread over the hall. Already opinions were being formed, and questions flew in all directions. My Lord Bastard was asserting his view to Raoul de Gaucourt, Queen Yolande whispered in delighted success into the ear of her daughter, while of the royal party, Regnault de Chartres was deprecating her in his best episcopal manner. Her hair, he said, was sinfully exposed; not that he would condemn her for this, saints being always allowed some latitude, but she appeared vulgar and bold-faced. For one, he would remain doubtful.

The King rejoined his company of advisers, a look of beaming contentment spread over his troubled countenance. "I have been relieved," he said, "of a secret and burdensome worry that

has always oppressed me. I am deeply grateful to this girl."
For a moment, Jeanne was talking to the Bastard. Then at
a word from him, she turned and again saluted the King. At
the far doorway the heralds raised once more their trumpets and
blew a silver blast.

Followed by her two shabby knights, Jeanne, her head high,
marched serenely down the hall through ranks of peering wondering nobles to the great doors which swung open to receive
her. Without turning she passed between them and disappeared
from view.

As the gathering of welcome disintegrated and filtered gradually out of the assembly hall toward other points of interest,
Gilles de Rais felt a hand upon his arm. Georges de la Trémoille was by his side regarding him pensively.

"Well, Gilles," he said, "now that it is over what do we have
in our hand—a nun, or a wizard?"

"We have seen a saint, cousin, as real a saint as ever breathed.
Of these folk we are apt to expect an incorporeal being, but as
they live, they, too, are flesh and blood."

"The perfect convert?" La Trémoille inquired.

"She is moved, I know, by a force we do not understand.
Something beyond herself impels her. But just what it is neither you nor I can say."

"I am inclined to agree. For I, too, am moved by higher
things. My loyalty, for instance, always impels me. Wherein,
then, do we differ?"

De Rais laughed. "Young Jeanne," he said, "is virginal by
reputation."

"Fair thrust," grinned La Trémoille. "Personally I was quite
impressed, though our friend the Archbishop was not. She has
strength, that girl."

"And courage in her eyes."

"H'm," said La Trémoille. "Would you call her pretty,
Gilles?"

De Rais was suddenly at a loss. "Why, I never noticed," he
said.

CHAPTER VII

§ 1

To MEET the doctors of the King's Parliament, the girl, Jeanne, journeyed from Chinon to the capital city of Poitiers and there took up her quarters. Yolande had opposed this move. The Queen of Sicily believed that her appearance before the assembled nobles in the hall of Chinon had sufficiently substantiated whatever claims the girl had made, and had established her definitely enough as the future savior of France.

But the Archbishop of Reims objected. On professional grounds, he gravely distrusted the girl's claims to heavenly guidance. Should sorcery be ever proved against her, he had no desire to be mixed up in the affair. To have approved a false prophet, would wreak incalculable damage on his episcopal reputation. Let her be proved honest by the Parliament, he advised. He himself would take no responsibility.

On the whole, King Charles sided with his mother-in-law. Nothing, he could take his oath, was evil in this girl. With direct simplicity she had guessed the basis of his secret self-distrust, and had answered it with intuitive understanding.

"You are the heir," she had told him while the courtiers waited in the hall at Chinon, "the true and only heir of France. Take heart, gentle Dauphin, for you shall regain your kingdom through my aid." And with her words a new confidence was born within him.

La Trémoille, always incalculable to his colleagues, suddenly supported the reactionary Archbishop, and Jeanne was sent to Poitiers. At her side, as official guardian and as special agent of La Trémoille, went Gilles de Rais, happy and contented in her presence.

110

If Gilles de Rais proved himself her friend, the Parliament of shabby excited doctors did not. For six long weeks she faced the daily questionings of these lawyer-clerics, while they minutely examined her on all phases of her sanctity. Day by day they plied her with questions, set baited and logical traps for her to fall into, and badgered her unmercifully.

Yet as the days went on, her reputation as a saint grew and increased. To her piety there was added now stories of her triumphs over the learned scholars of the Parliament. "I do not know A from B," she had admitted, yet the clarity of her pious answers had confounded her examiners. And in those weeks she became, to the anxiously awaiting world, a saint without question, and a saint in triumph.

A further test remained to complete her case. She must be proved indeed a virgin. Already she had been thoroughly and completely exorcised, having undergone this process at least a dozen times; but the possibility of a past contact with the devil must be absolutely disproved.

In concluding a piece of business with the satanic powers, no maiden could (owing to the innate lechery of the diabolic make-up) retain her virgin state against the power of the satanic importunities. So that, if Jeanne remained as yet intact, she was untouched by sorcery. This was the case as it was presented to the world, and an excellent case it was.

Of course, the Cathari sect, heretics that they were, were completely chaste. They believed, among other and lesser errors, that intercourse in any form became a sin. For this they were, of course, persecuted by all devout and righteous Christians, and often suffered burning for their chastity. But the Parliament, in its questionings, took care of all the heresies; and of this sin too, Jeanne was exonerated.

There remained now but the examination by the committee of instructed women while the Court of France and the beleaguered city of Orléans awaited eagerly the verdict. The commission, itself, was above suspicion of dishonesty, partiality or ignorance. Queen Yolande, herself, was its chief figure, while

her assistants, Jeanne de Preuilly, wife of the Governor of Orléans, and Jeanne de Mortemer, the eighteen-year-old bride of
Robert le Maçon, were almost equally distinguished.

On the day of the ceremony, the ladies visited the girl in the
privacy of her apartments, while in the corridor outside, her
official guardian, Gilles de Rais, waited impatiently for them to
emerge. While waiting, he wondered vaguely how even so experienced women as those who had accepted this task, could go
on oath concerning a fact so difficult to establish.

The possibility of Jeanne's failure in this last and final ordeal
appeared before him. Suppose that after all the Queen of Sicily
should discover the saint to be a fraud, or to be one of those
whose silver skirts peeped out below the black cloaks of dancing witchcraft. He shivered with delightful terror.

But the door of the examining chamber opened, and with
sweeping skirts the ladies emerged into the hallway. Something
struck De Rais about their manner. Standing together somewhere between his bench and the room they had just left, they
were whispering busily together. Somehow they lacked the solemnity that was due to so important an occasion, while young
Jeanne de Mortemer was actually giggling. De Rais felt outraged. What right had these to treat of saints with levity? They
were jesting in the face of God.

He rose from his bench and approached the group, bowing
with stiff ceremony.

"I beg your Majesty," he said respectfully, "to communicate
to me the long awaited answer to our question. I await with
difficult eagerness the result of your labor, and with impatience
the further proof of the sanctity of the maid."

Queen Yolande turned toward him from the group. Her face
was serious, yet her eyes smiled. "Have no fear, my friend,"
she assured him. "Our Jeanne is indeed a virgin. Of that, upon
my honor, there is no possibility of a doubt." And then, as
though admitting him to their secret she added, "She could certainly be nothing else—at least as yet."

The ladies bowed sedately, and arm in arm swept down the

long hall to where their coaches awaited, leaving the Baron where he stood.

With this verdict, the six-week trial came to an end, and Jeanne was discharged by the doctors of the Parliament. A full report was issued to the world, and therein it was announced that Jeanne, the maid, was found in all respects devout and honest, pious, devoid of false pride and a virgin. While, to be sure, nothing had appeared to convince them of divine responsibility, nevertheless the girl had promised to give a sign from Heaven before the town of Orléans. For this reason, it was the recommendation of the Parliament that she be given the opportunity she requested. In fine, the report was a complete and favorable recommendation.

§ 2

At Blois there had come together a force of men and leaders who were determined to march to the relief of the beleaguered city of Orléans. From that city, De Gaucourt, Ambroise Loré and the Admiral de Coulant had been sent, and at Blois they were welcomed by the delegation from the Court. Queen Yolande was very much on hand; the Duke of Alençon, blond and good-natured, had arrived from Chinon. Regnault de Chartres, the refractory Archbishop, had been persuaded to quit for a moment the Councils of the King. Even De Boussac, La Hire and Poton de Xaintrailles were included in the gathering.

Within the city there awaited the command to march, an army of seven thousand men together with an imposing quantity of supplies. There was a great volume of corn donated by the Queen of Sicily herself, there were steel and saltpeter, various arms and weapons, several wagon-loads of sulphur and a few hundred head of cattle. These were donations largely of the loyal towns and cities of the kingdom. For it was hoped that now began the last and final attempt to free the mighty fortress of Orlèans from the vicious band of half-starved besiegers who still clustered in their muddy, isolated bastions about the city's edges.

At the head of his army of Breton and Angevin troops, Gilles de Rais, handsome and majestic upon "Nutcracker," his great black horse, entered the city with the escort of the saint.

For the first time, Jeanne was wearing her suit of white (undecorated) armor, which had just been made for her at Tours. Over her cuirass, she wore a loose cloak open in front, which fell in graceful curves against her horse's flank. She carried no shield, but instead she held upright a banner such as all commanders used to employ before their lavish use by the rascally free captains had practically driven them out of fashion. This banner, however, was distinctly odd, unusual to say the least. It was made of a coarse, stiffened linen cloth upon one side of which was painted the image of God the Father, and upon the other, a silver dove sitting sedately upon a field of blue.

On her side hung the sword from the Church of St. Catherine de Fierbois, the existence of which had been revealed to her in a dream. Never, she had promised the priests who had sent it to her, should it be put to use. But even saints forget their promises; for, at a later day, when many things had already happened to the saint, it met its end, broken in anger across the rump of a miserable camp-fire harlot in the public square of St. Denis.

The Army was, in fact, an armed provision train, and for this reason the wise commanders had thought it best to run no unnecessary risks along the march. This was especially important, as the most valuable item of their cargo was the miraculous maid whose goodness and value had recently been vouched for by the learned doctors of the Parliament of Poitiers.

Now both Blois and Orléans lay on the northern bank of the River Loire, while between them, along this side, were the English garrisons at Beaugency and Meung. In this territory also, there was rumored to be a large English army sent to aid in the attack upon Orléans. The south bank, save for the English encampment in the ruined suburb of Le Portereau, was obviously safer and almost as direct. It was by this route, therefore, that the convoy planned to proceed. Arriving near Le Portereau, they planned to make a large circle inland and so avoid being fired upon by The Turrets. A few miles beyond the city there was a ford, and by this they could again cross the Loire, after loading the provisions upon barges sent from the city.

Slowly they rode from Blois, clattering across the wooden planking of the bridge into the flat plain beyond. About half the cargo was being taken, the rest being left behind for a second trip. There were, then, six hundred wagons of supplies to say nothing of cows and sheep and goats, which marched along in herds attended by their peasant drovers. The army of fighting men which surrounded them was almost as heterogeneous a herd as were the animals. There were soldiers of all breeds, from the well-equipped troops of De Rais to ragged town boys joined up from the taverns and street corners of Blois and Poitiers. There were also some priests of the Chapel of Champtocé and a company of monks belonging to the saint. These latter bore a banner she had given them, and as they marched, sang lustily to heaven.

In the forefront rode the saint, looking intently before her, a very symbol of the victory they desired. From time to time, De Rais, who rode beside her, regarded the girl curiously. In talking to La Trémoille, he had gilded upon his remembered image of her a nimbus and a glow of saintly light. Even at Poitiers, she had been to him miraculous—so fluent were the stories of her triumphs and divine, though innocent wisdom. But here in the sunlight, that silly vision vanished. Riding easily beside him, she seemed as much a part of the conventional army as was the profane La Hire. A pleasant, clean-looking country wench, she resembled very much any young lad of good estate newly commencing his career of war.

Gilles de Rais was twenty-four, and Jeanne was seventeen. They talked easily as the convoy rolled and clattered behind them, discussing the countryside, their native provinces and the war upon which they were engaged. He was not surprised that she knew little about maneuvers and military tricks, her one idea being to locate the enemy and give him battle. This was,

De Rais knew, not considered in the best of taste by expert commanders, but he preferred this method. But as for sieges she was as ignorant as a choir-boy.

"I shall raise the siege of Orléans," she said, whenever the question of strategy was mentioned. But when pressed for details, she evaded the question with a reference to her council of saints.

De Rais fell silent, a little annoyed by this confident claim; for the existence of this council was hard for him to swallow. His own belief was real, but on a plane far removed from the possibility of casual angelic conversations. The Heavenly Powers were approachable, he knew, but approachable through the psychic ecstasy of holy mass or through the subtle essence of the churchly music. They did not speak directly, yet this was what she claimed.

The day was warm and sunny, and riding in heavy armor, even at the slow pace of the convoy, was tiring. De Rais' head began to ache and his tongue was dry, but the girl beside him showed no signs of fatigue. Upon her upper lip only, De Rais discerned some tiny drops of perspiration.

"God's Throne!" he exclaimed fervently, "but I should enjoy a glass of beer; and not an inn in sight."

Jeanne turned in her saddle. "My Lord de Rais," she said sternly, "you must not take the name of God in vain. I command you to take back your words."

De Rais looked at her astonished. In her eyes, he saw a blaze of angry rebuke. It was indeed a command that she had uttered, and to calm her he retracted his unmeant over-emphasis. Jeanne, however, was started upon a sermon that was earnestness itself.

No achievement in this world, she told him, no slightest success was possible without the aid of God. In His hands reposed our lives and reposed our awful fates. To blaspheme, even lightly, was a sin against this kind and long-suffering Deity and an insult to His honor. From here she elaborated her view, growing eloquent in the sincerity of her belief. For its sins, her beloved country had been afflicted with the plague of the English, even as locusts had descended upon corrupt Egypt. The blasphemies of the army of France, its cruel looting of the holy places, its forgetting of the duties to the Church had brought down, at last, the righteous wrath of Heaven.

"I wish," she said, "to cleanse my men of sin, to purify their lives and to lead them into the forgiveness of confession. It is a part of my mission and a part very great indeed, for without grace we shall never prevail upon our enemy."

De Rais was impressed. He knew that she meant what she said, and that to her this phase might well be more important than the knowledge of the tricks of strategy. The sinfulness of France was widely admitted to have caused its downfall. What other reason was there? But like so many heretofore, he had considered these sins as national weaknesses, inherent and inescapable.

From theory, Jeanne became eminently practical. For her conversion she intended to commence with her men, these very soldiers of the convoy whom she already considered her own. From this purified and consequently invincible force as a nucleus, the task of purging the rest of the army could be prosecuted. Blasphemy, profanity and evil thoughts should be banished for ever from the chivalrous field. Repentance and contrition should come to all, and last of all, the trailing crowds of prostitutes should be removed that the flesh be not tempted. In the shadow of death, the soldier had need of grace. This was her hope for the delivery of France.

It was a mad and hopeless plan; one laughable in its impossibility had another person ventured it. But from the lips of Jeanne, it became logical and important, a worthy truth whose realization she could actually achieve. As she spoke, he felt again that surge of real enthusiasm that had at first sight attracted him. She knew as well as he the difficulty of her task, but was not one jot deterred.

They camped that night in the fields by starlight. At the maid's command, mass was performed and was attended by the soldiers. Jeanne, herself, received communion and made a speech to her men, begging them to confess their sins—a curious time and a strange place for an appeal to righteousness. But as she spoke in her simple, direct language, understandable and understood by all, there was no laughing at a peasant girl, but a dawning belief and confidence in a saint.

On the twenty-eighth, the army passed the towers of Orléans, easily seen from across the river, and came up the Loire to call a halt a few miles beyond the city, while the wagons proceeded on two miles farther, to a spot well selected for the unloading. From Orléans, through the Burgundian gate on the east, the Lord Bastard of Orléans and certain of the captains left the city and, circling the wall and the Great New Tower that was washed by the river, took a boat and sailed up-stream to where De Rais, Ambroise Loré and the maid were waiting.

It was now decided that the troops which had accompanied the maid should return to Blois by the route they had taken for the purpose of bringing on a second trip the remainder of the supplies which it had seemed·wiser to leave behind. Jeanne was to enter Orléans through the Burgundian gate in company with the Bastard and Ambroise Loré.

Jeanne was upset. She felt that she was being ignored and treated cruelly by these high-handed commanders, and she refused to enter the city without her men. She had struggled over these, and she knew that for the most part they had all confessed. They were, moreover, her own troops, and they knew her. Within the city, at best there lay another force unrepentant and filled with sin, futile therefore in the face of the English. At the worst, there would be no army at all for her to command. If she deserted her own troops, she knew well that all her labor would have gone for naught. Human nature is refractory stuff and without her guidance the troops would only too surely relapse into sin. No. She was decided. If they went, so should she. In vain. My Lord Bastard pleaded with her, employing with all his skill his suave tongue and persuasive manner. He told her of the waiting Orléanais and begged her not to disappoint them. But after a while he left her unaffected.

In the end, it was Gilles de Rais who persuaded her. She felt that he had understood her plans and that in him she could well entrust the safety of the converts.

He, in turn, faithfully promised to continue her work of conversion. The mass was to be said regularly and confessions were to be encouraged. Of this phase he swore to take complete and interested control, and to return with his men as soon as possible. As an aid to his work, Jeanne sent with him her own confessor, Brother Pasquerel, in whom she had great confidence.

The army went into camp beside the anchored barges, while Jeanne, in company with the Bastard, the Marshal de Boussac and the unfortunate La Hire, crossed the Loire to spend the night in the little town of Checy upon the opposite shore. La Hire found the saint a most oppressive companion, for his vocabulary, though amazingly extensive, had been practised almost since infancy upon the field of battle. In this way, save for a few simple nouns, his language consisted simply of the finest collection of assorted oaths in the divided kingdom, his Lorraine and Dauphinois profanity being especially prized. After heroic, yet despairing, efforts to converse, he was forced by sheer lack of words to fall into silence. This painful quiescence must have shamed the girl a little; for she granted him her permission to swear at all times by his baton of office, and happy in this boon, La Hire was again able to complete his thoughts.

§ 3

True to his word, Gilles de Rais returned to Orléans with his army and the balance of the supplies, arriving above the city on the morning of the fourth of May. By the river he was supervising the unloading of the wagons and the restacking of the supplies upon the waiting barges. As before, these boats were intended to slip down-stream to the city unhindered, the only obstacle in their path being that of the wooden bastions of the English that lay between the loading-place and the Burgundian gate. This fort, however, was some distance from the river to the north, and hidden from it by the trees and bushes along the water's edge.

There was, therefore, every prospect of a safe voyage, as a dummy attack was already in progress against this St. Loup bastion while the other English outposts were too far away either to interfere with the barges or to give assistance to the garrison of St. Loup.

The trip from Blois had been tedious, and De Rais had been surprised by the fact that in the absence of the girl commander he had been thoroughly bored by the details of the march. Supposedly, he was fond of the profession of war for its own sake, but on a new examination he found it to be, in reality, a dreary business. In the excitement of battle, surrounded by the clamor of conflict and the shouts of the wounded and dying, he rose to a state of sublime contentment. And by the side of Jeanne, he shared her idealistic enthusiasm. Alone, at the slow head of the marching convoy, he was restless and discouraged.

From the city there issued forth My Lord Bastard of Orléans, De Boussac and La Hire. In their company, De Rais and his men returned and entered the city in time for their midday dinner, leaving the business of the barges to the competent under-officers.

My Lord Bastard was in excellent spirits. Like De Rais he was young—twenty-six in fact—and eagerly enjoying his meal. With a pleasant smile he turned to La Hire.

"I should like your opinion, Vignolles," he said, "about our pretty mascot. But be careful with your tongue, for De Rais here, is her staunch admirer."

"Certainly, I am," said the young Baron. "Who could fail to like her?"

"The English are not overfond of our saint," said De Boussac. "They call her bad names."

"Which is more than I may do," lamented La Hire. "The wench has made me forswear all my pretty phrases. By Saint Aignan's lung, I shall be unable to command. How in the name of Saint Ursula's virgins can I even order a charge? By the time

I have thought up a polite phrasing, the enemy will have fled."

"In compensation," consoled the Bastard, "your retreats may be equally retarted."

La Hire banged the table. "Blast my retreats," he bellowed. "I can run as well as any man. Do not forget that—tongue-tied or not."

My Lord Bastard rose from the table. "I am going to pay a visit to the wench," he said, "and to encourage her in her good work. Every day, I am told, she ascends the walls and calls upon Mollyns and Glasdale to surrender. Some day they may heed her."

"They called her a harlot yesterday," remarked De Boussac, "and threatened to burn her at the stake."

"What did she reply?" asked De Rais.

La Hire slapped his leg. "A good reply," he laughed. "She shouted back like a ninny, that she was no such thing, but a modest virgin and so certified by the Parliament of Poitiers."

"If nothing else," said the Bastard, "she has put heart into these sniveling Orléanais; and heaven knows that that alone is a valuable service." He looked about the room, counting the three commanders. "I shall expect you all before the St. Loup Bastion within an hour," he said and, bowing formally, quitted the room.

§ 4

The St. Loup Bastion lay some two miles and a half east of Orléans and formed, on this side, the sole blockade against the Burgundian, or Eastern Gateway. From St. Loup, also, the English maintained communications with Jargeau and the other forts of the upper Loire. In itself, the bastion was a strong wooden structure, set upon a little hill close by the ruins of a dismantled church, and surrounded by a ditch.

About this fort some fifteen hundred French soldiers were scattered in the flat surrounding fields, making feinting attacks, or firing their crossbows aimlessly. Within, a garrison of three hundred English, well protected by their stout fortification, replied with burst of bullets or arrows whenever a company of attackers came within range. Inside the bastion they were safe enough from such an attack as this, but it annoyed them that while they remained thus cooped up, the barges of provisions were passing close by in the sluggish current of the river just out of sight beyond the visible clump of trees along the bank.

For the French, the attack formed a most pleasant occupation for a warm spring afternoon. De Rais' Bretons had arrived but that morning and were, in consequence, still tired from their march. They were deployed in groups about the green plain while keeping, as a general rule, well out of bow-shot from the fort.

The attack was not intended to be a serious encounter, but rather a chance to stretch one's legs and to enjoy a little mild and gentle exercise. De Rais was sitting upon his horse somewhere in the rear watching the maneuvers with slight interest, while keeping his eye turned at frequent intervals toward the northernmost tower of the walls of Orléans, around which must come any reenforcements that the English might send from St. Laurent Camp at the other side of the city to relieve the bastion.

Near him on the grass a half-dozen men were sprawling lazily, withdrawn temporarily from the skirmish under the pretense of restringing their bows. One of them had taken off his shoe and was making ineffectual attempts to repair it. Out of the corner of his eye, the commander saw a bottle pass surreptitiously from one soldier to another. This was, of course, a minor infraction of the rules of war, but the men were Angevins from his own estates, and he blindly looked the other way. Had they been from Touraine, however, it might have gone badly with them, but to his own vassals he believed in allowing special favors.

The amateur cobbler was staring to the rear. With a sudden cry he sprang to his feet and ran hobbling across the stubble of field to the spot from which De Rais was regarding the battle.

Forgetting his military manner, the soldier clutched at his

master's bridal. "Messire Gilles!" he cried excitedly. "Look what comes, in Our Lady's name! There, see behind you—and riding at a gallop!"

De Rais turned in his saddle to look where the peasant pointed. From behind the scattered field of combatants, coming directly from the city, he beheld a group of horsemen riding furiously in a cloud of dust out of the charred remains of the Burgundian suburb. There were, perhaps, a dozen of them; and the foremost was clad in new armor and was carrying a tall banner. Without a doubt, it was the saint.

"See, Messire Gilles," cried the half-shod one in a sort of triumph. "It is the holy maid, indeed!" And without awaiting a reply, he set off in a hopping run in her direction.

And now occurred a phenomenal thing. From all the great field, men were running in single lines converging at the point where already the girl was drawing rein. They seemed like filings moving upon an enormous sheet of green, attracted by an irresistible electromagnet. Men in the ditch before the bastion dropped their implements and ran. Men resting upon the grass sprang to their feet. Men in the act of winding their crossbows dropped them carelessly to earth; even the skirmishers reappeared from behind the fort. And all were running to the maid.

Jeanne had halted in the center of her little group of followers and was waving her preposterous standard slowly to and fro. About her, as he watched, Gilles de Rais saw the crowd of men-at-arms grow and swell with rapid accretion, gaining almost miraculously with each new addition, and becoming quickly a horde of milling eager soldiers, while the great field emptied itself as though the soldiers were being poured from its surface, leaving here and there oases of almost deserted commanders.

From the center of the crowd came now the blasts of a trumpet, and from his place De Rais beheld the girl, erect in her saddle, fervently exhorting them. He knew instinctively that this was a religious and not a military address, and wondered what would be her next move. Like a good captain, he waited where he was, gathering about him a body-guard of men, snatching at them by the command of his voice as they fled past him.

The multitude of soldiers opened a little, and through this aisle Jeanne rode slowly to their head, while they in turn fell into some sort of rude formation behind her. Slowly the re-formed army got under way and headed directly toward the bastion. There was no longer need to hold back; De Rais gave his command and set out to join her.

He came up just at the edge of the moat. Jeanne had halted for an instant, still waving her banner. "Now is the time," she cried in a clear voice. "Attack boldly and the bastion is ours!"

With a cry, the army surged into the ditch unmindful of the shower of arrows and bolts that fell upon them, stumbling over one another, slipping and scrambling down the steep walls. In another moment they were out swarming up the other side, fall-ing over one another in their haste. The skirmish had become a storm.

With a mighty crash the army hurled itself against the barri-caded portals, crushing all before them in the weight of their impact. From the massive doors they recoiled, thrust back by the very force of the encounter, only to charge again, breaking the doors inward with a splintering of heavy wood, and upon the fallen timbers, the Bretons and Angevins of the army entered the bastion, pushing, fighting and driving back the defenders. And in the thick sat the maid upon her horse, waving her ban-ner and shouting encouragement.

The bastion of St. Loup had fallen, and with it the whole at-tack of the English to the east of Orléans. That side was freed at last. To the north of the city, a company of English on their expedition of relief from the western camp of St. Laurent, halted before the Paris Gate. A thick cloud of smoke ascending in a column into the cloudless sky told them that their march was useless. What need now to fight their way through the troops of De Boussac, who had issued forth to intercept them. St. Loup had fallen, and they were cut off from their supply fort of Jargeau. The first step of raising the siege had been accom-plished.

The army of Orléans, now beyond doubt the army of Jeanne, was still engaged in finishing the day: For a few of the English had fled the blazing bastion and had hidden themselves in the half-ruined belfrey of the demolished church which lay close by. The task of dislodging them was tedious, but for the victors exceedingly pleasant. A huge fire was built in the base of the tower, while green branches were thrown upon it to give forth clouds of biting smoke. And the English, at last, descended.

Evening was falling when the victorious army returned in gay triumph to the city, bearing in the van their hundred prisoners, the sole survivors of the garrison. Among her troops the saint rode in silence, a look of great unhappiness upon her face. It had been her first day of fighting, and the sight of so much suffering had saddened her.

Before she left the field, Brother Pasquerel had heard her confession and given her his blessing and thereafter she had addressed her men, telling them to pray their thanks to God for granting them their victory, and begging them to confess their sins lest she abandon them for ever; yet despite the fulfillment of her duties to her mission, she felt distressed and melancholy —dazed in her heart now that it was over.

"I weep for them," she said to De Rais, "for they died, poor souls, unconfessed."

Upon her bed in the house of Jacques Boucher by the Renard Gate, she wept indeed; for even though she shut her eyes, she saw again, impossible to eradicate, the picture of a mass of men—sons and fathers—and lovers—lying upon the grass in death.

But while their saint was living again her day, praying in the darkness for the comforting presence of her heavenly council, the city, outside her fastened window, roared its celebration. Music and dancing and shouting in the public squares, great processions of beggars and merchants, drunken mercenaries and pretty barmaids, arm in arm swung through the streets singing and shouting and relating tall stories as they strode. The market-place swarmed with soldiers and citizens mad with joy. For hope was again restored.

In every section, the doors of the taverns stood wide, invitingly, while within beer and wine were poured out freely to the thirsty heroes. And among these celebrants of victory, these folk who loved the maid and were so thoroughly confessed, the harlots of the town and camp reaped a magnificent harvest.

By the south wall, built against the ramparts past which flowed the waters of the quiet Loire, the chapel of Notre Dame was silent and deserted. An ancient priest moved softly through the darkness, walking in gentle meditation and fingering his rosary. Before the shrines, a multitude of candles blazed, giving forth soft golden spheres of light isolated in the darkness and melting gently into the obscurity of the nave. Before the lighted shrine of the Blessed Virgin, knelt a figure in armor, his face, uplifted in the light of the tall tapers, glowing with an inward ecstasy.

Gilles de Rais was praying; for in the victory he had seen the sign Jeanne had promised and had at last believed.

CHAPTER VIII

§ 1

THE night of revelry was succeeded by the peace of Ascension Day. There was, of course, a truce; and for twenty-four hours the fighting was discontinued while the folk of Orléans attended their prayers and observances, or rested from the rigors of the night. Jeanne took off her armor as a sign.

But while the city was at rest, My Lord Bastard had called together a council of war to discuss the further prosecution of the campaign, and at the meeting the entire high command was represented. The Lord Bastard was full of hope and encouragement. Moreover, he had already worked out a plan.

"To-morrow," he announced, "we shall retake The Turrets."

De Graville nodded approvingly.

La Hire, the practical, grinned in derision. "With what?" he asked. "The town bands?"

"With our own knights," explained the Bastard, "and with the well-tried men-at-arms, that our friend De Rais and the rest of us have brought for the purpose."

It was Loré who interposed. "I do not wish to object," he said, "but being a man of low habits, I have many acquaintances among these crazy Orléanais. To them The Turrets is their own prize jewel, and they would no more allow us to take it for them than they would allow us to surrender their saint to the enemy. If we attack, they would follow us to a man."

La Hire sprang to his feet shouting: "If you think, any of you," he bellowed, "that I am going to attack any blasted fort, any double blasted bastion, or any unfortunate, God-forsaken, triple blasted earthwork with a pack of howling cobblers at my elbows, you are all crazy as hell."

127

My Lord Bastard smiled suavely. "Exactly my own sentiments," he said. "Like the rest of you, I too love the Orléanais
as though they were my brothers. I have, perhaps, an even
more personal and family interest, but also like you, I do not
like them around me when I am busy. Hence to make this attack, we must get rid of them. I propose that early in the morning we pack them off by the Renard Gate to the west with the
purpose of attacking the English camp of St. Laurent down the
river. When they are safely out of the way, we can go out by
East Gate, circle the New Tower and cross the river by the
islands. Then having gained the south bank we can come at
the far end of the bridge through the village of Le Portereau,
and so attack The Turrets in peace."

With this agreement reached, Jeanne was summoned to the
council and the plans were laid before her. She was not told at
first of the plan to take The Turrets; but suspecting—partly
from their manner and partly from the fact that on the day
before she had been kept in ignorance of the St. Loup attempt,
until she herself had found it out—that they again retained a
secret for themselves, she demanded full details, and the Bastard indulgently told her of their plan, adding, however, that
such an attempt was extremely unlikely unless The Turrets
were largely deserted by their garrison.

Even the best of councils are apt to err; and while the conference of captains discussed the strategy of war, the city
without their doors stirred with a new-born confidence. The
capture of St. Loup had revivified the hopes of the besieged. A
refreshed eagerness suffused the guilds and townsmen as they
chatted in little knots about the market square or paraded
boldly along the ramparts, telling and retelling the stories of
their glorious victory and magnifying the event beyond human
credence.

The towered gateway of the Porte du Pont became in some
way the center of interest, and its ramparts and parapet grew
black with people. From here and from the adjoining walls,
they looked down enviously upon the deserted roadway to the

bridge that stretched between the rows of slant-roofed houses which marked its edges. Near the end of this sadly empty lane, they saw the rival barricades separated by the gaping hole in the pavement where the arch between had been cut away. And farther on, past the chapel and past the mid-way tower of St. Antoine, they beheld in sadness the battered towers and the stone gallery of The Turrets.

Out of the vagueness of their feeling, a determination in the burghers' hearts articulated itself. Wordlessly the decision spread among the citizens. To-morrow they themselves, under the guidance of their saintly leader, would retake alone this coveted fort. They were tired of waiting for the knights and professional defenders to take action.

Some one looking down upon the city gave a cry of surprise, and the watching crowd rushed to the edge of the parapet to see what went on below.

The maid, without her armor, was descending the steep street that led to the ramparts and to the great gate which led through the Porte du Pont to the bridge itself. Slowly she made her way, accompanied by Brother Pasquerel, her confessor, and a small number of archers. Through the crowd she went and was hidden under the portcullis that was raised for her to pass. The gates themselves opened, and she emerged on the deserted alley of the bridge.

From the ramparts, the crowd beheld her clearly, walking with her followers down the length of the bridge. About the middle, she halted and took from Brother Pasquerel a letter to the English. It was her last demand, written in the name of the King of Heaven and signed by His agent, Jeanne. In it, she commanded her enemies to abandon their forts and to return to their native country.

Carefully she tied this letter to the shaft of an arrow, and caused it to be shot in the direction of several English who were sitting peacefully upon the bridge just beyond the broken arch. They watched the flight and, after the arrow fell, undid the missive and read it carefully. What they shouted in return

could not be heard upon the ramparts, but the watching throng
saw their saint turn sadly away and retrace her steps into the
town.

§ 2

The morning which followed the day of rest found old De
Gaucourt and a company of men-at-arms by the Burgundian
Gate in the eastern ramparts. According to the agreement between the leaders, the Governor was guarding this gate against
any of the townsfolk who might be so ill-advised as to wish to
go out. But the ill-advised were legion, and De Gaucourt was
having a difficult time.

Overnight, the hope of storming The Turrets had become an
overwhelming and universal resolve. About this gateway there
milled, therefore, a tumult of would-be conquerors. Townsfolk, armed to the teeth, arranged in their own companies of
defense, the local militia; even the non-military guilds were on
hand, filled with courage and with a determination to set forth
and capture their beloved citadel of The Turrets.

Finding their way barred at the very outset by their Governor, they became angry and turbulent. At any moment, they
threatened to sweep him and his handful of soldiers from their
path. Until this actual moment occurred, however, De Gaucourt
held his place and, in the face of the angry citizens, refused to
budge. Somewhat at a loss, the town bands sent for their saint
to advise them.

She came at last, surrounded by a body-guard of rabble, and
listened with earnest attention to the cause of their discomfiture.
As their leader, she at once took their part. There was no reason, to her mind, why the townsfolk should remain against their
wishes within the gates. In the eyes of God, these citizens of
her flock, whom she knew to be but freshly repentant of their
sins, were surely as wise as the captains who wished to control
them. They were, moreover, much nearer to a state of grace.

Faced by the opposition of Jeanne, De Gaucourt knew that

resistance was hopeless. Reversing his position, he offered to put himself at the head of the burghers, and followed by the emboldened citizens, he led them through the gateway, along the eastern rampart and around the circular base of the New Tower to the river.

Here, by a bridge of boats, they crossed to the islands in mid-stream. The pontoon bridge was now brought around and made to stretch from the Ile aux Toiles to the mainland of the opposite shore. Again they crossed the bridge, and marched down-stream to the wooden bastion of Les Augustins that guarded, upon the Le Portereau side, the entrance to the stone bridge and the fort of The Turrets.

Jeanne returned from the Burgundian Gate into the city to find the military commanders. The commanders, especially My Lord Bastard, were furious. Not only were the careful plans of the day before utterly destroyed, but the wretched citizens had gone out alone and without consulting them. Angrily the Bastard refused to interfere. Let them spear themselves upon the pikes of the English for all he cared. And the other captains agreed.

On the far side of the river, the town bands were disporting themselves much in the way that the scornful La Hire had anticipated. With wild whoops of bravado they charged the English earthworks before the Augustins bastion like a herd of buffalo, to be met with determined resistance and a discouraging cloud of arrows.

Whereupon, the valiant burghers gave vent to whoops of a different sort and fled howling to the river where their bridge of boats allowed them to cross again to the safety of the Ile aux Toiles. And here they remained in vast numbers, quaking with fear, while old De Gaucourt, on the mainland, held his ground with his handful of soldiers upon the top of a small hill.

It was early afternoon before Jeanne could persuade the grumbling La Hire to go with her to the aid of the embattled De Gaucourt. With La Hire's submission, the remaining commanders, a little shamefaced, consented to follow as soon as they could collect their men.

From his position on the hillside, De Gaucourt saw the girl, accompanied by La Hire, cross to the Ile aux Toiles, where she was received amid wild and enthusiastic acclaim. From here she led the Orléanais again across the floating bridge to the south bank. Once there, Jeanne and La Hire mounted their horses and charged upon the enemy.

Behind them came the townsfolk, refilled with confidence and fairly bursting with courage and daring. Again the English retreated to their earthworks and reopened their deadly fire. And again, despite the leadership of their saint, the townsfolk fled shrieking to the river. Alone with a few of his own men, La Hire pressed the attack while Jeanne, her white cloak flying in the wind, galloped madly back and forth between the English and the river, calling in vain upon the burghers to rally.

As she shouted and encouraged the refractory attackers, the banners of My Lord Bastard and of Gilles de Rais were seen appearing around the corner of the New Tower and approaching the river. With them, they brought their own troops and much of the artillery from the town. In good formation they crossed the river and, coming up to the earthworks, took charge of the attack. The earthworks were swiftly overrun, but already it had begun to grow dark and the Augustins bastion had yet to be taken. Although the troops were almost at its walls, a palisade of stakes yet barred their entrance. No one had as yet passed this, and as darkness always concluded the day's work, the fervor of the attack was already dwindling.

Jeanne and Gilles de Rais were in the front rank, working with a youthful enthusiasm to complete the capture of the wooden fort. Suddenly a shot from a culverin crashed square against the palisade tearing a great hole. Into this breach sprang two men-at-arms tearing at the sides of the aperture. Right behind them entered the girl and De Rais, calling for their men to follow. With a cry of triumph, Jeanne placed her banner against the wooden wall as a signal of victory, and surging past her, the attacking army entered the bastion.

Night fell while the men-at-arms were yet scouring the buildings of the adjacent ruined monastery, where like their compatriots of St. Loup, the remnants of the English had taken refuge.

The day was a partial success. The wooden fort had fallen; but beyond, The Turrets and the entrance of the stone bridge remained as secure in the hands of the enemy as ever. As nothing further could be accomplished in the darkness, it was necessary to wait for morning.

Early on the second day, the attack was resumed. The leaders came again from the city and took up their command and, deploying about the end of the bridge, the army seriously took up the work before them. From out of the field there came groups of hardy warriors who for a while attacked viciously the walls before them. Being at last repulsed, they retired among their fellows to watch with interest some new, though similar, company repeat their own efforts. For the most part the crowd of soldiery waited patiently, scattered about the field watching these would-be heroes, awaiting their own turn at the fortress or discharging a random shot in its general direction.

The storm resembled, more than anything else, a huge open-air fair at which various local strong men successively tried their strength, watched by their friends and neighbors, and each time failed to ring the gong.

At noon, with a blare of trumpets, the combatants retired for lunch, and the scene became a vast picnic in the open. Men-at-arms strutted about, their mouths full of fowl or joint, boasting thickly. Little groups lounged upon the grass mending broken straps of armor between bites. Some, exhausted by their efforts, slept upon their backs in the sunshine, while upon the near-by hillside a number of townsfolk were attending to the wounded, setting dislocated shoulders, treating wounds with hot oil and plasters of rough parchment upon which had been written proper spells or fragments from the Gospel of St. John, and generally making themselves useful.

Bugles blew furiously across the field and lazily the army rose and stretched its legs. Ho hum, it seemed to say, back to work.

From all parts of the hill, men were running easily down the slope toward the stone towers at the entrance of the bridge, carrying in their arms, their shields, their scaling ladders and all the various accouterments of their trade. With a rush, they came upon the stone defenses, Jeanne in her white armor at their head. Snatching up one of the ladders, she threw it with her own strength against the ramparts.

A volley of arrows greeted the renewed attack, falling like a cloudburst among them, while stones rolled down the straight walls and bounced off into the crowd of soldiers. In the thick of the bolts and bullets, the troops pushed on heedless of danger, leaping into the ditch and swarming up the other side like a wave of advancing ants.

Suddenly the wave stopped, spread sidewise and wavered in its rush. Among the startled soldiers a terrible thing had happened. In their midst, the maid was down. She had fallen backward into the ditch and lay there, in her white armor, sprawled awkwardly upon the ground. Worse than this, the crowd that grew around her, anxiously protective, saw projecting from her shoulder the naked shaft of an arrow.

With great care, they picked her up and carried her back, away from The Turrets, to the quiet hillside where the wounded were being tended. And as they carried her, she wept.

Throughout the long afternoon, the fight went on, stubbornly attacked and as stubbornly defended. Neither was the fortress taken, nor were the assailants driven off; and at sunset My Lord Bastard sounded the retreat. A good day's fight had been fought, and the men already were showing signs of fatigue.

But as My Lord Bastard rode slowly from the bridge back toward the hillside, he met Jeanne descending toward him, pale and shaken from her experience, but otherwise unharmed.

"Sunset," he greeted her; "time to stop until to-morrow."

Her face was set and a look of great determination showed in her eyes. "No," she said earnestly; "very soon we shall enter The Turrets, and to-night we shall return to Orléans by the bridge. Let us rest for a little and eat and drink; then attack once more and the fort will be ours."

My Lord Bastard shrugged and gave in. Already, like the rest of his forces, he had begun to believe in this determined mascot of his.

Jeanne mounted her horse and rode away up the hill toward the vineyards which had been untended since the siege began and were overgrown with weeds. Here she dismounted and, in the quiet of the late afternoon, gave herself up to prayer.

Returning, she found the attack again well under way, and in the forefront she beheld her banner waving encouragingly in the hands of some unseen soldier. As she reached the ditch, those in front had already mounted the farther bank and were at the walls. From above, the rain of arrows had dwindled by the shortage of ammunition to a feeble shower, while at the same time, though she did not know it, the army of De Boussac was already emerging from the Porte du Pont and advancing along the bridge from the city to attack The Turrets from the rear.

Upon the bank of the ditch, Jeanne raised a valiant shout. "Look to my standard," she cried. "When it touches the rampart, enter, for the place is ours."

Almost as she spoke, the banner nodded and struck against the wall. A new energy seemed to enter the attackers at the sound of her voice, and a sea of men, bristling with arms and waving a host of scaling ladders swept across the ditch and swarmed against the gates and ramparts.

From the walls of the city, the cannon and culverins were hurling great bullets of stone and lead upon the fort, while in the river a giant barge was anchored below the arches of the bridge. Upon this barge blazed a roaring fire, sending up cloud upon cloud of stinging, choking smoke. For upon the fire had been thrown a great mass of pitch and sulphur and garbage and old shoes. Blinded by the fumes filling the fort so that they could hardly see to defend themselves, and almost overcome by the hot stench that rose from below, the English, their faces still turned toward the army of the maid which had already entered The Turrets, retreated slowly out on the narrow alley of the bridge.

In good order they continued their retreat, crossing over the wooden planking that spanned the broken arches, only to find before them a new enemy. For directly in front, even as they crossed the temporary planking, they saw advancing the army of De Boussac newly issued from the Porte du Pont.

As they hesitated, the fire from the barge below leaped up and caught the planks of the temporary span across the broken arch. With a terrific rending, it splintered and broke in two, sending up a crashing shower of sparks. With its collapse, the rear-guard of the English, who were yet upon it, fell headlong through the cavity into the river below. Loaded with their heavy armor, they struggled briefly and sank to the bottom, Glasdale, the commander of the fort, among them.

Those left upon the bridge were fairly caught. Before them advanced De Boussac and his men, while behind yawned the great black hole of the broken arch. In the struggle that was for them hopeless from the outset, all were killed or taken prisoners.

The impossible had happened. At last The Turrets, fortress invincible that it was, had fallen to the Orléanais. And fallen— as all before its walls who had heard her cry of encouragement well knew—into the hands of Jeanne. The triumph was to her.

In the dark of the evening, the arches of the bridge were repaired; and by that path, the army returned in glory to the city.

§ 3

With the capture of The Turrets, the siege of Orléans was at an end. Brave as they were, the English of the bastions sprinkled about the walls and of the St. Laurent camp, had no desire for further defeats.

From the ramparts, the folk of Orléans watched the departure of the dreaded foe with joy and with a deep sense of gratitude. For to Jeanne, and Jeanne alone, belonged the credit for their deliverance. Although they cheered and laughed and even wept with joy, there was also more than a touch of sadness, for with the attack, the defense, as well, was over and partings were in progress.

All the antagonism of their ordeal had ended with the capture of The Turrets, and one by one the captains, suddenly become old friends, were saying farewell and riding forth down the narrow streets to the gates of the city. La Hire had gone, cheered with mighty cheers as he led away his efficient company of grizzled veterans. Jeanne, their saint, was preparing to depart for Tours, summoned by the King. De Rais was on his way to the triple fortress of Chinon to confer there with Georges de la Trémoille.

Disbanded at last, the troops of the defending commanders were on their way home, traveling across the flat country of the Loire, each in the manner that suited him best. They marched alone or in little groups of similar destination, poor in pocket for all their gallant defense, yet immeasurably rich in their hearts of the glory of war and of the sweet reward of victory. Within them, too, reposed a wealth of stories of the fighting and of the white-clad girl who had led them to victory and to peace. Tales, these were, of miracles and simple valor destined to be told and repeated again and again, living on in the hearts of France long after the tired men who brought them had for ever ceased to be.

At Chinon, Gilles de Rais discovered his cousin to have grown. The face of the Chancellor was sterner and more determined, though his barrel of a body was increased in grossness. He greeted De Rais with pleasant cordiality, and seemed truly glad to see him.

"Your reputation, my cousin, comes before you," he said

kindly. "Overnight this affair has made you one of the great captains of the realm. And there is no question but that in due time your talents will be well rewarded."

"I have done my duty, cousin. Who could do less?"

"Who, after all, could do more? You have, I am told, indeed earned your laurels. I congratulate you."

A flush of deep pleasure overspread De Rais' face. "We have conquered, my Lord," he said, "by the grace of God."

"Perhaps," La Trémoille admitted. "Nevertheless, it is, rather, your advice that I seek concerning the next step. The war is by no means over, even though certain stupid folk have this idea."

"There is much to do," continued De Rais. "Charles, the Dauphin, remains uncrowned; and between Orléans and Reims remain untaken half a dozen powerful cities."

"She has made a deep impression, that girl," said La Trémoille, "even to your language. 'Dauphin' and 'crowned'; not king and anointed, as we at Court are apt to say. I have been talking of late with our friend the Bastard, and even now I am awaiting a visit from the holy Archbishop, whom for all his robes, I wish would catch the plague. Every one has his own idea so that in any case, the decision of procedure will be difficult."

"There is, my Lord, but one direct and natural course. Recollect the army and march boldly to Reims."

"There are difficulties."

"Of course. They must be surmounted."

"Naturally it is a noble plan, and one of great appeal to the people of France, newly awakened, I am informed, to courage. Let us consider it for a moment. It is Jeanne's idea, and she is at present our goddess. But remember that between here and the city of Reims, there lie, essential to be captured, the fortresses of Jargeau, Meung, Beaugency, Gien, Troyes and even Reims itself. There is also within this territory the great and unbeaten army of Sir John Fastolf lying in wait. Consider again the effect of one defeat, one failure before these hostile walls.

Again we are beaten, disheartened, pushed back below the Loire with nothing gained but a moment of triumph for us to remember. And one defeat along the march destroys as well that other hope and buoyant confidence, the maid herself. Even the English failed before the city of Orléans. Can we in our new enthusiasm, count surely upon Troyes and Jargeau and Reims?"

"Yes," said De Rais, "for the tide of victory has turned, and Jeanne herself shall lead us to success. Men who know her will follow her again even against the army of Fastolf."

"It is a hard decision, Gilles, and one that as yet I have been unable to arrive at. Caution is difficult for conquerors to understand. But I have seen many victories, and even more defeats."

De Rais was silent. What could La Trémoille know of saints?

"Another plan," mused the Chamberlain, "is to march into Normandy, for it is through this duchy that Bedford maintains his communications with his native land. It might be wiser to cut his blossoming at the root, nor is there an army of any size along the English road."

"It would be a sad disappointment to us," said De Rais, "for we have heard her say that the King shall be crowned at Reims, even as she said that she should deliver Orléans."

"Tell me, Gilles," asked La Trémoille with great seriousness, "how strong, really, is your confidence in this girl?"

"I have a great and a secure faith, my Lord. I have been with her on the field of battle, in the midst of victory, of retreat and of death. I have seen her fall and lie stricken with wounds upon the earth, and I have seen her rise, her face shining with a divine light, to lead us again to glory. She is not as you and I, nor is it within the power of our worldly minds to comprehend her. I believe in her, my Lord, with a great belief."

"She is, then, a saint," said La Trémoille simply. "You rather convince me."

"Indeed a saint, cousin, and one whom we as men of war

can comprehend, for she is also a brave girl, pure and humble and strangely human. The girl, Jeanne, is my friend; but there is also Jeanne, the saint, in whom I believe as I believe in God the Father, for I know with a secure knowledge that her strength is derived from Him. Never has she hesitated in her courage, nor ever abandoned what she set out to do. Let us do as she says, cousin, and place in her hands the fate of France, just as I and all who know her would willingly place our lives, our hopes and our very souls. Let us go to Reims and place our King upon the throne of France."

For a moment La Trémoille was silent. "A fine appeal, De Rais," he said softly. "I am impressed, cousin, more so than you realize, perhaps. One does not stand often in the presence of such true devotion. But you are not the world. Even among the captains, I have heard other and quite divergent views, while at Court—well, it is a difficult matter. Truly I am troubled; for among other things we are desperately poor. Orléans, even in victory, was not cheap, and for the moment I can not see where another crown can be raised."

"Let the King borrow," suggested De Rais naïvely. "There are rich men in the realm who can well supply whatever is needed."

La Trémoille smiled. "We have already borrowed, as you very well know," he said. "Queen Yolande has lent vast sums. I, myself, am almost beggared, while your own generosity has been more than strained. It is difficult to ask again; for neither you nor I can afford much more."

De Rais rose proudly. "Allow the maid to go her way," he said imperiously. "And I for one shall supply an army, though to do so I may have to mortgage my estates."

"I honor you, Gilles," said La Trémoille, "but I shall take you at your word. If I accept this dangerous risk I shall demand fulfillment of your promise and shall expect an army, freely donated, to take its place before Jargeau."

De Rais bowed and left the chamber, walking in an exalted mood. In this interview he had had a chance to put in words

the emotion that lay in his heart. If he had overstated his belief, he had also understated his feeling for the human girl.
More than to La Trémoille, he had articulated to himself his
own opinion and his essential verdict upon the maid.

Alone in his study, the Chamberlain took up a red account
book and idly opened it upon his knees. Leaning back in his
chair, he scanned pleasantly its lists of agreeable figures. Here,
in black and white, reposed the record of the sums he had so
generously advanced to the Treasury of the impoverished monarch, and opposite each item was written a date with annota-
tions of the interest charged. Herein, upon the pages of this
book, he beheld vast sums increasing and doubling themselves
with almost terrifying prolificness. A tapping on the outer
door announced the visit of My Lord Regnault de Chartres,
Archbishop-in-exile of the city of Reims. With a sigh, the Grand
Usurer of France put away his accounts.

CHAPTER IX

§ 1

REIMS, the goal, having at last opened its gates to the army of King Charles, prepared with reluctant excitement to witness and attend the spectacle of his coronation. As the heavy gates swung open, the tired waiting army of France and of the maid breathed a sigh of prayer and of relief. Here they knew was the fulfillment of their hopes and the compensation for a generation of defeat and humiliation. The dreary period of pain and exile was at an end, for success had laid its hand upon them.

Hither they had come from the country below the Loire, spurred on in hope and courage by the determination of the girl commander. Nor had their path been easy, for along this road they had traversed had lain the fortresses and armies of the English, ever powerful and ever filled with menace. But despite the dangers of the way they had arrived at last in triumph.

To their banners of victory had fallen Jargeau, taken by assault though stubbornly defended; Meung between Orléans and Blois; Beaugency, the near-by fortress, at whose assault the exiled De Richemont had suddenly and briefly lent his aid; and upon the heels of Beaugency, they had met, on emerging, the enemy upon the field at Patay. In the great and terrifying battle that ensued, the victory had been to France, and on that day there met with utter demolition the vast and terrible army of Fastolf, Talbot and the English.

From Patay they had marched to Gien and then Auxerre, light of heart and filled with boundless courage. Sweeping northward, the army of success had camped before the town of Troyes and had arrogantly demanded its surrender. Without

142

a struggle this city had given in, granting its submission and its loyalty to the King. To the northward Chalons also had offered no resistance; and in the end they came unchecked to Reims.

Jeanne was their commander, even the captains had long ceased to dispute her right, yet in the actual fray she had taken little part. At Patay she had been the inspiration, the mother and the saint, the generals had been the fountains of command; yet upon the march she was supreme, and by her wishes, the lives of war were lived. Blasphemy decreased, no harlots, squabbling viciously for a share of loot greater than they justly deserved, upset the balance of the baggage train. In their place were women, surely, but these were prophetesses and holy folk, self-appointed satellites or rivals to the maid. A company of monks and traveling priests kept pace, singing their psalms and carrying out the wishes of Jeanne in regard to mass and the frequent confessions of the troops.

As they marched through mile after mile of dangerous and once hostile country, there had emerged from towns and villages as they passed great crowds of simple folk eager to touch the hem of Jeanne's long cloak, and to beg humbly for her blessing. At first she had been pleased by this devotion but as the devotees increased in numbers and in frequency, she grew alarmed. For, to orthodoxy, these folk were dangerously adoring.

Once there had come out from the ruined hovels of a tattered village, a troop of aged women. None else came. Perhaps the village, ravaged by the war, was deserted save for these. In ragged garments they swarmed about the girl, hags of hideous age, snatching greedily at her robe, kissing it and holding it against their faces. A murmur of vague sounds whispered through toothless gums hung above the withered cluster. No one could understand their mad senility.

Something in the vision shocked De Rais. The contrast with his saint distressed him. He crossed himself and rode in silence long after they had disappeared. But Jeanne had no such feel-

ing. "Poor creatures," she had said, "I pity them." And then
she too guessed at more than age: "May God who is ever com-
passionate, have mercy on their souls."

Reims, too, admitted the army without a siege, watching them
curiously as they came, and recognizing the leaders as they entered. From the vantage places on the walls and ramparts, they
saw the competent De Boussac; Ambroise Loré; La Hire, the
terrible, swearing doggedly by his staff; the King himself, smiling with a renewed confidence; the Admiral de Coulant; My
Lord Bastard of Orléans, and Gilles, Baron de Rais, ecstatic,
upon his horse Nutcracker. In these campaigns he had become,
almost incomprehensibly, a curious visionary blinded to everything by a superhuman devotion to what he thought was
Jeanne.

They stood now at the end of their journey, a great concourse of gallantry within the shadows of the vast cathedral,
joined together in the mighty ceremony for the King, in whose
honor they had come. Here, gathered in the holy dusk of the
dim old church, were assembled the leaders of the cause of
Charles; the men and captains who had fought upon the field
in failure and in conquest, men who had fled in terrified retreat and had advanced triumphantly to victory. There stood
here, too, the statesmen of the Court who had aided in their
way, devising stratagems and treaties. Among the throng stood
ladies of the Court, whispering idly to one another, and elsewhere here and about, appeared a considerable sprinkling of
clerics, princes of the Church and theologians.

The morning sun poured through the windows of the apse in
a flood of jeweled light upon the altar, while from the great
rose windows and from the narrow ones high in the clerestory,
there descended upon ranks of patient nobles, standing row
upon row in silence down the nave, another heavy, rich and
supplementary illumination.

Behind the crossing and under the vaulting of the apse,
King Charles stood, his head bowed in proper reverence, awaiting his anointment. Close about him stood the pick of his com-

mand, and those as well whose names were great in France. Here were the Counts of Clermont and of Vendôme; My Lord Bastard of Orléans to become Count Dunois; the blond and vacant Duke of Alençon, who was to bestow upon his King the arms of knighthood; Guy and André de Laval who with their cousin had been the first to acclaim the saint; Jeanne herself, still in her undecorated armor, holding her standard in her hand.

To one side and a little withdrawn, the bulk of Georges de la Trémoille sweated in his lavish garments, watching the progress of the spectacle with narrow detached eyes. Near him four great men, signaled that day to special honors, waited, self-conscious and important. Upon them had descended, at the royal bidding, a vast distinction; for it had been left to them to journey to the Abbey of St. Remy and to bring back in their charge the crystal flask, the Ampulla, in which for centuries had reposed the holy oil that had once, long ago, been sent from Heaven to anoint the Kings of France. The four stood haughtily in silence, aware of their glory and justly proud. Nobles they were, these men and high commanders; but to-day, in the eyes of all, especially great. Four there were—four only: the Marshal de Boussac, Sire de Graville, the Admiral de Coulant and Gilles, Baron de Rais, richest noble of the Breton duchy.

But greater even than these, there stood behind the Archbishop of Reims, beside the altar, the bishops of Chalons, Laon, Seez and Orléans, ecclesiastical peers—for the moment—of the realm.

In his hands, the Archbishop held the crown provided for the ceremony, raising it with outstretched hands and giving it his blessing. From the brilliant crescent of the secular peers of the realm, Charles stepped forward and with dignity knelt upon a velvet cushion. Regnault de Chartres lowered the shining crown and, impressive in his gorgeous robes, pursued the ceremony of the solemn coronation.

For a moment all heads were lowered, while the Archbishop, with deep and ritualistic reverence, bowed over the kneeling figure of the King.

From the rear of the cathedral came the cry of silver trumpets as the heralds greeted the new-made King, and upon this joyful blast, a cheer roared out, shaking the very walls and piers of the great building. But through the noise of shouting, there poured from the organ and from the lusty choir the solemn rolling of the hymn of victory, and in this song the voices of the shouters melted, joining one by one its thundering music.

Through the surge of vibrant harmony, Jeanne alone was silent. Her standard trembled in her grip, and her eyes were filled with tears. Oblivious to the tumult that raged about her, she felt alone, filled with an overwhelming and frightening joy. To her saints, to Margaret and Catherine and to Saint Michael, she addressed her soul. For her happiness was due to them. They, it was, whose councils she had followed, and to them belonged this triumph. As the music of the hymn enfolded the girl in its ecstasy, she lifted up her inward voice and called upon them (as throughout her life she had always called) beseeching that they listen to her secret heart and heed with private ears her grateful and unspoken prayer.

But as Jeanne, her head lowered in humble reverence, prayed in silence, another woman surveyed the scene. Behind the semicircle of peers, Queen Yolande smiled a satisfied and happy smile. Here at Reims, she saw the fruition of the latest and greatest of her schemes. It was she, she knew, who had commenced the long and winding course. It was she indeed who had guided and directed at every turn—De Richemont; in a way, La Trémoille; Gilles de Rais; the Breton troops; the allies of the south; Clermont; Guy and André de Laval; Jeanne, this curious and doubtful saint; Charles, the anointed King— all of these were fragments of her planning and creatures of her vast imagination. The scheme was not yet ended, much in fact remained to be accomplished, but Reims was theirs, filled with glory and with promise of feasting and of wine. Rewards were at hand and rewards were merited; for a campaign was over, and to-morrow was another day.

With a pleasant satisfaction, the Queen looked back upon

the course that had been followed, a course that from her return from the south until the present moment of delirious song, she could regard with clarity and with completeness. It lay before her eyes, a beautiful and intricate pattern spread across the land of France. A pattern it was of scrolls and delicate design of leaves and branches miraculously intertwined, and garnished with a tree of lilies, while among its interlacings there dwelt, appropriate and decorative, a host of gargoyles and grotesques.

§ 2

Reims and the splendor of the coronation had marked indeed an ending of the phase of victory. Once more there had arisen the uncertainty of plan and the disheartening confusion of a thousand councils. About the person of the maid, had formed an eager and enthusiastic corps of ardent soldiers, committed to battles and to sieges; but in the Court, intrigue was again in favor.

There resulted a period of inconclusive marchings back and forth across the new-won northern country. Soissons, Château-Thierry, Crécy-en-Brie, Provins and Compiègne were occupied without the loss of blood. An English army had appeared, but had not been attacked, while through the ravaged country had marched the army, hungry and ill-fed, scouring the stripped cities for victuals and for plunder.

Restlessness and discontent spread throughout the army, and Jeanne herself became a little downcast. It was to protest this intolerable situation that Gilles de Rais made upon his cousin, Georges de la Trémoille, a visit.

In the Governor's palace at Compiègne, the young Baron found the all-powerful Chamberlain, become, since the coronation, a count of the realm.

"Come in, come in," said the fat man cordially, "and allow me to congratulate you. Since our last meeting you have been made, I am told, a Marshal of France."

"And you, a count of the realm, and our friend the Bastard

of Orléans, likewise a count, under the name of Dunois. But I can not see that we are in any way better off."

"No?" asked La Trémoille. "Why not. Is not glory its own reward?"

"I have come," said De Rais, "upon Jeanne's behalf, to protest against this policy of inaction."

"You have become a great partizan of this girl, Gilles," said La Trémoille, "which is in its way very fine. But you are forgetting that though she is perhaps the greatest of my pawns, it is I, George de la Trémoille, who plays the game. A fact, I may add, always valuable to keep in mind."

"So you once told me before I, too, began to play. I believed you then, but now I am no longer sure. It may well be that you also are a pawn, while it is the hand of God who plays."

"I am always interested in your views, Gilles, but I am surprised at a new quality in your tones. You are very peremptory to-day. Why?"

"Because I have brought an ultimatum. I am sick to death of this intrigue, of truces emptier of meaning than the promises of a serving wench, of delay while Normandy becomes consolidated by the English and Paris daily grows stronger to resist us. Since we have left Reims, what have we seen of glory? There has been compromise and treaty, pretended advancing and stupid retreat, and what has been the result? Nothing. Are we nearer Paris? No! Do we take Artois and Picardy though they would fall into our hands at the mere presence of an army on their frontiers? No again. What have we seen? An endless series of estates, counties, governorships lavishly bestowed upon the folk at Court as rewards for futile and unhappy plottings that have brought nothing save ridicule and dishonor upon us."

"You hint rather closely at me, cousin. Do you suspect me of riches?"

"Yes. Of riches and graft and of usury; nor do you dare deny the charge."

"I should not wish to. I have, I am proud to say, removed from the royal treasury more gold and lands than all of Louvet,

Giac and Du Chastel put together. But remember this, Gilles de Rais, I am worth it."

"While you have been so notably engaged," said De Rais severely, "I have mortgaged my estates and have served my King with loyalty as my sole reward. Nor has Jeanne received, for her pain and suffering, so much as the price of a horse in recognition."

"Do I hear envy, my friend?"

"Disgust."

"To me the sound is similar. There is a pretty estate in Bar and a barony in Maine. Both are vacant."

"I am not interested in bribes."

La Trémoille sighed. "Too bad," he said, "but then I might easily use them both. Perhaps it is just as well."

De Rais, by the window, turned suddenly toward the Chancellor. "What about Paris?" he demanded.

"There is a truce, as you know."

"Does it forbid attack?"

"It hints, my young friend, at surrender. Capture, if you will, by means of these talents of mine which you so foolishly despise. Capture as Chalons, Troyes, Reims, Soissons, Senlis and Compiègne were captured, by my wits and without the loss of blood. I am no fool, Gilles; and do not forget that more has been gained by honeyed words than with a thousand scaling-ladders."

"You refuse, then, to take action?"

"I refuse to be dictated to by my agents."

"Dare you refer to me, sir, as your agent?"

"Why not? You are. Keep your place, Gilles, and all will be well. I am not a good man to cross; and this I can promise you—I do not care for disobedience. As I once told you, I can watch with equanimity the casual dropping of the pawns from my board."

De Rais drew himself up angrily. "To-morrow," he said, "we shall leave Compiègne for St. Denis, and from that city begin our attack upon the walls of Paris."

"Is this mutiny at last?" asked the Chamberlain easily.

"If you wish," De Rais returned defiantly.

La Trémoille gave in easily. "Then good luck," he said genially. "We may even meet before the gates. I have already commenced a little treachery within the Paris fortifications."

De Rais paused at the door of the room, and the Chamberlain added a final word of parting. "By the way," he said amiably, "if you meet De Richemont on your travels, give him my regards. You remember who he was, do you not?"

§ 3

The march from Compiègne to Senlis and thence to St. Denis (which is almost at the gates of Paris) differed greatly from the long procession that had swept from Orléans in a tremendous crescent to the east of Paris, circling it with magnificent disdain, passing through Troyes and Chalons, to achieve its end in the coronation spectacle at Reims. It differed yet more strongly from that new and hopeful journey from Blois to the besieged city; that first gay convoy which had brought as a commodity, among the other provisions, courage for the tired citizens of Orléans.

The difference was one of spirit; for a reputation had been established, and reputation is a precious talent. Gone was the spontaneity of new and surprising victory, for success had become a habit. That Paris was ordained to fall, was already a settled fact, inevitable and expected.

Behind the girl commander, rode her old and trusted troops (many of them being of a privately paid army that Gilles de Rais supplied). These were her own personal soldiers, owing a singular devotion to the girl. Hers they had been, devoted and without question, since that first night when, under the stars by the Loire River, she had caused them to confess their sins and to make their peace with God.

But even these had changed with victory. From baffled country lads new to the pride of war, from rusty farmers and

From the *Froissart* of Louis de Bruges (Bibliothèque Nationale, Paris).

View of the Paris of De Rais' Time

from foolish townsfolk, they had become old campaigners, filled with the wisdom of experience, hardened by their service and arrogant in victory. From an unimportant convoy led and commanded by a country noble, they had grown to be the army of the maid, commanded by a saint and directed by a Marshal of France.

As a sign of this new sense of pride, it could be noted that despite their famous state of grace and condition of well advertised and chronic repentance, there had crept back, combatted by the saint herself as well as by her cohort of monks and holy women, those evidences of painted sin, the harlots of the camp.

Dignity had spread itself to the high command. Here we no longer found the bellowing good-hearted pirates of the road. The soldiers of fortune, La Hire, Ambroise Loré and Poton de Xaintrailles had gone for ever. Nobility of the highest rode in front. Jeanne was surrounded by a company of haughty princes, nobles in whose veins ran royal blood. There was the Count of Clermont, heir to the Dukes of Bourbon, proudfully forgetful of his cowardice at the battle of Rouvray; the Duke of Alençon, cousin to the King; René of Anjou, now Duke of Bar and brother to the wife of Charles, forsaking his books of hours and his dabbling in the art of paints for a brief experience in the company of a saint. Count Dunois, for all his left-hand claim to Orléans nobility, was semi-royal, while Guy and André de Laval, with their cousin, Gilles de Rais, were of the old and ducal Breton family. This was the council of the chief command, and Dunois, My Lord Bastard, was by virtue of his twenty-seven years the senior member. Over them, supreme in confidence, ruled the maid, approaching eighteen, keeping her own and private council with her saints.

From Senlis they descended, passing through the heavy forest to the town of St. Denis, in whose old church lay the bodies of the Kings of France, guarded over by the sacred Oriflamme, the banner of Saint Louis. In this church too, there reposed the head of Saint Denis, brought by its former owner from the gates of Paris. This saint, the patron of the Kings of France, had been beheaded when he was yet Bishop of Paris long ago, upon the martyrs' hill. Disliking this height, he had risen miraculously from the execution and, carrying his head before him in his hands, he descended the slope and walked to a proper place of burial at St. Denis. He was a very great saint indeed. So great, in fact, that there had appeared in Paris (presumably sent from Heaven) a duplicate and equally authentic head, to be held there in reverence for the veneration of the pious.

They entered St. Denis unhindered, the empty pavement echoing to their marching tread and to the clatter of their hoofbeats with hollow resonance. Through vacant streets and thoroughfares streamed the troops, and halted in the silent marketplace. A melancholy city lay about them, deserted by its inhabitants and stripped not only of its treasures, but of its very supplies and furnishings. From the darkness of a muddy alley, a dozen half-clad children emerged, a part of those thousands of homeless and forsaken ones that were so common a spectacle now in France. For a moment they stared dull-eyed from the shadows, watching the brilliant army of the maid; then suddenly frightened, they turned and made off in terror.

From the square, selected companies set forth to scour the shops and houses, searching out supplies and quarters for the men. In the whole of the empty city no people remained to greet them, save this tiny band of abandoned children and a few old people, isolated and moving aimlessly about, mumbling sadly to themselves, and searching in the vacant dwellings for forgotten scraps to eat or a few small sticks for their fires. It was a dreadful empty city, cloaked in the stillness of death.

An unease attacked the army. They were nervous and curiously distrustful. Firstly, they had come unblessed by royal authority, even, it was said, against the wishes of the King; and secondly, the aspect of the city was ill-omened.

From the entrance to a filthy alley, Gilles de Rais rode out into the public square. In the center of this bleak stone space he saw Jeanne on horseback conversing with the Count of Clermont. Automatically, De Rais drew rein. He had conceived a strong dislike for this elegant weakling, and did not care to enter his society. Wishing to talk to Jeanne, he waited, surveying casually the half-emptied market-place. The bulk of the army had gone to search out food and quarters, but a few remained, scattered in groups about the flat stone flagging.

Between him and the girl there stood a group of men close together talking secretly. In the heavy silence of the windless air, a laugh broke out among them. It died and was followed by a shrill and solitary peal of female mirth.

Of a sudden he saw Jeanne wheel about and pause, her back to the startled Clermont. Then leaning forward, she dug her spurs into her horse's flank. Out of the group that laughed there burst a woman of obvious ill-fame, running like a flushed rabbit across the paving. Down upon her rode the maid, shining in her polished armor. The knot of soldiers broke and scattered from her path, and before her ran the harlot, scurrying away in terror.

As he watched, tense with the interest of the chase, De Rais saw Jeanne draw from her velvet scabbard the miraculous sword from the votive Church of St. Catherine de Fierbois, which Jeanne had promised never to employ. Across the square ran the two flying figures, the harlot afoot and Jeanne upon her horse. Yard by yard the horse of Jeanne ate up the distance between them until they came together.

The fleeing harlot ducked her head, running desperately. But the saint was already upon her. With a whirl of shining steel the sword descended in a flashing arc. From the old façade of the carved cathedral there echoed back the impact, and the harlot reeled and fell upon the cobbles. A sharper cry of breaking steel shouted through the clatter, for the sword of blessed power was broken.

Jeanne, motionless upon her horse, regarded with amazement the broken hilt that remained grasped within her hand, while across the pavement danced the point, skipping and clattering foolishly.

The harlot, unharmed, picked herself up and limped away into the waiting darkness of a narrow alley mouth. Involuntarily De Rais crossed himself with fervor, and while the saint retraversed the square to where in its center the Count of Clermont waited, De Rais turned his horse and left the marketplace in silence. He had no wish to talk to her just then.

§ 4

With the arrival at St. Denis, skirmishing had begun almost at once. An easy march brought contingents of men from the army base to the walls and ramparts of Paris, and here they circled about in a desultory fashion exchanging pot shots with the townsfolk who paraded boldly among the parapets casting down a few arrows and stones while hurling a large volume of insulting language at the occasional attackers below. One could scarcely consider that Paris was in a state of siege, but as a precaution the city gates were naturally kept closed and well barricaded, while defenses were being rapidly repaired and kept in readiness for an attack.

Within the walls, city life went on much as usual. The prices of food quite naturally rose upon the ancient plea of wartime exigency, and those who trafficked in the necessities became, as is customary in war, very prosperous.

The change which had recently taken place from English to Burgundian rule was greatly approved. Philip of Burgundy was popular with the Parisians. He had a way of doing things in a grand manner that appealed to the honest burghers, and they liked and admired his handsome appearance, his almost royal dignity and his bursts of splendor. He was a fine prince to look at, and his authority was professional.

Yet even in Burgundian Paris, there existed a loyalist, or, as they secretly called themselves, a French, party, largely encouraged by devious means and supplied with the sinews of war, by the Court of King Charles. Especially were they the protégés of that monster of corruption, Georges de la Trémoille.

It was by necessity a secret party, moving quietly about the city, conversing in whispered promises and making here and there important converts. While Charles delayed and waited at Compiègne, it grew with quiet insistence and gathered strength. Even the parliament, always strongly of the Burgundian party, was touched with Armagnac gold. The flying wedge of La Trémoille's intrigue consisted of monks, especially of a chapter of Carmelites who had their monastery at Melun. One by one, these men filtered into the city and established themselves unobtrusively at strategic points within the town.

These monks and plotters counted largely upon utilizing the human symptom of panic—so powerful a force in time of stress —to induce into the citizens a paralyzing terror of the forces of King Charles, much as the Orléanais had been afflicted with a similar terror of the besieging English. By this means they hoped to be able when, at the proper moment, the gates were opened treacherously from within, to stampede the citizens into frightened and helpless confusion.

Under their direction, tales grew overnight of loyalist cruelty and ruthlessness. Old yarns of past pillagings and outrages that took place during the civil wars before the advent of the English when Paris had been menaced by the Gascons of Count Armagnac and by the Duke of Orléans were dug up. These stories were collected, reburnished and spread out before the citizenry. A report, apparently well substantiated, that King Charles had promised the city to the mercenaries in lieu of back pay, gained credence.

There was too—and of this the schemers made special point —a report that a sorceress without the walls, attired shamelessly in male clothing, achieved unnatural victories by means of a pact with Satan, while in her company traveled a troop of evil women and apostate monks well versed in sacrilege and magic. This was, thought the Carmelites, an excellent attack. For sorcery was a common thing, a horror that any burgher could understand. Involved and curious as the black art was, the basic principles are simple enough. The worship of God needs only to be inverted (somewhat as an object in a lens is inverted) to become in very fact the worship of Satan. In all his qualities and manifestations the devil (said the scholars) is the ape of God.

Jeanne's new confessor, a certain Friar Richard, had been, before his fall, a well-known figure in Paris. He had preached then with astonishing violence upon the subject of human vanity, of luxury in general and particularly against the immorality of feminine headgear. By the fury of his tirades, he had become notorious and popular, but now, seeing him beside the Armagnac witch, the Paris burghers nodded wisely and recognized the source of his inspiration.

At St. Denis, Jeanne's army grew impatient. Since July it had been held together and kept in readiness for war. Yet it had marched back and forth across Champagne and Ile de France receiving the submission of peaceful towns, avoiding hostile country and even retreating before an unseen English force which had happened to block its path. A restlessness was overtaking the entire corps which could hardly be allayed by the ineffectual skirmishing and pecking at the walls of Paris. It was time, the soldiers felt, for a blow to be struck. Once more it was demanded that their saint should lead them into victory. Their morale and her reputation demanded it.

Regularly to St. Denis came messages from the King, promising to come at once and join the maid in her attack as soon as this or that bit of business had been concluded. At length the negotiations with Philip of Burgundy were dropped. It was seen that Paris was his ace and that he had no intention of giving it up despite his pretenses and counter-propositions. Besides, the plotting of the Carmelites was nearly ripe.

In the very midst of the intermittent skirmishing about the city, the army of the King, marching in royal state, entered the town of St. Denis, and the decision was made to attack. For once, the visions of Jeanne and the cold strategy of La Trémoille were in agreement, and between them the day was set. This day decided upon equally by the plotting monks and by the saints of Heaven, fell upon the eighth of September which happened, curiously enough, to be the Day of the Nativity of the Virgin, a most ancient and holy festival. By the custom of wars, feast days were usually kept holy, and to fight on such a day as this seemed, to say the least, unprecedented.

Nevertheless, the great army set forth, ten thousand of them, under the leadership of the Count of Clermont, old De Gaucourt, the Duke of Alençon, the Marshal de Rais and De Boussac, and of Guy and André de Laval. With them, they carried all the necessities for a storm—mortars, cannon, culverins, scaling ladders, bundles of fagots, extra crossbows, food and drink and various other supplies.

The attempt was strangely ill-planned. Strictly speaking, it had not been planned at all. While awaiting the King, the skirmishers had circled the walls, practically without orders, merely pleasantly passing the time without the slightest attempt at proper reconnoitering. Nothing definite was known, in consequence, of the condition or even the geography of the fortifications. Jeanne in her exalted mood had scorned such mortal methods, while the young princes of blood royal knew nothing of details.

De Boussac, My Lord Bastard and the other practical soldiers were not relying upon success by force. It was impossible, they well knew, to capture Paris by assault, and for them two hopes remained: either success by means of the saint and the divine intervention of Providence, or capture by means of the treachery of the Carmelites and their other allies within. Beyond a sudden storming of the gates, therefore, no other plan had been prepared.

From St. Denis they marched to La Chappelle, and from here they moved upon the gates of Paris and halted behind a slight hill that rose between the St. Denis and St. Honoré Gates. On this rise of ground they established their artillery and opened fire upon the city—a fire that was returned at once, though rather feebly, by those defenders who were on the ramparts.

Between the artillery and the two near-by gateways of the city, there existed a double moat, separated by a narrow mound of grass. Of the two gates, that of St. Honoré was selected as being probably the easiest to attack. It opened in the wall between two small gate towers, and before it, on the narrow strip of grass between the city and the innermost moat was built a barricade of wood similar to those which had protected the bastions of Orléans.

Leading their army, Jeanne and the Marshal de Rais rode out lengthwise from behind the shelter of the hill. Behind them came the troops of Anjou and Brittany laden with fagots and scaling-ladders. Along the line of the outer ditch, men appeared as if from nowhere, pouring into the moat and emerging on the narrow mound before the second obstacle.

With a cry of dismay, they drew back suddenly and halted in perturbed bewilderment. To their surprise, the inner moat was filled to the top with deep, black, unpleasant-looking water. As they hesitated in uneasy confusion, there descended from the walls above a shower of deadly darts and arrows.

Upon the mound, Jeanne shouted at the defenders her demand that they surrender to her in the name of Heaven. From above, there came the usual reply of curses and missiles; and the storm began in earnest.

Fagots were brought and thrown carelessly into the water, but a slight current carried most of them away, and the moat remained unfilled, and as deep as ever. The artillery behind the eminence now commenced its bombardment, and gradually the fire from the walls slackened as the most of the defenders deserted their posts.

In the afternoon there came to the walls a vast crowd of citizens, newly armed; and poured down upon the besiegers a flood of arrows. Those below held their places, keeping up a desultory exchange of shots with the walls above, or throwing a few hopeful bundles of rubbish into the moat.

Upon the parapet, boldly exposed to view, a man appeared opposite the spot where Jeanne was standing. He became at once the target for a hundred archers as he stood there unconcerned and winding carefully an enormous crossbow. All at once he knelt, and fitting in his arrow, he took deliberate aim and fired.

From his hand his arrow flew, watched by the fascinated eyes of both the armies. Straight it came, well-aimed and true, and with a little metallic cry, it found its mark. Jeanne staggered, lost her balance and fell backward into the ditch.

Through the ensuing confusion, the Marshal de Rais rode furiously, while men-at-arms ducked from his path. The crowd about the fallen girl opened at his approach as he sprang from his horse.

"Back to your posts!" he shouted. "Leave the girl to me."

The wound was in her thigh, painful of course, but scarcely serious. De Rais propped her up comfortably against the escarpment so that she was safe from the arrows, yet at the same time near enough to give her commands. And here she remained with Gilles de Rais beside her throughout the day, while from time to time the other commanders came to visit her, bringing her cheering news of the progress they were making.

Yet though she continued to issue orders and to cry encouragements to her men, the moat was never filled nor was a bridge across it made.

"We shall enter this night in spite of everything," she told De Rais. Yet in this prophecy she was completely wrong.

Within the city the Carmelites and other hirelings were at their work.

"Flee for your lives!" a monk cried loudly, running down a narrow street.

"The Armagnacs have entered. Flee!" shouted another in a market-place.

A soldier on the ramparts suddenly threw down his arms. "Flee for your lives!" he yelled in mock terror. "The St. Honoré Gate has given way!"

"Flee, flee, all is lost. We are betrayed," echoed the Carmelites in a thousand strategic places. "Paris is in the hands of the enemy!"

In her ditch, Jeanne could not hear these cries, nor could De Rais, resting faithfully at her side, but in the camp behind the artillery, the noise was clearly audible to La Trémoille, who listened through the ears of spies.

Another noise followed at once upon the shouting of the Carmelites. A louder sound, stronger and more determined.

Through the city rang the counter-cry: "To the defense! St. Honoré holds! Down for ever with the Armagnac witch!" There were bursts of panic. A single street went mad with terror. A space of rampart was hurriedly deserted. But the bulk of Paris remained undisturbed, and the defense went on.

Treachery had failed, and from the camp behind the culverins there came the order for retreat. In the darkness the besiegers gave up the fight, and crawled back across the outer ditch to the safety of the field beyond. In tears and protestations, Jeanne, her miracle unaccomplished, was carried sadly away upon the shoulders of De Gaucourt.

The hopelessness of siege was manifest, and on the thirteenth of September, leaving behind him garrisons and governors for the country of the north, King Charles withdrew from St. Denis to Gien across the Loire, and there disbanded the army which he could no longer afford to pay. With him, by specific royal command, traveled Gilles de Rais; and Jeanne, herself, had promised to follow.

"Allow me, I beg of you, to remain with the girl," he had petitioned of La Trémoille; but the Chamberlain was obdurate. "You have shown yourself headstrong," he said. "I can not trust you in such unreliable company, nor must you disappoint the King."

Sadly he departed, threading his way through the city in a roundabout fashion. Though he did not admit the thought, he was searching for Jeanne, hoping that by some last vision she should destroy two pictures that were before his eyes. For he saw her now in these two pageants: standing, nonplussed, in the market square, her broken sword clutched firmly while, like a rat, a harlot ran unharmed into an alley; again, lying in tears across the shoulders of De Gaucourt as he bore her from the failure before the gates of Paris. Passionately he longed for a revision of his ideal. But Jeanne was not to be found to grant him the miracle that he craved. In discontent, he rode away in the train of his King, surrounded by an unpaid army.

And at St. Denis he left the maid for ever.

CHAPTER X

§ 1

WITH the disbanding of the royal forces, there scattered to the ends of France the bold company of knights and nobles who had fought in one another's company ever since the battle of The Turrets. Some returned to their homes. La Hire was already engaged upon the conduct of his trade, his corps of seasoned veterans seldom lacking an employment. Regnault de Chartres, rich in governorship, remained at Senlis. De Boussac, De Coulant, the Count of Clermont and Ambroise Loré were also in the north guarding the newly acquired territory.

Alençon was again in Brittany where he was planning a conquest of Normandy. For this purpose, he begged La Trémoille for the assistance of the saint, and was refused. Gilles de Rais had also asked for service with the girl, but the Lord Chamberlain saw in the possibility of this combination of Jeanne, Alençon and De Rais too great a force of will and popularity for his own safety.

From Mehun-sur-Yèvre (where seven years before had come a tired messenger from Paris announcing the death of the mad King Charles VI), La Trémoille sent out the news that he had other plans for Jeanne. She was destined, he announced, to aid D'Albret in an attempt upon St.-Pierre-le-Moûtier.

To De Rais' personal appeal, the Chamberlain was almost harsh in his refusal. "It is thought wiser," he said firmly, "that you and she be not together. In her company you disobeyed the wishes of the King in going before the gates of Paris. We do not wish the risk of any repetition of disloyalty."

De Rais stared at the Minister in angry silence.

"Furthermore," La Trémoille continued more confidentially,

161

"there are those at Court who, I regret to say, have linked your name with treason. I do not, of course, believe the charge, nor does His Majesty The King. Yet I suggest, and most sincerely, that a little quiet, such as a minor part in the curbing of the Constable, would do you no political harm."

Turning on his heel, De Rais went out, furious at what he saw as his reward for years of loyalty.

Nevertheless, he obeyed the recommendation which La Trémoille had made and buried himself through the rest of 1430 and all of 1431 in the minor, inclusive struggles that were taking place in France.

To his camp there came regularly the full accounts of the progress of the foreign war. Though he knew himself to be in exile, he accepted easily this period of waiting; for Jeanne herself was suffering a slight eclipse. A distressing amount of ill-fortune attended her. He heard of her success with D'Albret before St.-Pierre-le-Moûtier; of her disastrous rout before La Charité; of her wearisome marches and countermarches, her expeditions from Senlis to Compiègne; and of her futile sally in the hope of disrupting the Burgundian base at Pont l'Evêque.

Gradually the English were being driven out, but not by feats of arms. No longer did they flee in terror before the steel-clad saint. They seemed, rather, to slink away, starved by a lack of energy or by a dearth of gold.

For Jeanne also, he felt, this was a filling in of time wherein she waited the moment when again she should boldly raise her head and accomplish the remaining of her promises. And when, at length, she should expel the final company of English and bring about the rescue of the Duke of Orléans, then, as in the past, De Rais would be at hand.

To De Rais in banishment who had known her in her glory, the stories of her progress came as a dim unpleasant dream. He felt quite sure that like himself, she also was biding her time awaiting a new and more glorious emergence. And yet the accounts saddened him; for with each one, another check was added to her ever-growing list.

Since the day when, in the square of St. Denis, the sacred sword of Saint Catherine de Fierbois had been broken upon the miserable carcass of a fleeing camp follower, disappointment and compromise had attended the saint that he adored. Her year of war was one of slow and dull adventure—a year of battleless campaign, of gloryless victory and of miserable defeat. News came of a growing schism among her corps of monks and holy women; of shortages in money and in men; of supplies that were withheld and of opportunities that were not seized.

So remote had she become, that the news of her capture barely stirred him. He recognized it merely as a further prolongation of the nightmare. Of its vital reality, he believed nothing. Captures were part of the business of war, like defeats and wounds; and for the worthy, ransoms were easily paid. Pierronne, the prophetess, who had served with Jeanne, was already in the enemy's hands and was to be tried for witchcraft. But who would wish to ransom Pierronne?

Yet Jeanne, herself, remained unransomed. Nor was there any attempt made at rescue. This latter fact heartened him, for it indicated that La Trémoille was already negotiating for her release. Otherwise, a horde of men would already be bursting down the gates of Rouen. Nevertheless, the affair distressed him.

About this time, his camp was invaded by his cousin, Gilles de Sillé, who came catlike and smiling, unannounced, from nowhere. Upon his face was again that sly, secretive smile hinting at secret knowledge and of mysterious communications that he might be induced to make.

De Rais was glad to see him. The little priest was a friend out of the past and was, moreover, an excellent and unabashed companion. They talked endlessly of the wide-spread facets of the world they knew, and dipped often into the secret phases of which De Sillé was so fond.

"Tell me, Cousin de Sillé," De Rais once asked banteringly, "you who know so much can easily answer this question: Why do not our friends at Court pay up the ransom and let the maid go free? Surely they are not entirely impoverished."

"In such matters," confided the priest, "one does not move without advice."

"That is obvious enough, surely. I suppose you mean to tell me that La Trémoille has forgotten to remind the King of this very minor detail."

"It is the Chamberlain who is waiting for advisement."

De Rais laughed. "You do not know him," he said. "My cousin is more than apt to act alone. He follows no one's instructions, save where they agree with his."

"Yet in this case," said the priest, "the Chamberlain has asked permission to effect the rescue of the girl, and this permission has been refused."

"You young fool," burst out De Rais, "do you suppose that the King or even La Trémoille must be granted leave to rescue from the English one of our own generals?"

"Jeanne does not come within this case. It is doubtful whether she was purely of the military leadership. But, more important, is the fact that she is now awaiting trial."

"Every one knows what sort of trial! A mock tribunal held by bribed judges."

"Do not forget that whatever be the nature of the Court, it is not secular. Jeanne is a prisoner to the Church, accused of a very serious charge."

"There is, I know, a ridiculous and trumped-up accusation intended to raise the price of her ransom."

"The accusation is serious enough to demand the presence of the Bishop of Beauvais," said De Sillé, "and of the Vice-Inquisition of France."

"Nevertheless, the charge itself is nonsense; the wearing of armor—as though she could fight in petticoats; the stealing a horse from a thieving bishop—when she paid more than the brute was worth as I personally can swear; and the breaking the Sabbath—what rubbish!"

"The charge," said De Sillé soberly, "is sorcery."

"Even more groundless. My God, she is no more a sorceress than I am; nor could any one but a miserable bishop even consider so insane a notion."

"The English have always called her a witch," said De Sillé.

"So I have heard."

"And the English hold her prisoner."

"So they do. But they must prove a case, and I defy even you, cousin, with your fluent imagination to do that."

"I do not speak from imagination, cousin," said De Sillé. "I, too, am of the Church, and there are many episodes in the life of our little saint that are, to say the least, strange. In the light of these, there may well be wisdom in awaiting the outcome of the trial."

"Like all churchmen, you speak both wildly and with vagueness. I invite you to make your case."

"It is not mine, but the case of the Church itself."

"What is it then?"

"Would you like to hear?"

"Of course, if there is any sense to it."

"Very well then, cousin. Firstly, the country from which she comes enjoys an evil name for sorcery, and abounds in evil spirits and demons."

"What of that?"

"A certain tree near Domremy is sacred to these demons."

"Well?"

"It was near this tree that she first heard her voices."

"What rubbish!"

"She is accused of definite crimes. She attacked Paris on a feast day."

"So did many others."

"She stole a bishop's horse. She consented to the death of a prisoner of war at Lagny. His name was Franquet d'Arras."

"What of that?" burst out De Rais. "Who has not condemned a prisoner to death? It is no great offense."

"Thou shalt not kill," quoted De Sillé, "save in war, or in self-defense, or in quarrels, or in punishment for crimes or heresy, or for some other lawful reason. In addition she attempted to escape from the benign hands of the Church. Sacrilege," he asserted briefly.

"Is that all?"

"As a child, she disobeyed her parents, thereby violating a commandment. She wore male attire, which is counter to the teachings of the Church and she has performed false miracles."

"Go on."

"The miracles are well attested. A cup was lost and discovered by her by means of a revelation. In the same way, she discovered a priest living in concubinage, and she restored, at Lagny, a child to life."

"If miracles, then, are evidence of evil, why was not Saint Remy himself burned as a witch?"

"There are miracles both true and false. The Church maintains that Jeanne's are false."

"Does it deny Saint Catherine, Saint Margaret and Saint Michael?"

"It calls them Belial, Satan and Behemoth, and cites the fact that they have deceived the girl. They promised the delivery of Orléans."

"And she achieved it."

"And they promised the freeing of the Duke of Orléans. He is yet a prisoner. They promised the fall of Paris. It remained untaken. They promised Jeanne's rescue, and she remains a prisoner. There are other things that lead the Church to suspect that she is not devout. She has placed small crosses—symbols of Our Savior—on letters whose counsel she wished disregarded. She has, at her trial, refused to swear upon the Gospel, and more than that, she refused to repeat the Pater Noster in open court. It is thought that she wished the inviolable seal of the confessional in order to admit, in its safety, to the bishop that she was not of our faith. She has made no denial of this."

De Rais got up angrily. "Not a word or hint is true," he said. "Having known her well, I can swear to her piety, her devoutness and the pureness of her heart. More than that, the charge of sorcery is baseless; for she has been found and certified a virgin by Yolande of Anjou at Poitiers, and by the Duchess of Bedford during her captivity."

De Sillé shrugged. "Catherine Suave," he said, "was a false prophetess and was burned over thirteen years ago. She also came from Lorraine, and was a virgin. Do you not know that there is power in virginity that is not always holy? Scrofula may be cured by a virgin who keeps vigil at night naked upon her knees, repeating a ritual that is not of Christ?"

"The case is worthless as even you must know."

"Yet even La Trémoille must hesitate before it. You are, perhaps, too confident."

The Baron regarded his cousin sternly. "I have heard sufficient of this nonsense," he said. "Good night." Turning his back upon the priest, he left the tent.

For a while the priest remained where he sat. He had well remarked the change that had come over the face of his auditor, and he smiled to himself well pleased by the skill of his discourse.

§ 2

During the time that Jeanne Darc was undergoing trial in the English city of Rouen, and for a considerable period thereafter, Gilles de Rais continued in the pursuance of his inconspicuous campaigns, living the life of war without pleasure and without satisfaction.

At Court, King Charles continued his existence in the towns and castles of the Loire country, living an easy and reputedly pleasureful existence of wine and ladies, such as was fitting for a king when not engaged upon active service. He had left the war to take care of itself, and the progress was not at all unsatisfactory.

France was becoming a giant field of war traversed by marching unled bands. For where the knights and captains of the dying chivalry had failed, the degraded peasant and villager had taken hand. What need now for shining saints or brilliant nobles? No force could long persist before an angry nation. And France had been aroused.

More than Orléans, more than the triumph of the coronation, this had been the work of Jeanne. Enthusiasm had been awakened and, through her leadership, the peasants and the citizens had learned that they, as well as knights and nobles, could fight and play their part in war.

The ultimate course of these events was plain to Philip, the Burgundian. The English, he knew, had nothing more to give him, and it became only a matter of time before it would be wise to break for ever with the foreigner. On that day Duke Philip, demanding great rewards in lands and power, would gracefully withdraw from the English alliance and would allow King Charles to enter upon a much curtailed inheritance.

Toward the end of May of the year 1431, the messenger who traveled regularly between the headquarters of Gilles de Rais and the ecclesiastical court at Rouen, clattered into camp. His path had been lengthened by a long circuit which he had been forced to make in order to avoid a marching English army and several walled cities that had lain in his path. Though he was late, his news, he felt, was good, while the hardships of his journey should well merit the bonus of an extra crown.

Dismounting from his horse, he found his way through the camp to the headquarters of its commander. At the entrance, a man-at-arms lounged in casual guarding, his lance resting its butt upon the ground while its point leaned against the taut cloth of the tent. As they chatted amiably together, another man, a priest, approached, walking from the opposite direction. The newcomer saluted the sentry and spoke a few words of confidential command. The guard saluted and allowed him to pass, while barring again the entrance to the messenger.

Gilles de Rais looked up from a rough plan that he was studying and saw his cousin standing in the doorway.

"Come in," he said, "and tell me what brings you on so pleasant and so unexpected a visit."

De Sillé advanced to the table and seated himself comfortably beside it. "I have come to you," he said, "because I have some news to break."

"What sort of news?"

"That I will tell you later. Some days before my departure from the city of Rouen, I saw your messenger who at this moment stands outside your tent, quit that city with a story of the trial. Another messenger is already on his way, yet it seems better that you hear the truth from me, a relative, than from a vulgar man-at-arms. For this reason I traveled quickly, going direct by virtue of my garb, where messengers must be more roundabout."

"Tell me your story," said De Rais, "and I shall not listen to the soldier."

"It would be better to hear his tale. To it, my own may then be added as a complement or a conclusion."

"Do you conclude the tale?"

"Not quite, I fear. Call in the messenger."

The Baron signaled to the guardian, and the man was ushered in. Humbly he bowed before the Marshal, and began his report.

"I have come from Rouen, my Lord," he began.

"I am not surprised," commented De Rais. "Speak on."

The messenger became suddenly embarrassed and, in consequence, diverse. The journey had been long fraught with danger. Twice he had been forced to turn back, and once but narrowly escaped assassination.

"I fail to find interest in your private life," said De Rais sharply. "Give me your news quickly and begone."

"It concerns, my Lord, her who is on trial before the high ecclesiastical court of Rouen. The maid, Jeanne Darc."

In his precise, circumstantial manner, he gave forth the details of the trial, of the questionings and conferences between the churchmen and the girl, and came at last to the abjuration that was given her to sign.

De Rais had risen from his seat in excitement. "Tell me,

man," he shouted, "what did she do? Did she sign or no? Never mind details—tell me at once—did she sign?"

"Yes," said the messenger, "she signed."

"Thank God. And they let her go?"

The soldier looked down and hesitated. "No, my Lord," he said, "she has not been released. Instead she was condemned to the perpetual prison of the Church to eat there the bread of sorrow, and to drink the water of affliction, so that she may weep over her offenses and commit no others which may give her cause for further pain. Such is my report."

De Rais was silent until the messenger had left the tent. Then he turned to Gilles de Sillé, his face suffused with joy. "A victory," he breathed. "Who now will fear to work for her release? A thousand petitions will be dispatched to Rome, and in a year she will be free."

De Sillé, looking at his cousin, said: "Perhaps," but was not heard.

"So it has come at last," went on the Baron. "For she has won success before a hostile court. Throughout the length of this ordeal, I have sat paralyzed in spirit, and weighted down as by a night of fear. Even I, whom she has called her faithful and valorous companion, have been shaken in my faith. But now, once more, I can believe. It is, my cousin, as if the fear of death were lifted from my heart, and I can breathe again.

"For a year, I lived in dread, filled with a nameless terror at each advent of news. Willingly, and with gladness in my heart, would I have stormed the city where she was (as I have been begged to do by Alençon and by La Hire). Yet even they knew well of its futility. At an attempt at rescue, the English had promised to destroy her, while even a success could only mean escaping from the Church itself, a sacrilege into which she would not willingly be led.

"But now she will be free. Once more she shall appear before us leading us again in glory and success. Through the furnace of persecution, she has emerged, sanctified in victory. I could weep, De Sillé, from the surge of joy which runs across my soul. But I am long past tears."

The little priest rose silently. "I shall leave you your moment, cousin," he said softly. "Even I have not the courage to intrude. In a little while I shall return, for I am yet unheard."

Without awaiting a reply, he slipped almost unnoticed from the tent. De Rais had seated himself and dropped his head upon the table in ecstatic prayer.

In time, the priest returned, and found his cousin pacing up and down his tent in unhappy restlessness.

"Tell me, De Sillé, what news you bring," cried the Baron. "I am terrified by the vagueness of your words. Speak, in the name of God, for my joy has been destroyed by apprehension."

"Jeanne is not free," the priest began. "I feared to interrupt your happiness."

"Tell me what remains untold," commanded the Marshal. "Although I fear to draw even a breath, I have the strength to hear."

"Do you fear God, cousin?"

"I fear the treachery of man, created in His image."

"Do you fear the power of Satan?"

"I fear the Evil One in all his manifestations. I fear his servants and those who act under his inspiration."

"Do you fear the terrors of death?"

"Less than these."

"For in death," went on De Sillé, "one goes to God for judgment. Do you fear this High Tribunal?"

"That, at last, I do not fear."

"Then listen, cousin, and in strength. Jeanne has recanted of her abjuration, and has been judged relapsed."

De Rais was staring at the priest, his face become a rigid mask of fear. His distended nostrils quivered faintly.

"This is the judgment of the high tribunal of Rouen, issued through the mouths of men who, though capable of human weakness, are judges in the eyes of God, and priests."

"Proceed," the Baron murmured in a lifeless voice.

"The words, spoken by the Bishop of Beauvais and repeated from memory by me, are these: 'We declare that Jeanne, who is called the maid, is a corrupt person, a prevaricator and deceiver of the people, a soothsayer and a blasphemer of God; that she is prideful, cruel and dissolute, and that she is, in essence, an invoker of devils, a sorceress, heretic and apostate. We are resolved to sever her from the protection of the Church; to tear her from its body, and deliver her to the vengeance of the secular arm: sorceress, heretic and apostate. In these words she has been condemned and for these crimes she will be burned.' "

As he listened, Gilles de Rais stood, contorted with anguish before his informant. And as the words fell upon him, each syllable became another turn upon the rack that tortured him—sorceress, idolator, apostate; invoker of devils and blasphemer of God—sorceress, heretic, idolator. With a cry, he took a murderous step in the direction of the motionless priest, then with a crash, he fell, borne by the weight of his armor, insensible to the floor.

Signaling to the man-at-arms on guard, De Sillé left the tent and set forth for Rouen. The news was broken, and he wished to see the execution of the girl who had caused him an unnecessary fear.

§ 3

On the thirtieth of May, 1431, Jeanne was burned at Rouen in the presence of a great crowd of citizens, soldiers and prelates. Having abjured imaginary crimes and repented of her abjuration, she died, deep in prayer, wearing upon her head a cap of indignity upon whose white surface was blazoned the damning words of her conviction. From the pyre, the sentence rang out upon the world.

Die, Jeanne, upon the flames—Heretic, Relapsed, Apostate and Idolatress. Die, Jeanne, who have called thyself the maid, in the purifying fire of the Church, so that at last the fester of your soul shall mercifully be cauterized.

Far from Rouen, engaged with his armies in futile and meaningless wars, Gilles de Rais heard the cry of the execution and, shuddering as with an ague, closed his eyes upon the memory of his saint. For a year he continued, blindly fighting, plunging deeper into the cruelties of war in an effort to continue his dullness of feeling. Furiously he fought, gaining new fame at Lagny, totally uninterested in either victory or defeat.

The death of Jean de Craon in November of 1432 recalled De Rais to life. He became now the sole master of the huge estates in Brittany, in Anjou and in Maine; the heir to the name and power of the triple family of Craon, Rais and of Laval. The importance of his position was forcibly recalled, and he was made to look upon himself.

What, in the vague background of his mind, he had imagined to be the splendid warrior, Marshal of France and brilliant noble, he saw now as a dingy soldier, boasting in apathy upon a sorry steed.

The wars, he knew, had beaten him. The flashing courtier whose prodigality had been the marvel of the world, the faithful valorous companion, had vanished with the death of Jeanne, forgotten in a shabby army, even by himself.

This he now realized, and he knew also that his military enthusiasm had long since died. The wars had served their turn without ennobling him and, despite the flashes of exciting interest, they had been, since the coronation, a dull career of hopeless tedium.

In their midst, De Rais had marched, giving freely of his wealth and of his loyalty. Of his own devotion, he had mortgaged his estates for the taking of Jargeau, and throughout the affair he had given, with lavish generosity, his courage and his faith, unasking of reward. As a result, he had become a puppet, another captain of the fat and greedy Chamberlain, playing a mediocre part within a dying war.

Out of the field of warlike France, Jeanne, alone, had achieved greatness. Brave, honest and pure of heart, she only was worthy of his respect and homage. Unselfish, unsparing, as he had been, of loyalty and of devotion, she too, had given freely of her soul. In the considered clarity of his new awakening, she loomed yet bigger, vaster and more important upon the horizon of his inward vision. Condémned by the tribunal of the Church, she had died, capped by the words: "Sorceress, Idolator, Apostate." Yet to De Rais, she remained the glorious figure which he once adored.

To the hideous charge, the petty schemers of the world had not replied. So much, they muttered in their beards, for the sword whose edge is blunted; newer blades remain.

From the office of the Chamberlain, there came an order to the camp of Gilles de Rais. The Marshal was requested to lead his army to Savoy to meet the Duke of Bourbon and give him military aid. The tone of this command was peremptory and showed yet more clearly the true position into which De Rais had fallen.

Angry and resentful, filled with a great disgust, the Baron considered his reply. For him, he knew, the wars were over, nor could he be commanded. Upon the ashes of a minor life, he was resolved to build a new career, so shining and magnificent in scope, untrammeled in its splendor and its freedom as to wash out the tarnish of the past.

A scrivener was summoned to the commander's tent. "Write," ordered De Rais, "to My Lord Georges de la Trémoille, instructing him to send me the sum of twelve thousand reaux of gold for the campaign in Savoy."

But to his lieutenants he gave a different order. "Prepare," he said, "for the disbanding of the army; for we are through with war, and shall return to Brittany."

The twelve thousand reaux were spent in feasting and in the payment of his troops; and, without so much as deigning an answer to the royal council, Gilles de Rais set face toward Champtocé.

For his disobedience and for his squandering of this handsome sum, De Rais was banished from command and removed from royal confidence. In his place, his brother, René de la

Suze, traveled to Savoy and gave his service to the Duke of Bourbon.

Safe in his fortress of Champtocé, De Rais laughed loudly at the anger of the King; for even monarchs were powerless on such occasions. In Champtocé, the Marshal was under the protection of the Anjou duchy and only through the Court at Angers could he be attacked. Even if King Charles should dare this course, it would avail him little; for there remained always the fortress of Machecoul, quite safe within the Breton frontiers. And royal interference had never been tolerated in that proudly independent duchy.

Gilles de Rais had made his exit from the world of France, and the manner of his passing had pleased his heart. To his own satisfaction, at least, it showed his mood. Pretense was over. From now on, he should be himself.

PART THREE

CHAPTER XI

§ 1

IN THE late autumn of 1432, at the age of twenty-eight, Gilles de Rais returned definitely to his estates, having spent the greater part of a decade at the wars. He settled himself at first in his Anjou castle of Champtocé, and began the commencement of a new existence.

From Lagny he brought his cousin, Gilles de Sillé, who had become steadily a closer and more intimate companion. In the mind of this curious little priest there was a facile daring quality that delighted the Baron. After the heavy hypocrisy of the Court, his tacit admissions were remarkably refreshing.

Together they set about the rearrangement of the vast estates. Old retainers were discharged or sent to lesser castles. Catherine, the Baroness de Rais, was banished with her daughter, Marie, to Pouzauges and to other places to which her husband had no intention of ever going. Champtocé was entirely reservanted, so that nothing remained from the régime of the late Jean de Craon to connect the Baron with the past. Without giving coherence to the thought, De Rais was clearing the slate to leave it free for what he wished to write.

There came into existence almost from the first, an inner circle of confidential friends who, in their different ways, advised and aided the whims and fancies of their master. Of this coterie, De Sillé became the chief.

Roger de Bricqueville attended to the rents, the management of the estates, the supply of ready cash, and the supervision of

the castle staff. Henri Griart, lately from the University of
Nantes, librarian and scholar, assisted in the matters of the arts,
advising upon the value and selection of brocades, buying handsome manuscripts and superintending the redecoration of the
castles.

There appeared about this time another figure, one Eustache
Blanchet, a priest and a man of great ability and discretion. He
became quickly the executive arm of the organization; the purchasing agent, the emissary and the procuror. Under the directions of De Rais, he scoured the country for treasures and for
those other functionaries whose presence was required for the
artistic and creative work of embellishing a noble and a feudal
existence. Under his direction, a corps of assistants and associates labored ceaselessly.

About the person of De Rais these men made up a sort of
cabinet, advisory and executive and, in varying degrees, intimate with their Lord. Later other men were added. But in the
beginning the four sufficed.

To Champtocé they brought special cooks enlightened in
methods of extraordinary dishes, who lent their genius to the
kitchens. Under their guidance the private army was reduced
in size, yet added to in dignity by new armor and by the addition of new officers selected for their size and their ferocious
bearing. A barracks was constructed for this guard from a wing
of rambling, disused stables which leaned against the outer
walls. Some of these warriors, however, lived in the village and
regaled the wondering peasants with bloody tales of war.

In the castle itself were installed poets and actors for the
dramas given in the central hall; designers of scenes and costumes; embroiderers of fine silks; illuminators of books; musicians skilled in playing and composition; priests for the
chapel; choristers blessed with liquid voices; and even a small
company of alchemists, intent upon their search for gold. For
these a laboratory was fitted up with furnaces and odd-shaped
vessels, while for their art there were supplied newts and toads,
mercury and silver, and the blood of fowls.

Under the resurrected castle life, Gilles de Rais flourished. He could look back with quiet scorn upon the decade of the wars. There, he felt angrily, he had been a monstrous dupe, betrayed into a foolish and degrading humility and robbed even of his proper recognition. What welcome had they given him in France? Why was the Count of Clermont given the supreme command in the country of the north? He had been discriminated against, he thought, and forced into subservience to lesser men, princes though they were.

In France he had been put upon basely and without justice, but here at Champtocé lay his revenge upon a heedless world. Was he not richer than any of these—greater in spirit and more powerful? Surely he could eclipse in magnificence the royal princes and, if need be, the very King himself.

The remolding of his castle became a manifestation of his mood. Denied the Roman Triumph which he thought he merited, he set about another triumph of his devising.

Into the organization of the externals of his life, he threw the entire force of his tremendous energy. From his past experience, he knew the inevitable result upon himself of idleness. Morbidity and depression had been his companions in the days before he had escaped to war; but they had vanished from him in the struggles of campaigns. He had never, of course, been inert. Even in his early days of married life, he had rushed headlong from one minor interest to another, never ceasing in the flow of his activity. But to be occupied merely for its own sake, was for him futility itself. Always he had needed a deep, believed-in purpose.

Contentment had followed upon the wars. From the first, he had made a passion of loyalty. In the service of France, it had been an ideal of patriotism that had given him life, though it had also caused the execution of the prisoners of Rainfort; and under Jeanne, his passionate devotion had raised him to a spiritual and to an emotional ecstasy.

To recapture the illimitable enthusiasm that he had had, was no longer possible. The verdict of the Rouen court—"Witch,

Idolatress, Apostate"—had laid upon any such potential hope a black and suffocating pall. The whole bright fabric of his momentary exaltation had been his faith in her. He had not been born a mystic, and the worship of an abstract godhead was beyond his spiritual reach. He had been trained instead, a devout and feudal youth in a land where fervency was rare and apt to be discouraged by the Church. Jeanne had supplied the necessary touch of earth that had enabled him to believe, but with the judgment of the churchly court, this faith had lapsed and was, within his heart, as dead as was the maid herself.

In her passing, goodness was proved vain; purity of heart, tenderness and piety were shown as worthless things before the judgment of the Church. Once more to him were verified the old instructions; render to a just God his feudal rights; obey the rules and letters of the Church; pray, attend mass, confess, and live your life to suit yourself, in freedom.

And with relief, he followed these commands. At Champtocé he enjoyed now to the fullest the pleasure of a new and complete freedom. To himself and to the entire world that surrounded him, his whims and minor wishes became laws, and his brief ideas sprang overnight into accomplished facts. Jean de Craon had disapproved of his extravagance, and he was dead. Catherine, his wife, had looked with frowns upon his revels, and she was bidden from his presence. The august power of the King had commanded harshly, and had had to fume in helpless anger in the face of flat refusal. All these restraints had vanished in his life; Gilles de Rais had become the sole and only authority, and the joy of it overpowered him.

Days were spent in drinking and carousing with his cousin, Gilles de Sillé. Feasting continued late into the night, while lights blazed in the halls, and from the cellars exhausted lackeys brought up bottle after bottle from the dusty bins below. In all these orgies, the reaction of De Rais' mind was similar. As the excesses continued, he would emerge gradually from his first intoxication into a state of nervously exhausted clarity that demanded cessation and an abrupt change. At a sudden command, the affair would terminate and the revelry would cease. He was one of those unfortunates unable to drown himself in drink.

These carousals, protracted and violent as they were, had no effect upon the energy which he expended in other directions. The duties of his household never lacked his attention, nor was there ever a flagging in his acquisitive and constructive program. Merchants were received and entertained. New treasures, constantly arriving, were unpacked and studied with minute attention, discussed and compared, and distributed among his many estates. For Champtocé was not alone in its embellishing.

Laden with these rich new furnishings, he made a series of state visits to Machecoul, to the great fortress of Tiffauges, and to the Hôtel de la Suze in Nantes, distributing his purchases among his many treasure-houses. Once, out of spite, he paid a visit to Pouzauges merely for the purpose of causing inconvenience to his wife. Catherine, apprized beforehand of his coming, was ordered to take herself elsewhere lest the sight of her should offend the sensitive eye of her husband. At each castle, the reception became a ceremony of pageant and of revelry, to which all comers were welcome. In whatever place he was, De Rais ordered the doors to be thrown wide to whoever wished to enter, while within, food and drink and relaxation were free to all who asked.

At Champtocé dramatic productions were often added to the entertainment of the guests. After the profusion of hypocras and pasties, the travelers and merchants who had claimed the bounty of his hospitality were admitted to the great hall to witness there spectacles which, in their richness, left the watchers gasping in amazement.

In these productions, De Rais took an intense interest. He had always loved this art for its own sake, but now that it fitted so nicely into his plan of a magnificent career, the theater became even doubly cherished. No pains were spared in the perfection of these dramas, nor was time or money counted. Into

the work, he threw his energy, his taste and his wealth; writing
the dialogue in part; designing the bits of scenery; arranging
the music that was played before; selecting the actors, and even
directing the piece and playing rôles himself; so that in every
aspect of their form they should be perfect.

The first attempts after his return had been small, jewel-like
achievements, exquisite in detail, intended for the pleasure of
himself and his small company of intimates. But in pride of
workmanship, and in the craving for wider and more universal
acclaim, he enlarged their scope, increasing them in richness
and magnificence and admitting, first, his retainers, the monks
and priests and captains of his household; later, the servants
and men-at-arms, the guests of the night; and finally, all who
came to Champtocé for any purpose whatsoever.

The theater was at this time just emerging from the domina-
tion of the Church and in consequence had already achieved an
immense and growing popularity. The ceremonial drama of the
preceding century was on the wane. Popular interest demanded
now a more human aspect. The more or less literal recital of
acted Scripture was passing from the fashion, its place taken
by mystery plays dealing with episodes of religious history, and
by the more symbolic morality dramas, both of which included
much that was not strictly piety.

There were produced as well, plays that were purely secular.
Histories, popularized, were presented with a variety of scenes
and with a wealth of realistic detail of costume, properties and
language. On holy days, special stages were set up in the cities
for pageants wherein were seen in the flesh views of the Nativity, the Flight to Egypt, or of the Marriage at Cana. Here, too,
one found regular theater halls for smaller efforts, farces and
sotties, both of which types were successful and well patronized.

Even in the villages and county districts, the dramatic art
was not unknown. Traveling actors journeyed from fair to fair
carrying their paraphernalia upon their backs. Arrived in the
market-place, they secured an adequate space among the farmers, merchants and produce venders, and set out across the

town clad in red coats and beating upon their drums to notify the world of their advent.

With the opening of the market, they were again at their places, surrounded by the stalls of vegetables and crockery and goats. Upon the ground a carpet was unrolled and with this as their stage, tragedy heartrending and terrible, tender drama replete with sentiment and tears, or roaring bawdy farce was presented to all who, having paid their penny, could crowd into the magic enclosure.

The show was generally well performed, though no one thought to ask for much historical accuracy. Such a thing is on the face of it absurd; for however much the Three Kings are disguised with lace and tinsel, they are, red-nosed and snuffling upon the stage, the identical Kings one could see later in the day drinking their beer in company with the fishmonger and the local wizard. Drama in modern clothes was never for a moment questioned. But excellent acting was demanded; for the theater must be ready always to compete with the conjurer's tent beyond the cabbage stall and with the trained Carpathian bear who danced behind the gaudy gipsy wagon.

The spectacles at Champtocé were of a different order. Lines and verses were polished to a cultured elegance by the castle poets. Diction and finesse in acting were achieved by experienced performers and expert coaching, and all was under the careful direction of a master hand. The costumes were magnificently designed. For them De Rais was satisfied with nothing but the richest stuffs and laces. Embroideries on cloth-of-gold, yards of furs and cloth-of-silver were employed, being draped about the figures of the actors and cut into fantastic curves and shapes.

Servants stood beside the great doorways welcoming the guests with goblets of wine and slipping on over their worn or drab garments, robes worthy of an emperor. So that even to the audience, the spectacle in the hall should not be marred. For a single such production Roger de Bricqueville, quill poised speculatively above his book of accounts, figured a cost of fifty thousand crowns in gold.

Being for ever faced by the necessity of finding an occupation for his mind, De Rais in his newly acquired retirement, seized upon the theater as a medium of expression, and into this art he poured the fulness of his superabundant activity. In his earlier life, before the interlude of wars, he had found solace in the details of ornament. Perfection of the spoken lines, elegance of gesture and a certain jeweled brilliance which he imparted to each comedy or drama had been sufficient to entrance him. But thrown again on these familiar resources, he discovered that mere dilettanteism no longer offered any satisfaction. Vaguely he was preparing himself for some future outburst, and in this light his comedies took on some meaning. They were experiments in perfection, growing gradually in size and scope.

As he played with the mechanism of magnificence, he realized the trend that he was following; so that slowly a plan which satisfied the diverse needs of his vanity took shape.

To obtain the utmost of applause, he planned a spectacle so gigantic in its dimensions that it would cause the whole of France to resound with his glory. Nor should this entertainment be cramped by castle walls or minor gardens. A public square must serve as an auxiliary setting, while from behind the stage there ought to rise the towers of a high cathedral.

Orléans, of course, must be the scene and, as he thought, he knew that Jeanne, the damned, should be its subject.

§ 2

As yet the spectacle at Orléans was far away; for, in his renewed life of vanity, he was not quite established. Though he had deserted the world, he wished for its applause which, with a godlike scorn, he could discard. In making of himself a standard of comparison by which all others could be judged, he set himself upon a giant pedestal of self-esteem. Just now he tot-

tered slightly upon his lofty perch, a little insecure in balance.
The base whereon he stood was new and scarcely stable. The
stones of solid fact were infirm in their setting.

At the unveiling of this mighty structure, he knew that he
must rise to startling heights, and meanwhile much detail must
be perfected. One of his many interests was his chapel, and to
the organization and embellishment of this phase of life he devoted many hours. It was necessary that in his worship of his
God, the great De Rais should kneel amid the richest of magnificence. It became, therefore, a part of his avowed existence
to fill the letter of the divine law, rewriting the characters of
adoration in marvelous and richly wrought illumination.

Alone in his walled garden, between the great donjon and the
smaller structure of the chapel, he walked slowly to and fro
meditating upon a new perfection of his choir. Superb as he
knew it to be, he thought that recently he detected a certain
over-sweetness which needed a correction. To his slight annoyance, an excellent voice had suddenly cracked and come forth
during a quiet passage with a blare of baritone maturity, so that
the boy had had to leave the castle service. His departure was
felt musically, and De Rais, as he walked, considered the in-
sertion of a new voice. Mentally he listened to three choirs: the
original, complete as it had been; the actual, missing a certain
timbre; and the ideal, which he was in the process of creating.
Under his tonal analysis, he was able to isolate the voice he
wanted. Alone it would be incomplete, too shrill for ordinary
pleasure save in the circumstance for which it was required.
Satisfied, at length, of its exact character, he let fall his
thoughts. The actual finding of the human owner of the mentally created tone was a task for Blanchet who was well able
to search the country until this music should be found in life.

Against the dark shrubbery of the garden, De Rais, in meditation, presented a handsome and a striking picture. In his ath-
letically active figure with its broad shoulders and slender waist,
there was an inherent gracefulness. His neck was large and
straight, and his legs were well-muscled. There was, indeed,

much to counteract the effect of his somewhat enlarged chest
and of his rather too wide hips.

He was dressed on this day in white. White skin-tight
breeches covered his legs; while above, he wore a shirt of soft
white wool over which there was a waistcoat of the same material. Above this was worn a doublet of pale gray silk, stiff with
the arabesques of gold embroidery. Upon his feet were boots of
glazed white leather and on his head a cap of ermine. Of color,
there was a sash of scarlet knotted about his waist through
which was thrust a short poignard whose hilt, projecting above
the band of red, was carved of gold and was encrusted with
sparkling gems. About his neck there hung a reliquary elaborately chased, suspended from a chain of gold.

Even in abstraction, there was reflected in his face a look of
cultivated and imperious pride that proclaimed to others and to
himself the existence of the great and haughty noble. A high
broad forehead rose above a slightly prominent and delicately
aquiline nose which terminated in his large, thin, mobile nostrils. Below them was a handsome cruel mouth which curved
easily into a smile of refined sensuality. His eyes were black,
changing quickly from lustrous depths into a flash of biting
anger. His hair and beard were also black, reflecting in certain
lights a metallic, bluish tinge. Of his beard he was rather proud,
being as it was a new addition to his features. Like his hair, it
was peculiarly soft and silky and lent him, he thought, a pleasantly sinister quality.

The face was interesting and contradictory. Immensely mobile and capable of great distortion, it could leap without warning from restful aquiline repose into a mask of hideous fury. At
rest, one saw a touch of Satan or of madness in its finely chiseled
elasticity. It was a face, one felt, on springs held in rest by the
most delicate of catches.

Having disposed of the problem of the choir, he turned idly
toward a stone gateway in the hedge, which led down a narrow
walk to the chapel. But seeing his cousin, Gilles de Sillé, coming through this gate, he changed his mind and joined the priest.

In the leisure of the afternoon, he wished for pleasant conversation.

"You look exceedingly complacent," remarked De Sillé.

"I am. I have been considering your mistress."

"Ah," said the priest, "the Church is flattered."

"I have been thinking of the blessings of our civilization and of the enormous part that has been played by the Church in the perfection of our lives."

"Yet I can not help feeling," said De Sillé, "that considerable has been lost ever since ancient times. Certainly in many respects we are behind the men of Rome. Examine for a moment our cities compared to theirs. Where, in our narrow lanes and dirty market-places, does one find the columned squares, the marble palaces and the baths of tile? Where does one find the individual freedom which the classic folk enjoyed? Surely we are more cramped in conscience and more limited in individual genius."

"On the other hand," went on De Rais, "our civilization, grouped about the central motive of the Church, is a thing complete in its own character, drawing to it whatever different genius God has bestowed on man. Our world is, in conception, as well ordered as a cathedral which in its construction receives, employs and directs all talents toward the end desired. For instance, our music—the psalms, hymns of praise, the sonorous chants unsurpassed in ancient times—are all of a religious character. Our literature is largely of a theological nature as is also our philosophy. Saint Augustine and Abelard both were churchmen. Our painting, carving and other arts received their encouragement in the quiet of the monasteries and, until recently, were almost wholly ecclesiastical. Who ordered altar-pieces or illuminated books but clerics, before this present generation? Who, indeed, wore gold brocade save bishops or, at most, a king? The very theater is of churchly origin and still deals largely with devotional subjects."

"That may or may not be true," said the priest, "yet art and literature and theater are older than the Church. The truth is that we are compressed into this mold and that we have lost, in consequence, our individuality."

De Rais laughed. "Not in our lives," he said. "There is a similarity between the altar-pieces, I must admit, yet do I live like Charles, the King?"

"In some ways, yes. You have identical fears."

"Therein you lie," returned the Baron, "for I am as devoid of fears as ever was a Cæsar, while Charles, the King, lives trembling in his boots. I tell you, cousin, I fear no man; for in my wealth I am secure. From this château I could defy the world. My walls forbid attack. I possess an army that is old in war, and my determination is acknowledged. More than that, I could buy outright the souls of all the captains of the world whom Charles could send against me. For every crown he offers for my capture, I can pay ten for my release. So, being independent of my King, what have I to fear?"

"I can see," said the priest, "that it is you and not this wretched Charles who is the direct and lineal descendant of King Nero. I bow in mock humility before the august power of imperial De Rais."

The Baron became, suddenly, a little angry. "Watch your tongue," he cried, "or like this Nero I shall slit your throat and have you dropped into the Loire."

"Only to find," went on the priest with gentle irony, "that, unlike Nero, you should be damned for the offense. And that is the point of my discourse. Despite your physical immunity, you would not dare that action. It is the weakness of our unified existence. Nero could dare without a tremor, but to Gilles de Rais, the Christian, the Church is powerful enough to command. The sin would rest upon your soul."

"It would be, of course," speculated the Baron, "a sin and directly against the teaching of the Church. I wonder, De Sillé, how great a sin?"

"One of the greatest, I am told. God is the King of life and death."

"A greater sin than lust, adultery or pride?"

"Human life is sacred to the Church."

"Yet I have already killed. The men at Rainfort met their deaths through me. Blackburn himself fell by my hand. Were these not sins as well?"

"The deeds lay in the course of duty, and so were not strictly sins."

"Suppose I thought that death became a duty to my being?"

"What priest could you convince? Who would absolve you?"

De Rais laughed suddenly, struck by a new idea. "Why, many priests," he said. "You would, yourself."

"I certainly should not."

"Grant me, then, half an hour among the clerics of my employ. A dozen would obey my wishes."

"And yet, though practically absolved, you hesitate, my Emperor."

The Baron regarded his cousin seriously. "I am not sure just why," he said, "yet I can not imagine any man who, without motive or passion, would have the hardihood to take a life for the sake of slaughter."

"That is because you lack the power over conscience. Like King Charles, you share the fear of sin. Find one who is free from a conscience which is church-imbued, and you will see the man who, like the emperors, is free."

"Where is such a man?" remarked the Baron idly.

"Not far away," replied the priest. "Touching your arm, in fact." He brushed the Baron's sleeve and bowed slightly.

The Baron smiled. "How dare you make the boast?" he asked.

"Because it is true. I, for one, am little bound by fear of clerics. I am one myself although, as you have probably guessed, I am not quite devout. Sin to me has little meaning. Nor should I hesitate to kill."

"You have worshiped the fiend and are contaminated," said De Rais sternly. "You have tried to lead me into heresy; nor is this your first attempt. You had better leave my sight before I lose my temper."

De Sillé bowed with deep respect. "You accuse me harshly," he said, "of unjust things. There are many secrets you do not understand, and you forget that I am still a priest of God."

De Rais turned from him and walked quickly toward the chapel gate. Under his hand there rested the carved surface of his reliquary. Crossing himself at intervals, he left the garden; but his mind was troubled.

§ 3

In his vast bed, Gilles de Rais experienced that night some difficulty in achieving sleep. The mattress was soft and comfortable; the room was warm and dimly lighted, while about the bedstead were drawn the heavy curtains intended to protect the sleeper from any current of night air which might penetrate the chamber. Despite these aids, the Baron remained awake, his limbs oustretched, and his mind alert.

His thoughts were turned in the direction of his cousin, and he wondered how far the little priest had slipped from grace. He knew that in the past De Sillé had come in contact with what he called the Other Faith and that, by his own admission, he had danced at midnight beneath the shadows of the Breton oaks in the company of the Satanists. With the advent of Jeanne, however, there had been a return to faith, and De Rais recalled the terrified remorse that had racked the little priest within the chapel at Orléans.

But Jeanne had passed and was discredited. In the light of the garden conversation, it became obvious that, to some extent at least, De Sillé had relapsed. The righteous horror which the Baron had expected failed him miserably. Instead he felt himself a prey to a startled and fascinated curiosity. Many times during the course of his career, De Rais had glimpsed the tentacles of Satanism lying half-hidden below the surfaces of every-day existence; for though it was a secret and a dread fraternity, it spread itself in a huge network of organization that could not be entirely concealed.

Just now, he had slight interest in this unfamiliar portion of the world of fact. Being awake and sleepless, he concentrated upon his speculations concerning the lapses of his cousin. How far, he wondered, could one wander from the Church of Rome? Was it conceivable to be lukewarm in faith, or to take up two worships?

Pleasantly aloof, he felt a thrill of delightful and imagined horror before the proximity of a secret evil, and on this point his thoughts turned from their course into a drowse of wild imaginings. Half asleep, he put himself into the part of De Sillé and became, vicariously, untrammeled by his own fears and limitations.

In this mood, he fell asleep and dreamed a curious and ugly dream. Once again, he was at the wars which he had left behind, camped before La Lude, although he knew that city to be already taken. Somehow the corpse of Blackburn had risen from the field and crawled into his tent, where it stood poised against the doorway. Against the figure of this resurrected dead, a maniacal rage consumed the dreamer. Springing from his cot, De Rais attacked his enemy with superhuman force. The spectral Blackburn, beaten and overpowered, subsided into death, and Gilles de Rais returned to bed.

Once more the corpse arose and tottered against the doorway in inert menace. In cold fear, De Rais seized him, murdering him afresh, cutting and tearing at the lifeless flesh with frantic dreadful terror. Interminably the fight continued. Blackburn, the corpse, lived on, hideous and passive, and refused to die. Together they rolled upon the floor in horrible proximity from which there was no freeing. The dagger in the dreamer's hand became the hand itself, immensely sensitized, plunging itself helplessly into the soft body of the enemy in a rhythm of fear, while both were bathed in blood.

The dream lapsed suddenly, slipped and widened out. Blackburn was dead at last, and the dreamer stood in satisfaction within a jeweled hall. Vaguely he recognized it as his chapel, grown vaster, quieter and more subdued. The motive of the stabbing arm had ceased, and De Rais was pleased with the event.

Standing motionless before a sort of altar, he felt himself suffused by a supreme joy of satisfaction, as though he had achieved the task for which he had been made. Triumphantly and filled with peace, he raised before the altar the bleeding figure of the corpse. With infinite tenderness, he held it up to a divine congratulation. No longer was it Blackburn, the hated Englishman, but was instead the form of Rossignol, a choir-boy he knew and loved. Compassionately he laid a kiss upon the quiet brow. "This I have done for you," he murmured. "You are delivered to delicious death."

Waking slowly, the Baron lay in peace within the softness of his curtained bed. A sublime relaxation of soul and limbs embraced him, while the mood persisted. Content with its remembrance, he closed his eyes and fell into a dreamless sleep.

§ 4

This dream was not forgotten, nor did it vanish with the morning. The Baron rose, still filled with a remembered rapture, to which his mind returned continually. The scene before the altar became a waking vision and an obsession of desire. Gradually the details faded, but the mood remained.

In the early morning he rose and came out into his dewspread garden. As he approached the chapel, there issued from its dark interior a flood of golden music from a single voice. In the sunlight, a ray of sanity descended on De Rais. The beauty of this morning music sufficed to clear his brain.

The singer was a boy from La Rochelle: the very Rossignol of whom he dreamed. Seeing him for the first time in the church of St. Hilaire at Poitiers, the Baron had been captivated by his appearance. At once he pictured the blond and classic beauty attired in the gorgeous chorister's robes of Champtocé, become a living copy of a young angel stepped from the tempora of an Italian altarpiece.

Then, suddenly, the boy had opened up his throat and sung, pouring from his young lips a veritable cascade of music that was superb in limpid ease. Trembling with the joy of his discovery, De Rais had taken him into his service, promising him a great office of trust, and bestowing upon him the pretty estate of Rivière. To his awed parents were given three hundred golden crowns to compensate them for their loss.

Nor were the promises left entirely unfulfilled; for at Champtocé, he became more than one of many choristers. Almost at once, he took his place among the groups of intimates who were emerging from their service of a noble master into the place of confidential friends and allies. Into the cabinet of De Sillé, Henri Griart, Roger de Bricqueville, and the priest, Blanchet, Rossignol was partly admitted.

Halted by the singing, De Rais stood still before the open portal of his chapel, listening with rapt attention to the voice within. Upon a sudden unexpected impulse, he knelt upon the grass and raised his eyes to heaven. "Merciful Father," he prayed with quiet fervor, "protect this nightingale from harm. Grant him, I beseech Thee, the right to live. Forbid, I pray Thee, that I ever wreak my passion on this voice of gold, and save him from the vengeance of my sinful hands."

With this unconsidered and curious prayer, the voice of Rossignol was stilled; and rising from his knees, the Baron entered the confines of his chapel.

The light of day came softly through the stained glass of the windows, diffusing itself in mellowed reds and blues over the dark carved benches and choir stalls, falling with subdued beauty upon the Eastern rug that covered the stone floor, and lighting up with added color the magnificent richness of the hangings which, above the woodwork, completely covered the painted walls.

This chapel was a treasure-house; a visual contact between the Baron and his God. In its luxuriance of wealth there was a double tribute. God was honored by the gifts; and De Rais, for having given. Here were found priceless vestments and yards of cloth-of-gold. A pair of orphreys, pieces of cloth-of-gold heavily embroidered, for which he had paid three hundred crowns, lay carelessly upon a corner of the choir stalls. In this chapel reposed a quantity of gold and silver plate, of almost unheard-of-value. There were chandeliers of silver, crosses, censers, monstrances and patens upon whose surface precious stones blazed and glittered like bits of fire or like minute fragments from the brilliant windows, reduced by microscopic means in size, only to grow by compensation in their value and intensity. Immense gold candelabra, unmatched in France, held in their septifold arms the scented candles of devotion.

To administer this place of holiness and repose, he had created an ecclesiastical staff worthy of a cathedral church. There was an archdeacon, a dean, a vicar; there were chaplains, coadjutors, cantors and clerks. For his corps of choir-boys there was a schoolmaster; and over them there ruled a bishop, veritable in dignity, yet holding his appointment through no other sanction than that of De Rais himself. Outside the walls of Champtocé, his bishopric ceased to exist. Eighty there were in all who, clad in robes and surplices of rich brocades and rarest furs, and bearing behind them scarlet trains edged with velvet and embroidered with threads of gold, moved through their duties, well-fed with costly delicacies, quietly, and in hushed majesty.

Impossible as it was to display at one time all the treasures of this chapel, he alternated them as he alternated the voices of his choir: selecting the singers in fresh groups and combinations for each service. With his material objects he did the same; varying the display endlessly; purchasing anew and for ever augmenting, eliminating and purifying his collection. From chests filled with a variety of hangings and vestments, he selected for different occasions, schemes of color and design that pleased him. The mass, in its potentialities, he regarded as an art similar in its quality to the art of music, yet deeper in its emotional basis and more amenable to artisic interpretation. He conducted his chapel with a brilliant and appreciative hand as, had he possessed the skill, he would conduct a splendid orchestra.

The air, the harmonies, the composer varied. De Rais, the artist, played and interpreted. For an apostle's feast, the vestments were of cloth-of-gold, the voices rich and slightly heavy, and the whole was done in antiquity and in reverential dignity. The feasts of the Virgin were white. Silk brocades embroidered with silver were tinged with faint blushes of color from the glass of the windows and mellowed by the flames from a host of tapers. Green was employed for confessionals. And with each variation, the decorations changed, even to the reliquaries of the saints which were designed of delicate and graceful proportions and wrought from precious metals.

But exaltation does not last, and the calmness of the chapel soon lost, upon that morning, its power to soothe. Nevertheless, he remained seated or kneeling within its depths, while for his pleasure the choir and the heavy organ performed their melodies. Restlessly, he enjoyed the declining Gregorian, pouring its majesty to the accompaniment of a full choir, the sacred Mass of Guillaume de Machault, already of a past century and an ancient Inviolata issuing from the clear throats of four young singers. Yet these served only as a temporary palliative to an unease that would not be allayed.

At noon, after a short prayer, before a handsome shrine, he rose and left the building. In the garden he met De Sillé.

"I have had bad dreams," he confided. "Must these also be confessed?"

"Assuredly. Yet dreams are easily atoned."

"Even the dreams of frightful sin?"

"Even to concourse with evil forces—succubi and vampires. Although this is a special error and separate from mere visioning. As to the nature of this sin, however, even the scholars of the Church are most confused."

"The sin I dreamed was of another sort."

"Our dreams," explained the priest, "are but the shadow of our lives."

"So that their sins are shadows of our waking sins?"

"Precisely."

"Then," mused the Baron, "if sins of sleep may be absolved, their realer brothers may also be forgiven?"

"When there is consciousness of evil, atonement is more difficult."

"Yet it is possible?"

"Always it is possible."

Though he did not ask the question, De Sillé was puzzled. What sin, he wondered, had his cousin dreamed?

The afternoon was spent in drinking and carouse. For a time, an alcoholic exhilaration served to grant the Baron a chance to rest. But as the sun went down, he sank again into a tortured and confused meditation. Already the restlessness that had attacked him was becoming recognized in origin and in form; and, as he sat among the emptying flagons, half deafened by the roared-out songs, he sounded within himself an emotion which he dreaded to understand. Within him raged a war between an overpowering lust and a tremendous fear.

Rising from the board, he left the dining hall, and craving solitude, he made his way to a remote tower where he had fitted up a strange apartment. It consisted of a cold bare room, stone-floored and devoid of carpet or hanging. In shape it was a rectangle, vaulted with stark ribs that met, like great curved spokes of some gigantic wheel, in a rough-hewn block in the center of the ceiling. At one side, a door led into a tiny cell-like chamber wherein he sometimes slept upon a cot that stood against the wall. The entire place was stern and utterly unrelieved in barrenness. For him, it formed a retreat of monastic solitude, and an escape from the oppression of his opulence. None came near it without his invitation.

Here he remained in thought until, in the night, the solitude became oppressive. Then he sent for Gilles de Sillé and for Henri Griart, his librarian.

With him Griart brought a book that he was studying. By the light of a thick taper he read, partly aloud and partly to himself, pausing now and then to examine more closely the beautifully wrought illuminations.

Across the room, half ignoring him, sat De Sillé and the Baron conversing idly or pausing in their speech to listen. A large flagon of wine rested on a table between them and eased their conversation. In the chimney-place a fire blazed, unneeded, for the room was already hot and heavy-aired.

In a drowsy monotone, Griart was reading with his scholar's intonations of the Roman Cæsars. He had reached the orgies of Caligula and dwelt carefully upon the depravity and the cruelty of his reign. Suddenly De Rais sat upright in his tall-backed chair; for Griart was picturing a scene of butchered children who died to please their king.

As the librarian read, the scene of these departed horrors rose before his master's eyes. Books to De Rais were truer than the words of priests, and what was written had to be believed. Colored by his brilliant imagination, the picture that was evolved leaped and danced before his eyes.

This was the scene that had been missing from his dream; and in the reading, it was given form.

Griart, glancing from his reading, saw a curious look upon his master's face. The black eyes were half closed as he regarded a goblet held unseen in his grasp. His nostrils, ever indicative of excitement, were spread and dilated, and his mouth was horribly smiling. The librarian put down his book and rose.

"Yes," said the Baron, "let the reading cease. I wish to think, and talk to Gilles de Sillé."

The librarian went; and slowly there began between the two who remained a long, a careful and a horrible understanding. Over a vast amount of wine they talked, entering gradually into a self-revealing drunkenness. Vague, twisted, involuted thoughts took form and grew into a plan of action which satisfied and shocked and terrified them both.

Some time before the dawn, a man-at-arms, acting under the orders of De Rais, entered the quarters of the sleeping choir-boys. In a loud and rousing voice he called a certain one by name. The boy rose unwillingly, demanding what was wanted of him.

"You are summoned," said the soldier briefly, "by our master, the noble Baron de Rais, Lord of Champtocé and of Ingrandes, to visit him in his apartment and to supply his entertainment. Hurry, my Lord awaits."

Surprised, the boy dressed quickly and followed his guide across the gardens to a small gate at the foot of a round tower. Together they climbed a stone stairway and paused in a little vestibule before a heavy door. The man-at-arms knocked loudly, and waited for reply.

A voice, curiously thick, answered from the farther side, and slowly the door was unbarred from within. As it swung open, the chorister entered, and it was shut behind him. Outside, the soldier turned and with ringing steps descended again the worn stone stairs. From the fireplace, there came a figure, red-eyed and swaying with drunkenness, toward the boy; while at his side another figure crouched. And in the hands of both were knives that glinted sharply in the firelight.

§ 5

Morning came again, and from the tower chamber Gilles de Rais emerged, wild-eyed and unnerved by his ordeal. From the bare room where lay the broken corpse, he descended to the empty dining hall, and there commenced a day of riotous carouse. Blanchet, Griart, De Sillé and a dozen others gathered at his command to aid him reassert control upon his nerves. Throughout the day they sat, drunk with wine, shouting out songs and jests, pretending to find amusement in the dice, and quarreling loudly over the chances of the game.

Across the table, De Sillé searched with sly inquisitiveness the face of his companion, appraising him coolly and wondering upon his state of mind. De Rais caught the look and shouted in defiance. "No, Cousin Priest, I am not yet afraid. We shall return to-night to the resumption of our sport." He rose with a gesture of finality. "I leave you to your pleasures," he shouted to the rest. "Come, Cousin de Sillé. Back to the chamber of the Cæsars!"

Days of revelry ensued, followed, at intermittent intervals by nights of murder in the solitary tower. The life of Gilles de Rais had become a strange debauchery, through which the blood lust traveled, insatiable and unappeased. Victim after victim entered by the heavy door, lured by commands, or promises, or bribes. Each was received, flattered briefly and destroyed.

Out of the drunkenness of his first attack, De Rais emerged into a maniacal clarity that invented for each new visitor a newer method of his death.

Upon the floor the Baron slept, sometimes, like a beast, unable, in his utter weariness, to drag his limbs to the couch that waited in the adjoining room. Sometimes reviving from the stupor of his trance, he would go out and pace the dark ramparts, muttering in madness to himself.

At last, exhausted, worn in mind and soul, he emerged one morning into a surfeited clarity. Strangely as it had come, the lust for blood had disappeared, leaving him weak, and dripping with the sweat of fear. Now that it was over, he could look back with living horror at his nightmare. Yet even he could realize but vaguely the extent of his enormities. Curiously, too, he felt no touching of remorse; although he knew how mightily he had offended against the tenets of his God. In the anguish of his terror, he hurried to his chapel, and in its quiet depths, he prayed with fervent passion to his Maker.

Beating his breast, and weeping tears of contrition, he sought the sanctuary of confession and, pouring out his sins, asked humbly of the unseen priest for divine absolution. Blanchet, within the confessional booth, turned white with horror, trembled, hesitated and, in the name of God, forgave.

CHAPTER XII

§ 1

ONCE it was over, the space of days which had comprised the orgy of the chamber of the Cæsars, had upon De Rais a strong reaction. An abstract horror of the deeds committed and of the place of sin overwhelmed him. He avoided with loathing the deserted tower in which he had held his abattoir of passion. In order to reclaim his soul, his days were spent within the velvet darkness of his chapel. For hours he remained in prayer, roused from his silent meditation by the celebration of frequent masses. With eagerness he took communion often, following the example once laid down by Jeanne.

His inchoate feelings were not entirely remorse. For the deaths that he had occasioned, he felt but little regret. There was, instead, an intense disgust, vague and overspreading, which had settled like a hideous blanket over a portion of his existence, covering with its fringes all of his life which touched upon the tower chamber.

By some freak, or by the very evasiveness of the man himself, Gilles de Sillé escaped contamination. Somehow he had managed to avoid direct association with the hideous deeds and, with his ever-changing moods, he wormed himself again gradually into favor.

But Champtocé, from dining hall to outer moat, suffered. Beside the vastness of the world, it seemed now small and cramping. Of a sudden, the gemlike quality of its decoration oppressed the Baron, and he fretted aimlessly within its confines, filled with a longing for size and majesty.

Without discovering to himself the true cause of his repug-

199

nance, he decided suddenly to leave, and to take up his abode
in the great fortress of Machecoul in Brittany. His motive was
escape. He wished to retreat from the brilliant scene of his debauch and to withdraw further into himself. Machecoul—
heavy, solidly made and melancholy—was, he felt now, more
appropriate a setting for his life.

The castle of Machecoul was a vast medieval sort of place,
filled with cavernous chambers, and honeycombed with ancient
lightless stairways curling upward between the walls. In comparison to the brilliant Champtocé, it was a place of shadows
and of semi-darkness, within whose dusk he hoped to find a
privacy of soul. Unspoken in his mind, there lay the hope of
further crimes; for, through the texture of his loathing, there
lay well shielded, though formlessly apparent, the specter of his
undefeated lust.

From Champtocé, the household of the castle rose and
marched in a long line westward across the Anjou roads in the
direction of the sea. In front of this procession rode heralds
and behind them the tall officers and men-at-arms of the body-
guard. After these came the retainers of the castle, the poets
and players riding or afoot, the troops of servants in dark livery, the monks and the eighty of the chapel, the singers, the
choristers and the musicians, while among them, beside a cart
laden with their tools, rode in an open wagon the little group of
tall-capped alchemists talking earnestly together. Directly following the heralds, traveled De Rais surrounded by his cabinet.

To this cabinet Rossignol and one or two others had been
added. For while the doings in the tower chamber had not been
flaunted, they were nevertheless not entirely secret—a fact
which linked yet closer those who were intimate with the Baron.
Some of the priests—a few terrified servants and one or two
officials—had fled. Yet the majority of the carefully selected
staff remained. They had been chosen, during the reorganization of the estates, partly for their lack of squeamishness, as
De Rais had almost unconsciously anticipated the commission

of possible and violent deeds. The tower, too, had been well guarded, and while many suspected, few had any certain knowledge. Even the choristers remained untroubled by certain defections from their ranks.

With great solemnity they entered at last the village of Machecoul whose crazy sagging rooftops seemed to huddle closely within its walls as though in an effort to escape, through close proximity, the cold fogs which rose from the tract of marshland that lay between the castle and the sea. As they crossed the narrow ill-smelling streets, the gaping villagers emerged from their hovels and cheered the spectacle while scrambling eagerly for the coins which their black-bearded lord tossed them from a golden casque which rested inverted and filled with gold upon the pommel before him.

From the village stretched a long avenue of elms leading from the crooked roofs of the town to the thick towers of the ancient castle of the House of Rais. The fortress had been constructed mainly toward the close of the eleventh century and formed a massive square of masonry from which there rose six enormous towers against the dark background of the Falleron forest.

Across the encircling moat a drawbridge could be lowered from between two heavy, flanking towers whose connecting arch was guarded by gates of oak studded with iron and braced by gigantic and rusty bolts, while the entrance was yet further protected by a double, spiked portcullis. The massive walls, machicolated and battlemented, were of immense thickness and descended below the ground where, deep in the earth, they widened out into a labyrinth of cellars and dungeons. In the walls themselves were numberless stairways leading in spirals and serpentines from the underground chambers to the ramparts above. These latter were protected by heavy parapets, flanked by loopholes and roofed by heavy beams. In the walls too were the foundations for the three towers that had been left unfinished. And at the corners stood the heavy towers of defense and the huge square donjon.

A solid heavy mass of masonry was the fortress of Mache-

coul, imposing by its weight and powerful construction, protected by gates and moats, battlements and turrets. Within the
walls were courtyards and terraces, vaulted chambers, and long
dark passageways, small gardens interlaced with walks from
which one could see the newer inside facing of the stone towers
where fine pointed windows, elegantly designed, were set upon
the face of the ancient stonework. Here, too, built against the
wall, close by the donjon, was a little chapel of St. Vincent.

As the master of this place approached, bearing with him the
army of his escort, the drawbridge was let down across the
moat, and out in welcome rode the majordomo and his staff of
servants. With embarrassed pomp, he knelt beside his master's
stirrup and, rising, delivered his halting speech of welcome.

§ 2

Immediately upon his arrival at Machecoul, Gilles de Rais
embarked upon the task of restoring, renovating and making
habitable this dark castle. The task was well worthy of his
abilities, as the place had remained closed and practically un-
used for many years. Nevertheless, beyond attending to a general redecoration, he took little interest in the castle itself.
Champtocé had been a jewel-box, a triumph of his artistic and
creative skill. Machecoul he wished to remain as a background
to himself and to his efforts. Though handsomely furnished and
richly embellished, it should not obtrude itself.

The winter of 1434 was spent in preparations for the series of
dramatic spectacles which he had originally planned at Champtocé. He wished to produce in the admiring cities of the Loire
Valley several Mysteries—plays dealing with the lives of saints
—whose magnificence should overreach in luxury any of the
dreams or farces which he had done at Champtocé.

Bourges and Angers were to be the preparatory witnesses,
and in these cities he intended to display his art to the fullest of
his powers. They were, however, merely preliminary to his
main objective.

For in the square of Notre Dame at Orléans, he intended, upon the fifth anniversary of the deliverance of that city, to present a spectacle so gigantic in scope and so lavish in detail that it should never be forgotten.

Essentially this was to be his tribute to Jeanne, and he wished in this production to link his name for ever with her own. For this occasion he caused to be written, complete and new, a drama, *The Mystery of the Siege of Orléans*, composed largely from his own memory and in which he himself was given a prominent part. Before the eyes of the very townsfolk she had once defended, Jeanne was to appear upon the stage a saint, valiant in purity, animated by a joyful courage and untarnished by the harsh decrees of priests.

During her lifetime, Gilles de Rais had been her faithful and valorous companion, and together they should appear in fantasy. Through the medium of the theater, De Rais wished to insinuate that whatever she had been—whether saint or sorceress, devout, heretical or apostate—he, Gilles de Rais, the rich, the powerful and the devoted, rode as ever by her side.

Yet even the complication of these preparations were not sufficient to take up all his time. Often from sheer weariness he would stop his work, exhausted, and lapse into a relieving carouse. Overstrained, fits of inertia would suddenly sieze him and he would fall again into a dissatisfied melancholy.

More than once, though almost against his will, he succumbed to the force of his curious and dreaded passion. Gradually, however, the loathing for his acts which had at first overwhelmed him, diminished until he could regard his sins with calmness that verged upon complacency. Mentally, this phenomenon filled him with a terror for his soul, and concerning himself he held a long and earnest conversation with his cousin.

"Am I," he asked bitterly, "one of those foredoomed to Hell?"

"A just God," De Sillé reassured him, "could not foredoom his subjects. Each man is born with his own complement of sins and virtues. To some, the virtue given is chastity; to others, courage; to others, faith—always in different combinations. Likewise are the sins allotted: one being accursed with sloth; while his neighbor bears the brand of lust. Each living being is well supplied—none escapes."

"Yet in some beings the sins outweigh the virtues?"

"Assuredly, the qualities are by no means equally divided."

"Then there are those who are by nature more sinful—possessed of more or stronger sins."

"True indeed, but as you know, grace is bestowed only upon the occasions of repentance, so that he whose sin is great, may also repent more deeply. It is a sort of compensation."

"But those whose sin is lacking"—objected De Rais—"surely you can not claim that they are barred forgiveness."

"Who is without sin?" asked De Sillé. "Come, Cousin de Rais, even in Jerusalem none was found."

"If God, whom we worship in our hearts," said De Rais, "is good in all His works, if too, He is (as we are taught) omnipotent, it seems curious to me that He has cursed His children from the days of Adam until the end of Time with any so hideous a taint. In sin we are born, and to sin again we are constantly liable in our lives, even though our Redeemer died upon the Cross to save us. I do not question wisdom that is beyond my understanding, nor have I any lack of faith, yet the question troubles me. God is the living essence of our righteousness; a symbol and example to our lives. Yet in a thousand years He has not forgiven save by temporary absolution, nor has He cleansed us of the stain of sin."

"Should we not be apt, without so constant a reminder," explained De Sillé, "to forget the presence of Divinity? We need this constant and severe rebuke to hold us to devoutness. Man is, I fear, a vile creature; and, let alone, would, like the very beasts, forget his God."

"That, I suppose," said De Rais hesitantly, "is true. Man is weak undoubtedly even in his higher thoughts; and vile, as you have said. Though I fear to think so blasphemous a thought, cousin, I wish to say this thing to you in secrecy. I have wondered if this very vileness is not a possibility only by consent of God. If, being Divine, He is able to purify our souls, why has He left us in this woeful state? We have been created in virtue and in sin. Why then has not our Creator, being beneficent and all-wise, made us pure and at the same time endowed with natural and overwhelming piety? What misery it would have saved!"

"Evil," said the priest, "emanates from Satan—not from God."

"Yet God is stronger than His enemy. How then can He in His illimitable goodness permit continuance to the works of Hell? I am terrified, cousin, by the depth of this enigma, and it destroys my sleep."

"From that enigma, all heresy has sprung."

"And is there then no answer?"

"A thousand, yet none are quite complete. One must perhaps reorganize one's values."

"How? Give me a clue with which I may go on."

De Sillé smiled craftily. "Man," he said, "is born in sin. If it is inconceivable, as you suggest, that an ineffable God could so create, whence then must come our being?"

"From Satan, by the logic of the argument."

"The Evil One is therefore our Creator."

"Which is of course absurd."

"Are we so sure it is?"

Once more De Rais resumed a confident expression. "Of that," he said, "we have good evidence. God created Adam in His image, and from the union of this first creation and of Eve, his wife, the world of man has sprung."

"Have you ever noticed," suggested the priest, "a certain difference of opinion between the God, Jehovah of the prophets, and the Christ who came to save us? Has not the latter scorned the old Commandments with the words, 'but *I* say unto you'? There is a conflict here that has a tinge of contradiction."

"God created the heavens and the earth."

"God is Jehovah?"

"Suppose it is Jehovah," said De Rais; "what then?"

"If we are created not by God, but by the Originator of Sin," said De Sillé, "what follows? Satan is not to be obeyed."

"I am bewildered," cried De Rais, "for now I know not which is God and which is evil; nor what is good, nor what is sin. Where can one be sure? Upon what foundation can one stand? My enigma has destroyed me."

"Lay your problem upon the altar of the Church," advised the priest, "and await your answer. Such is churchly and devout advice."

"But if they give me no reply, Cousin Gilles?"

De Sillé shrugged. "You might try the Other Faith," he said softly, "there being many answers."

De Rais studied the priest before him, looking sternly into the half-shut eyes. "You have hinted once too often of this Other Faith," he said directly, "and in reply I ask a question which demands an answer. In the eyes of God, where do you stand? Devout or evil—what is your position?"

Without moving, De Sillé returned his gaze thoroughly unperturbed. "Thou shalt not kill, cousin," he said suavely. "Thus has Jehovah commanded. Tell *me*, cousin, which, in the eyes of God, is yours?"

§ 3

In August, 1434, having completed his preparatory productions in the lesser cities, Gilles de Rais entered the city of Orléans on horseback accompanied by his brother, René de la Suze, and by a huge retinue of nearly a thousand persons. He was ready at last for the climax of his dramatic career. Fresh from his success at Bourges, he was serene in his assurance and in the experience of his showmanship.

Into the city they rode, a veritable army of occupation. First came his guard of honor, two hundred knights and squires, whose damaskeen halberds pressed back the crowds to make way for the entry of their master. Behind them, in regal maj-

esty, rode De Rais himself, sedate and almost motionless upon
his charger, while slightly behind, surrounded by heralds and
servants in the livery of Rais, traveled the courtiers and scholars of his household: De Sillé, Griart, the "Bishop," Roger de
Bricqueville and the rest. After them marched the entire organization of his chapel, from archdeacon to the crowd of
choir-boys, and in their train, a vast company of servants,
monks and actors.

So numerous was this host) that it filled to overflowing all the
principal inns. The Marshal with his personal suite, together
with their servants, filled the Hôtel of the Golden Cross. The
college of ecclesiastics occupied the Crown of St. George.
René de la Suze took over for his private use the Little Salmon,
while the Large Salmon housed De Sillé, the lesser councilors,
advisers and certain noble guests. Knights and several of the
more important prelates took up their quarters at the Image of
St. Mary Magdalene. Heralds, men-at-arms and minor folk
were quartered at the Black Head. Le Blond, the Vicar of the
chapel, De Rais' barber and certain others, were at the Sign of
the Armourer, in whose stables were also placed the horses of
the college. The rest spread themselves about the remaining
inns. Thormal, Court Illuminator of Champtocé, lodged at the
God of Love, a hotel singularly inept both in name and character for so austere an artist, while men-at-arms, actors and
vulgar hirelings sprawled about the Wild Man, the White Horse
and the Crown of Orléans.

For those who came to witness the spectacle, there remained
only the extra bedrooms of the townsfolk or the cold starlight of
the open squares. Once before, Orléans had learned to accom-
modate its guests, and this time the task was well performed;
for hospitality was no longer free of charge.

In answer to the invitation of the spectacle, came vast numbers of widely different folk. King Charles himself had promised to attend the opening, while the intimation of his intended
presence brought a crowd of princes, governors and lawmakers.
To the Episcopal Palace, Jean de St. Michel invited various

princes of the Church; and gradually the town filled up until, in truth, it much resembled the days when, packed with soldiers and deliverers, it awaited the arrival of Jeanne Darc.

It was the purpose of De Rais to display his spectacle before the eyes of France. Once again, he wished the world to see the girl who had delivered Orléans and France from their terror of the English. Dead though she was, at Orléans he should make her live once more. Nor was it his desire that any of those who had loved or followed her in war, or who had known her in her life, should be excluded from the joy of witnessing again the semblance of her presence. Rich or poor, mighty or humble, all of the nation was invited as his guest.

From Lorraine a priest had written of a certain peasant who, out of tribute to the memory of Jeanne, wished to walk the journey to the gates of Orléans. But this man was poor and unable to buy his bread along the route or to leave his little farm at harvest-time. In reply, De Rais sent gold sufficient for the journey and for the hiring of a laborer to care for the peasant's fields until their master should return.

Nor was this a solitary instance, and in result, the roads were filled with pilgrims. There came old peasants from the towns where she had fought, plodding slowly in the dust; scarred soldiers of her disbanded armies, marching in little groups from all the parts of France; merchants from Poitiers or Jargeau or Troyes; mechanics, beggars, thieves and bishops. There approached, too, many of the commanders who had fought beneath her standard, and a number of inquisitive princes with splendid retinue. The city became a carnival of cheering crowds through which the noble benefactor rode like a Roman emperor scattering largesse.

While Gilles de Rais held lavish court in his hotels, those in the lesser places were not forgotten. All who came to Orléans were treated as his guests. In certain streets and in several of the smaller squares, were set up tables for their use and here were served, freely and without charge, wines and meats, fruit and pastries. Hospitality was maintained and practised with a magnificence in keeping with the host.

In the square before the cathedral, the stage had been erected. It was in form a tall scaffolding comprising five stories, upon each floor of which a separate act was planned to be unrolled. Though its settings and scenery were already in place, the stage remained heavily curtained while carpenters still lingered about it finishing the final details of their work. Before it there crowded constant knots of new arrivals talking eagerly together and demanding of the workmen answers to their innumerable questions. At the sides of the stage were erected two balconies; one for the officials of the city and Church, and the other for the Court of Gilles de Rais. Like the stage, these structures were also hung in curtains.

On the morning of the scheduled opening, a herald in the livery of Rais, attended by a guard of men-at-arms, passed through the crowded streets of the swarming excited city. At intervals, he halted to blow upon his trumpet and to read with heraldic pompousness the announcement of the spectacle to which, through the grace of Gilles de Rais, Marshal of France, Lord of Champtocé, Machecoul, Tiffauges, St. Etienne de la Mer Morte, Pouzauges and other lands, all comers were invited to witness and to enjoy to the fullest of their natural talents. The announcement concluded, the herald folded again his parchment and marched onward to another point of importance where he commenced again his proclamation, cheered almost to deafness by his enthusiastic listeners.

From the portals of the Golden Cross, Gilles de Rais descended, arm in arm with his brother, and surrounded by his household there assembled. Behind his guard of honor, whose coats of gilded mail descended to the tops of their varnished boots of scarlet leather, he marched with slow majestic step across the city to the balcony beside the stage. Amid the cheers of the multitude he mounted the carpeted steps and took his place among the gorgeous entourage of his ecclesiastical attendants who, in their official robes of crimson and gold and silver, bowed with becoming deference at his approach.

As the cheers from the multitude that crammed the square and clogged the very streets and alleys of approach subsided, he moved quietly through his followers and unobtrusively descended a private stair that led to the space behind the stage. For in the drama whose act would soon commence, there was an important part concerning a warrior and a valiant noble who had fought beside the maid. The rôle of Gilles de Rais could not be filled by any hired actor. The Baron was to play this part himself.

So, for the delectation of France and for the glory of Jeanne Darc, the immense spectacle unrolled itself before the crowd that was massed before the stage in front of the cathedral. Under the eyes of the dignitaries and princes, seated in their elaborate boxes, and of the row on row of standing commoners, the one hundred and forty actors played their speaking rôles, while, in all, five hundred persons took up their parts upon the stage, strutting and posturing about its different levels.

Each wore a costume of magnificent design—gold and silver cloth, polished armor, embroidered coats, furs and velvets and gems appeared upon their figures—even the beggars whined in tatters made of silk or of brocade.

Nor were the scenery and properties far behind. No painted backdrops nor hangings of dyed canvas were employed. Each set might be transplanted to a royal castle without the substitution of a single article. Carpets, tapestries and hangings from Champtocé covered the walls and floors. The furniture from this castle and from the Hôtel de la Suze had been pressed into service. From the chapel of Champtocé there had been brought the ornaments for the religious scenes in which were shown the three copes for which he had paid so high a price. In no detail was there a diminution of this luxury, and through these scenes the actors, dressed in the magnificence of kings, paraded and spoke their twenty thousand lines.

The drama itself, for all its length and pompousness of

Gilles de Rais, Comrade-in-arms to Jeanne Darc

phrase, was simple enough in form. It opened with a picture of Jeanne tending her peaceful sheep in the village of Domremy. Into the scene, there came her heavenly council commanding that she go to war. Following this, she was seen appearing before the King at Chinon. It was a somewhat compressed Chinon, due to the limitations of the stage itself, yet in richness it surpassed King Charles' actual castle as the velvets of the acting monks surpassed the coarse wool of their living brothers.

So it progressed, through all the phases of the war. Glimpses of the enemy were given, such as the view of vast and mighty preparations being made in England, and of the English camps wherein (amid the boos and hisses of the audience) the Godons discoursed with proper awe upon the wonders of the saint. Orléans was at last relieved during a great battle scene, and there then followed in conclusion, the triumph of the city and of Jeanne.

Despite its stilted sentiments and somewhat over-elaborate staging, the theme was simple and devoid of great dramatic moments. There was no need before this audience to wring forth theatric tears. The remembered emotions were too true and close at heart to need dramatic emphasis upon the stage. Before these folk the bare recital of events they knew, sufficed to recall clearly the terrors they had suffered and the glory that they had enjoyed.

As the spectacle progressed, cheer after cheer burst from the throats of the spectators, packed so closely in the square, as familiar figures appeared upon the scenes. No one was slighted in the retelling: My Lord The Bastard, played his proper part; De Gaucourt nursed his injured shoulder; La Hire, a ferocious and an almost comic figure, swore in oaths that even he would fail to recognize. The chief performer was, of course, the character of Jeanne herself; while second in importance was the gallant, black-bearded figure, Gilles de Rais, who merited almost as many cheers. In gratitude for having given them the treat, they who watched quite easily forgave the slight aggrandizement which he had placed upon his part.

In the evening, the performance came to its conclusion, and tired from their efforts, the actors descended to a sort of cave below the scaffolding where tables were set with meats and wines of the finest quality for their refreshment.

Here gathered distinguished visitors from the audience such as Prégent de Coétivy, Admiral of France and Governor of La Rochelle, who had himself taken part in the production. At the banquet that had been prepared, Gilles de Rais received the adulation that he merited. Exhausted by his efforts, he sat back delirious with joy and listened to the enthusiasm of congratulations.

Throughout the city there was universal festivity. All doors were open, and in the streets and taverns food and drink flowed freely. Everywhere the guests were entertained, and where they wished, the burghers sent their bills to Roger de Bricqueville, Chamberlain and Minister of Finance to the lavish Baron.

§ 4

The cost of this performance of *The Mystery of the Siege of Orléans* upon the stage before the Church of Notre Dame, was staggering in its amount. Yet De Rais was not satisfied with a solitary presentation. While the general festivities within the city slackened, the production continued day after day, while there were served, still free of charge, supplies of food and drink to all who came and asked.

Unique of all the dramas of the world, this Mystery progressed with equal extravagance at each performance. No costume grew worn or faded upon its wearer's back, for each was daily replaced by another fresh and new, while with the evening closing of the scenes, these garments, worn but once, were discarded or sold to the dealers of silks at Orléans or in the nearby cities. The vender being Gilles de Rais, they brought but little, while for the new ones the highest prices were paid.

Finery and cloth-of-gold became in great demand, nor was there any haggling over values. Merchants were paid the sums they asked, and soon they learned that double prices for their goods were not too much.

To pay his debts, a very river of gold passed through the Baron's hands; for the accounts were endless. Besides the cost of the spectacle itself, the dozen inns required for his use sent in their regular demands. His personal expenditures were immense, while from all the lesser taverns came the bills for food and wine. In order to maintain this everlasting flow, Roger de Bricqueville toiled endlessly at his books. But even he was scarcely equal to the task.

In October, weary of the crowds of Orléans, Gilles de Rais moved to Montluçon where he put up at the Crown of France. From here he directed the production which still was crowding Orléans. An incident in this town showed the dangerous state into which his liquid finances had fallen. Tiring of the Crown of France, he sent for the innkeeper and the bill. The host, rubbing his hands apprehensively, approached with the account. A modest soul, he could appreciate the value of a dozen crowns, but this huge sum completely staggered him. He knew it to be correctly figured and only a little above a decent profit. With trepidation he presented his demand for eight hundred and ten gold crowns and awaited the expected outburst.

De Rais glanced at the figures and handed the slate to Roger de Bricqueville, ordering him to pay. The unwilling financier hesitated and asked the innkeeper to withdraw.

"My Lord," he said, "I can not pay this bill. There are only four hundred crowns remaining."

De Rais impatiently reached into his purse. A mere hundred crowns rewarded him. "Go to Machecoul, Roger," he commanded, "and raise the necessary money. Meanwhile we shall leave two servants as hostage for our debt."

From Montluçon they returned to Orléans and lived again at the Hôtel of the Golden Cross. But the expenses were not lessened. Into the greedy maw of the Mystery was poured unstinted treasure, while a huge amount fell into the hands of merchants, agents and hangers-on. To this burden was added the maintenance of a lavish court and a series of innumerable entertainments. No fortune could withstand this drain.

De Rais was not new at borrowing. Money had been raised by such means for the siege of Jargeau and for the payment of his private troops. Now, however, he was involved with a maze of complicated debts. Butchers, tavern-keepers and wine merchants supplied his feasts on credit, while drapers supplied the cloth-of-gold upon the security of his generous promises. To pay these folk, De Rais borrowed where he could, even taking merchandise in lieu of cash and selling the goods so realized at large reductions to the very merchants who had supplied them.

Yet gradually his credit became exhausted, and with it the cash supply of Orléans. Merchants commenced to worry and became insistent in their requests for gold.

Though the situation was serious enough, the Baron met it easily. In one lot, the furnishings of Champtocé were sold to give temporary relief. When again he was in need of funds, he continued this course of liquidation. Into the hands of money-lenders went his jewels. Other châteaux were stripped and emptied. With ruthless hands, he robbed the artistic treasures from his prized collections, while at high rates of interest, mortgages upon his lesser lands were freely given.

In December, Roger de Bricqueville was given a power of attorney to act in all capacities. No matter at what cost it was determined that the Mystery should go on. Though the effort should completely beggar him, Gilles de Rais refused to stop its course. It was, he felt, his justification of existence, and his entire purpose in life. To let it lapse would be admission of defeat and a severe blow to his colossal vanity. The spectacle was of his starting and at any cost it must continue.

Despite the pleadings of De Bricqueville, or the ruin that was facing him, he determined upon a bold and drastic course. To insure the necessary flow of gold, his estates themselves should be broken up.

In March, the details of these transfers and hypothecations were complete, and the current and other debts were liquidated.

During the course of these negotiations, Gilles de Rais received
a notice from an old friend, Georges de la Trémoille, calling to
his mind an unpaid debt of twelve thousand reaux that had
been lent supposedly to enable the Marshal to bring his army
to Savoy.

Georges de la Trémoille was now in exile eking out a satisfactory revenue from his various castles by means of his well-
known skill in highway robbery and in the capture of wealthy
travelers. Queen Yolande had been his downfall. It had
seemed to her, after the execution of Jeanne, that this Lord
Chamberlain had served his purpose. He, like Louvet, like Le
Vernet, and like the ill-starred Giac, must go; and like Louvet,
the same combination of forces was used against him. A party
was formed of Yolande, of the Constable De Richemont, and of
Jean of Brittany. In the Coudray tower of the castle of Chinon
Le Trémoille had his quarters, and to these apartments were
sent, in 1433, a band of twenty men-at-arms under four leaders. Without difficulty they forced their way into his bedcham-
ber and, with a mighty blow, Captain Rosières, one of the leaders, struck him with his sword. The Chamberlain was at the
moment in bed, the heavy coverlet pulled up about his ears.
Obstructed by the bedding, the sword hit the Chancellor in the
stomach which, being of enormous size, acted as a sort of cushion
causing the weapon to bounce upward and fly out of Rosières'
grasp. Before he could recapture his blade, another captain,
Jean de Bueil, a cousin of the intended victim, interposed, and
the fat man was carried off uninjured to Montresor Prison.
From here, upon the payment of four thousand crowns, and upon the promise to keep away from Court, he was released and
allowed to return to his estates.

Freed of his autocratic adviser, Charles VII was but little
better off. Almost immediately the governmental authority was
siezed by Regnault de Chartres, who certainly was little if any
improvement. Yolande, however, again interfered, and under
her dictates the Constable was restored to favor; while the management of the administration was snatched from the Arch-

bishop's hands and given into the obedient control of Charles of Anjou, who was the Queen of Sicily's oldest son.

Looking over the situation Yolande saw one flaw. King Charles, she thought, needed feminine inspiration. Marie, the Queen, was nice, easy-going and rather pleasant—but dull, and as a wife not much of a success. With careful skill, Yolande selected a bright and fascinating mistress and imposed her on the willing Charles. Under the guidance of this girl, Charles smiled and blossomed and became a king.

To pay his debt to La Trémoille, Gilles de Rais bestowed upon him a yearly income of twelve hundred reaux of gold, to be deducted from the rents of Champtocé.

This was, perhaps, the least of his many forfeitures. With the completion of the financial reorganization, an astonishing list of properties were found to have changed hands. Hardouin de Bueil, Bishop of Angers, obtained possession of Grattecuisse, Savenay and a large tract of forest land. A bourgeois syndicate bought Ambrières and St. Aubin de Fosse-Louvain. The President of the Poitiers Parliament took three small places; while another little one was bought by a Poitiers pharmacist. One of De Rais' own men-at-arms was able (largely through his commissions in the sale and purchase of commodities for the drama) to obtain the property of Voulte; while Confolens, Chabanais, Château-Morant, Lombert, Blaison and Chemillé passed to other bidders.

From the majestic confines of the castle of Nantes, Duke Jean of Brittany and his friend and partner, Jean de Malestroit, watched the antics of their mad and profligate vassal, engaged so fervidly in ridding himself of a large and valuable fortune. Before their eyes, they saw lands and villages slip from his fingers into the grasp of men of commoner birth yet more gifted with the appreciation of the solid values of existence.

Of all the possessions that De Rais controlled, Duke Jean coveted only two. These were the castles of Champtocé and of Ingrandes which lay just across the Breton frontier in the duchy of Anjou, guarding the road to France. As a means of defense against any such attempts as the late Penthièvres affair, or as the various expeditions of the two preceding Kings of France, they would be invaluable to his duchy.

To purchase them outright was manifestly impossible. In his extravagance, Gilles de Rais might easily dispose of lesser places, but he must be sorely pressed indeed, before willingly he could be induced to sacrifice his great and powerful castles. A careful planning must be made, and into the campaign of the Duke, the Bishop of Nantes was without difficulty enlisted.

Jean de Malestroit bore no love for the prodigal Baron. He remembered too well the affair of St. James de Beuvron when, Bishop that he was, he had been dragged unceremoniously from his diocese to the unpleasant dungeons of Chinon by this noble and by his co-commander, Arthur de Richemont, upon a charge of treason. The Bishop, though outwardly most friendly to De Rais, was not a man who easily forgave.

For himself, therefore, Jean de Malestroit bought the châteaux and lands of Prigné, the estate of Vuë, and the parish of St. Michel, together with other isolated properties within the barony of Rais. Through an agent, Jean le Feron, he purchased the estate of St. Etienne de la Mer Morte; while for the Chapter of Notre Dame at Nantes, he acquired the sumptuous and elegant Hôtel de la Suze for an enormous sum. At the same time, and with apparent generosity, the Duke of Brittany advanced large sums upon a blanket mortgage.

Of these matters, De Rais himself took little interest. Once the negotiations were complete, he felt secure in wealth, and continued, with a carelessness of spirit, the direction of his drama.

After a run of ten months, the spectacle came to an end, and wearied of the pomp of Orléans, Gilles de Rais sold the last of his costumes and returned to the quiet of Machecoul.

§ 5

At Machecoul, De Rais discovered a life of anticlimax. The purpose of the Mystery, in the management of which he had been able to free himself from the enticement of his sins, was at last achieved. During its continuance he had succeeded in losing himself in the details and spirit of this tribute to Jeanne. But now that it was over, he felt at loose ends—without a rudder by which to direct his course. It was the old story of recurrent idleness and of its consequent melancholic introspection. A new stimulus was needed; a fresh purpose for his extended existence must be found, and for the moment there was none in sight.

Even the possibility of war had vanished (although he knew that he should never again bear arms), for there had just been signed the Treaty of Arras whereby, in exchange for royal apology for the Bridge of Montereau, Philip of Burgundy had renewed his allegiance to the throne. The English were now upon the run pursued by Philip who, recompensed in advance by the royal gifts of Picardy, Maconnais and the country of the Somme, together with Amiens, Auxene, Peronne and many other towns, took up his task with spirit.

Into his troubled dissatisfaction, there burst upon De Rais a sudden and unexpected attack. Alarmed by the abandon with which he was scattering his fortune, his relatives issued now a formal protest to the King. A memorandum was drawn up wherein was stated the details of his fortune and his mode of life, from the vanity of his chapel, to the hypothecation of his properties. He was, they declared, unfit to handle his vast inheritance; and to this document René de la Suze, Catherine de Rais and Guy de Laval appended their signatures as heirs to the estate. The protest in this form was forwarded to the King with a request that he act to prevent further depredations.

At Machecoul, De Rais heard the protest with rage. It was to him an unwarranted and insulting attack upon his independence. He alone, he swore, was master of his lands, nor had any one the power to interfere with his freedom of action. It especially infuriated him that these people should call themselves his heirs; while the traitorous defection of his wife and brother was more than could be borne. He resolved in fury that they should be cut off from his inheritance. In some way, he resolved, he would so tie up his wealth that they should never touch a penny. Some plan must be formed whereby even royal authority could be defied.

He had another and deeper worry. If he remained without a task to engage his every moment, he should, he knew, be drawn again into the murder chamber. No force of his could avert the act. Again he would watch with pounding joyous heart the life-blood flow for ever from some dying victim. And again he would experience that stupor of delightful satisfaction as the severed head should droop and fall upon an inert chest. It was beyond doubt foredoomed. Yet though his passion was beyond his strength, he knew his soul to be in danger.

In his mind, a curious idea formulated itself. Born of inebriated melancholy, it developed into a plan of insane logic and coherence. Primarily it diverted his fortune for ever from his heirs into the only channel that was strong enough to hold it. The original idea had been to make the Church itself his inheritor, but this was quickly changed. Instead, the gift was to take effect at once and to be supplemented at his death. Nor was the general body of the Church to benefit. Instead an inner organization was to come into existence; an organization that would form an almost theatric monument to his piety, enduring for all time and interceding for him at the Gates of Heaven. Thus two purposes would be achieved. But more deeply cherished was an ironic tribute to his vanity which created this fund as a splendid and secret monument to his crimes.

At Machecoul, the Foundation of the Holy Innocents was established, and was dedicated in his heart to those bright souls whom, for his pleasure, he had dispatched to God. To its treasury he appointed Rossignol, whose golden voice had saved him once from death. By legal documents, Gilles de Rais conveyed to it his entire fortune and his revenues, together with whatever sums he should subsequently acquire, retaining for himself only the usufruct during the remainder of his existence.

With his death, the responsibility of its maintenance was to pass into the hands of some important and reliable nominee who was commanded to carry on his work. Various of these persons were selected in a carefully thought-out order. Charles VII headed the list. Should he refuse the trust, the duties were to pass in sequence to Jean of Brittany, the Emperor, the Pope himself, and finally as a last resort, to the order of the Knights of Jerusalem and St. Lazarus.

Although a former request for the papal recognition of his Bishop had been refused, he sent now a new petition to the Pope begging him to give official sanction to the enterprise, and to commend on pain of excommunication the strict fulfilment of its duties.

Immediately De Rais engaged upon the task of organization, and for some months retained his peace of mind.

One by one, however, the designated trustees of the Foundation refused to serve; while from the Pope there came no word of recognition. Then, almost without warning, a blow fell. An interdiction was laid upon him by the King.

In response to the protest of the heirs and relatives, a royal document, formal and absolute, whose only appeal could be made to the Supreme Council of State, was issued under the official seal. By its commands, Gilles de Rais was formally forbidden further to sell his lands, to dispose of his incomes or to alienate in any way the property that yet remained. Furthermore, all persons were ordered to refrain from dealings of a monetary sort with this Baron. They could neither purchase from him nor lend him for his use any moneys or goods lest they incur the stern displeasure of the Court. As a special precaution, the guardians and caretakers of his various estates were warned under heavy penalties to refrain from delivering, giving up, or otherwise vacating any of the properties of which they were in charge.

To insure obedience to his decree, King Charles ordered that this proclamation be read by heralds throughout the length and breadth of De Rais' domain. Readings were to take place as well in the cities of Orléans, Tours, Angers, and in the villages of Pouzauges and Champtocé.

The blow was severe and infuriating. It struck, moreover, at the Baron's very liberty of action which was to him the property that was nearest his heart. In baffled rage, he sought about him for a suitable revenge, but none appeared at hand.

One event, however, was unexpectedly in his favor. Jean of Brittany took his side and refused the King's herald entry into his duchy. Nor was the edict itself allowed to circulate. This attitude upon the part of Jean was of the utmost importance; for it confined the limiting decree to the very few estates that lay ouside of Breton jurisdiction. Once more De Rais could smile in defiance upon his King; and as a special mark of favor, the Duke bestowed upon his vassal the important post of Lieutenant-General of Brittany, creating for his advent a vacancy in that office by the deposing of its former incumbent who was, as De Rais learned with a joyful satisfaction, no other than his cousin, Guy de Laval, one of the signatories of the protest.

The motives of Duke Jean were scarcely altruistic in their entirety, nor were his actions caused by any great affection for his vassal. He coveted the fortresses of Champtocé and of Ingrandes, and to obtain them he must, he felt, defy the King. It was the second step of the ducal campaign, for the winning over of De Rais he felt was sure to be a ticklish business.

Nevertheless, the Duke had made what he considered to be good progress. During the affair at Orléans he had lent large sums secured by seemingly unimportant properties for which the Baron had no particular fondness. Yet most of these mortgaged places lay within the ancient barony of Rais. He held at this time liens upon St. Père-en-Rais, a fishing village; on Bourgneuf near the sea; and even on Machecoul itself; while he was owed, as well, the sum of thirty thousand crowns upon a blanket mortgage covering the entire barony. Besides these, were the estates acquired by Jean de Malestroit, while the latter had also in his possession the control of the Hôtel de la Suze in Nantes.

Duke Jean was sufficiently acquainted with his vassal's character to know that in the event of choice, the latter would be forced by his very pride of race to cling to the barony from which he took his name, even at the sacrifice of greater and of more valuable estates. A foreclosure would split the property of Rais and destroy for ever the inheritance of Jeanne the Wise.

At the appropriate moment, De Rais was explained the situation by a flattering and tactful letter from his Duke. Into the message was inserted a friendly sentiment of good-will and a careful mention of the greedy interdiction of the King, together with a reminder of the aid which Jean himself had given in defiance of the edict.

The proposition followed. For Champtocé and Ingrandes, one hundred thousand crowns were offered, while from this sum could be deducted the various liens upon the other properties. Should the offer be accepted, there would be restored Princay, Bourgneuf, La Benaté, the Island of Bouin and the like, while the barony of Rais should be reconstituted in its entirety and freed of obligations. Into the bargain was thrown the Hôtel de la Suze and certain other lands. Nor was possession of Champtocé to be claimed until the final payment had been made in cash. Of course, it was added, De Rais should do as he saw fit; but there remained the mortgage of thirty thousand crowns which shortly would fall due.

The full import of this communication was a little slow in reaching De Rais' mind, but a series of conferences with De Bricqueville showed him, with a cold dash of reality, the true condition of his resources. The supply of cash was at an end, and he was totally unable, he realized, to raise the necessary thirty thousand crowns without mortgaging yet further his estates. Nor, unless he accepted the ducal terms, was there a possibility of ever recovering for himself the integrity of the barony; for the interest paid already was more than were the rents received. Reading this document, he understood for the first time the extent of his extravagance.

Shocked by the interdiction of the King and by the failure that was consequent, which fell upon his Foundation of the Holy Innocents, he saw himself beggared and disgraced before the world. Impossible as it was for him to sacrifice the barony, there remained for him nothing but to accept the ducal offer and to search for other means whereby his fortune could be replenished. At least the sale would give him a supply of gold and a secure if very much curtailed income.

In the end, reply was sent to Nantes, and the proposition of the Duke accepted. One provision, however, was insisted on. Time was demanded before the sale should take effect. The Baron had small hopes of ever raising the thirty thousand crowns, yet before he gave up for ever the castle of Champtocé, there was a task that had to be accomplished.

Within an almost empty tower, there remained a certain cistern whose hideous contents he did not wish to be discovered.

Jean of Brittany acceded to the delay. In the face of royal prohibition, he had no desire for speed; while to all practical purposes, Champtocé and Ingrandes were already his.

CHAPTER XIII

§ 1

GILLES DE RAIS was now in desperate need of gold. The procession of estates that passed from his control took with them, besides castles, the lands and hamlets from which he drew his revenue. In his pride, he saw in the loss of these estates a blow to his prestige before the world. Furiously angry, he stamped about the castle of Machecoul in baffled rage, seeking in fury an outlet for his throttled anger. By the grace of God, by his own genius, or by the very powers of Hell, he resolved to recover his estates. In the past, he had done some minor pillaging out of his various fortresses, but this was, he felt, no time for petty thieving. A great and spectacular coup was in order. A recovery as surprising and magnificent as had been his downfall.

De Sillé, subversive and amused, had offered a solution, but before the horror of its major premise, the Baron had drawn back in fear.

Satanism, the worship of the evil forces of the world, existed in a greater extent than one cared to believe; drawing and attracting to its cause supporters from every degree and quality. To its ranks came peasants robbed of their homes and fortunes —dangerous, embittered folk; witches of the country villages; unmarried or sex-starved women; men ambitious for a secret recognition; princes; prelates; monks forbidden freedom by the strictness of their orders; tavern keepers; men of war and honest burghers' wives. There was no limit imposed on trade or station while in return for sacrifice, power, secret and of dreadful import, was bestowed.

Primarily the central object of this cult was the denial of God, and the worship of the Evil One, yet the variation within was very wide. Witchcraft, the name bestowed by laws and threatenings of the Church, covered, besides the covens of diabolists who danced in orgies about the figure of a sinful god, a wider organization. There were, bound loosely together, associations of wizards, sorcerers and alchemists, together with guilds and protective fraternities of certain supernormal trades. Healers, midwives, the village crones who, with mysterious herbs, cured one's ills or vented one's spite upon one's neighbor's cattle, were largely of this order. Under its protection flourished that tribe of Italian magicians who dealt in pseudo-supernatural death, carrying on, under the cloak of sorcery, a professional and semi-international trade of expert poisonings.

Although there was often a close connection with the secret cult, many practitioners of the magic arts remained secure within the Christian faith. Alchemy, for instance, whose purpose was the manufacture of gold by means of special and secret processes, was a well-established trade, patronized by many interested or curious persons. By nature, it was as exact and as theoretically practical as was medicine itself. Nor did it depend in many instances upon the evil forces of the world.

There were several basic schools of thought that differed more or less widely in detail and method, yet were alike in principle. It was usual for the individual experimenter to make his own combinations and, from his own experience, to develop a private and, usually, a secret theory.

In consequence, there existed all sorts and conditions of these practitioners, from the castle wizard who was, as well, astrologer, cooker of herbs, invocator, prognosticator, and specialist in charms, to the pure scientist who, though he employed the allied arts, never left his furnaces and instruments and, being interested in pure research, resented being classed with sorcerers and necromancy.

Nearly every prince, baron, or noble who made any attempt at a courtly existence, maintained within his household one

or more scientists who were interested in the yet undiscov-
ered phases of existence. Of these folk, the alchemists especially were popular. Their strangely shaped vessels and mysterious powders, their flames that burned in blues and greens,
were a constant fascination to the retired warriors whose extensive acquaintance with a practical existence demanded a
fresh and fabulous relaxation. The place of the alchemist was
more important than the Court armorer. He was allowed a
certain income and a more or less free hand within the walls.
He was, in fact, equal in social precedence to the illuminator,
the majordomo and the captain of the guard.

At Champtocé and, later, at Machecoul, Gilles de Rais, rather
as a matter of form than anything else, had had in his employ
several of these folk for whom he had set up a laboratory. Gold
he considered to be a commodity—like carrots. As a medium
of exchange, it was exceedingly useful, while as a material for
ornament, it possessed a rich brilliance that was most attractive.
As a substance to be sought after, however, it had never interested him; so that while he had been mildly amused by the
antics of his scientists, who by their conditions of employment
were also conjurers, he had never given much attention to their
efforts, beyond occasionally dabbling with their art much as
he dabbled at illumination and at verse-making.

In his castles he had also maintained a corps of astrologers;
mysterious mountebanks who wore tall peaked caps decorated
with the signs of the zodiac, and a look of portentous gloom.
Their prophecies, derived from stellar convolutions, were neither remarkably accurate, nor yet completely mistaken. In
general De Rais had found them helpful, though not by any
means infallible. They had prophesied that he should not die
in battle, and he had certainly escaped. They had foretold a
diminution of riches (not a very difficult prognostication in
view of his appalling and constantly increasing expenditures);
and that too had come true. On the whole they were almost
worth their salaries, besides being proper and quite necessary
(from a conventional point of view) ornaments to his estates.

Never regarding these folk with any seriousness, the Baron had not long kept them in his service. His turning again toward alchemy as a means of replenishing his fortune, came more or less by accident.

While staying at Nantes in the Hôtel de la Suze, lately recovered from the clutches of the Chapter of Notre Dame, he received a note from a man who stated himself to be a soldier by profession. This unknown requested a visit from the Marshal for the purpose of discussing a matter of importance. Apologizing in advance, he regretted being unable fittingly to entertain so powerful a baron, but, added the letter, circumstances forbade. The writer was, he regretted to say, in jail.

Gilles de Rais discovered the man in a pleasant cell within the ducal prison where he was apparently well-housed and respectfully served by his jailers. For a short time, they talked vaguely on general matters before the soldier came to any point.

"This jail," he said, "is very comfortable."

"You seem well enough treated," said De Rais, "and in that you are most fortunate."

The soldier shrugged. "Jail is like the world," he said with easy philosophy; "money buys comforts if not pardons. And I have been well supplied. My last campaign was most fruitful. However, I have spent considerable here, what with fees to the warders, extra wine and victuals, to say nothing of a fat bribe to the prison governor, so that I am at present a little short of cash. In fact fifty crowns would be most convenient."

"Why, then, should you think that I, of all the folk of Nantes, should aid you? Have I a foolish name?"

The soldier was unperturbed. "Because," he said, "you also are in need of gold."

Gilles de Rais sprang to his feet angrily. "Scoundrel!" he shouted. "Be careful how you speak of Gilles de Rais."

"Come, come," said the soldier, "every one knows that you have just sold a great estate to My Lord The Duke. Besides why should you not need gold? Most men do—not, perhaps, a beggarly fifty crowns, of course, but larger sums. Tell me, a huge fortune, a truly unlimited supply of wealth would not be disagreeable, would it?"

"Hardly," said the Baron, smiling. "Very well then, I am in need of gold."

"Good! In my late enterprise, I came across the house of a certain justly famous sorcerer. It is, in fact, his gold that has kept me so comfortable in this pleasant jail. But besides gold, I removed also a certain volume in which he had written down his secrets. During my rest here, I have read it carefully and have discovered in it this magician's formulæ. Among them there is a direction for making gold. Now this sorcerer was a wealthy man, and no doubt the gold which has been so fortunate for me is of his manufacture."

"It seems likely."

"You still doubt," said the soldier. "Probably you wish to ask me why I do not avail myself of this valuable revelation."

"I do ask, for it seems unlikely that if the book were not a fraud, you would offer it to me."

"And there we have the explanation of my actions," went on the soldier suavely. "To what use could I put such a secret in these quarters? Who would supply the crucibles and furnaces? Besides, I am not offering it for sale. You may take it and read it at your leisure, but it must be returned to me. I have no use for it just now, but I have use—and rather urgent use—for fifty crowns."

"Naturally I am interested. Let me see the book."

"By all means—as soon as I have fifty crowns."

"What exactly is your proposition?"

"Why, fifty crowns."

"I will buy the book."

"I refuse to sell. You must promise to return it."

"If it contains the secret that I wish, I desire to be its owner."

"I shall not sell," announced the soldier firmly. "Nor shall I permit you even to glance upon its pages until I have your promise that it will be returned, and the fifty crowns are in my pocket."

De Rais considered the matter briefly. He knew that valuable magical books existed, and his curiosity was aroused. Should, by any chance, the formula be of value, a trusted scrivener could easily copy out what was needed. After all, fifty crowns was no sum to haggle over. He produced the money.

"Let me see the book," he said. "I promise it shall be returned."

Armed with this precious treatise, he left the jail and rode back to the Hôtel de la Suze. Books of this sort were forbidden by law and condemned by papal bulls and royal decrees, yet they circulated among the trade of alchemists by various underground and surreptitious means. Many were purely scientific treatises concerning the mingling of chemical and biologic substances, but many more were tinged with the darker arts of evocations and sorcerous practises.

Many such questionable procedures were listed in this book, and with a superstitious horror, Gilles de Rais, in the privacy of his bedroom, passed them over hurriedly, only to return again and read them through with diligence and with a secret awe.

It was a fascinating volume, bound in heavy leather, and fastened by an iron lock. From its appearance, nothing was indicated of its secret nature, yet upon opening its pages, he discovered a maze of theories, incantations and cabalistic lore. The leaves were of black parchment written over in a reddish ink, with which were inscribed curious symbols, designs of circles and pentacles and much incomprehensible phrasing. As he pored over this treasure, he was baffled by references to unknown writers, and by the mention of unexplained procedure.

It was, nevertheless, a beginning; and in the exploration of its mysteries, De Rais felt that the way had at last been opened for him to reach his goal. With subdued excitement, he explored its pages, struggling over its seeming paradoxes, and unraveling, step by step, its hidden mysteries. He found here experiments for the raising of demons; advices for protective spells and, at last, the formula for gold.

Like most such recipes, this one left much to further research; nevertheless, De Rais received a working knowledge of the elements of this science, and a burning desire to experiment more fully in the seclusion of his castles, the theories which in his life the pillaged sorcerer had advocated.

In due time, the volume was restored to the cheerful soldier, who was soon released and disappeared at once from Nantes, presumably to study his cherished treatise at a profitable leisure.

§ 2

Arrived again at Machecoul, Gilles de Rais set about the creation of a laboratory, fitting it with furnaces and crucibles and supplying himself with the tools and accessories of his art. To Henri Griart, the librarian, he entrusted the task of collecting the necessary volumes of magic, and the written records of the more prominent sorcerers. Unable to work completely alone, he confided in his cousin, Gilles de Sillé, and in his special courier and secretary, Eustache Blanchet. Roger de Bricqueville was also enlisted.

Following the course laid down by Nicholas Flamel, he resolved to stick to the purely physical aspect of the art. Flamel had, reputedly, discovered the golden secret and was able when his work was done to thank his God that the treasures of the earth had been revealed. Gober, too, had blessed his work and had experimented without a touch of sin. Apparently the supernatural was not required.

Through the mass of references, directions and obscure formulæ, the Baron worked his way in some bewilderment. The business was not so easy as had at first appeared. Into the writings were injected a great amount that was irrelevant, futile and purely foolish. He had no interest, for instance, in the complicated cures for minor ailments, nor for the treatises that were no more than medical hand-books, strengthened by the addition of certain incantations; love philters did not concern him in the least. And these books were quickly discarded in disgust. He was further annoyed by the frequent appearance of such revealing formulæ as the following:

The eye of a Copprea fish worn in a gold ring arouses a sluggish intellect.

For general debility, a mandrake root worn over the navel is excellent.

Powdered salmon bones cure bad teeth.

Bury a lion's heart in the kitchen to ward off lightning.

Those born on the eighteenth day of the moon will be very healthy, but rascally and thieving. They are apt to be hanged.

A vulture's heart, split in two and well dried, carried in a doeskin belt, causes the wearer to shiver in the presence of poison.

For colic, eat heron's liver.

Much, too, was dependent upon impossibilities. An excellent formula supplied by a highly reputed experimenter, called for the eye of a basilisk and three pinches of powdered unicorn's horn; nor by all his searching, could De Rais discover any substitute for these ingredients, without whose presence the formula was worthless. All that he could find was a set of directions for the attainment of the necessary animals.

The unicorn was only to be snared by virgins, and these must be of noble birth. Upon seeing them before him, the beast was known to become subject to a great bewilderment and so was easily taken. The cause of his confusion was variously stated to be either the fact that the humans upon his line of vision were virgins, or that they wore no beards. The more virgins employed, sagely concludes this advice, the more the unicorn is bewildered. The basilisk was equally difficult

to achieve. He must in fact, due to his extreme rarity, be generated. To do so, it was recommended that a large rooster be
placed in a heated dungeon and fed upon fermented barley
mash until he became both fat and hot. Thus he was maintained until the heat (and fat) within him caused him to lay
an egg which was then buried at midnight in consecrated
ground. . . .

After considerable study De Rais grasped a truth. These
formulæ were either mystifications pure and simple for the benefit of the vulgar, or else in their directions lay hidden mean-
ings that were intelligible only to the initiate. He recalled Merlin's recipe for gold, so solemnly quoted by a reputed wizard:
"To make gold is not difficult," said the ancient sage. "In a
wooden bowl the experimenter is to mix the white of an egg
with a little salt—stirring constantly for five minutes without
thinking of the word 'Hippopotamus.' "

Obviously this was not a mystic formula for pure alchemic
research, nor was it, in all probability, a jest. It seemed more
likely to be a hint by the wise man that the hidden arts were
not so easy as the amateur experimenter might wish to believe.
The inverted theory that De Sillé had advanced concerning
the identity of Jehovah seemed to be justified in a paradox which,
with some firmness, stated that: "that which is above, is that
which is below; while that which is below, is that which is
above."

Already he felt that he was on the track of truth, and
through the curiously scrambled advices, he thought he saw
a glimmering of intelligibility. Obviously the science depended
on certain underlying principles the understanding of which
demanded much study and a knowledge of secret and hidden
things. In view of the difficulties in his path, he hesitated to proceed further without the aid of better-informed and more
skilful operators.

At Nantes, he visited a silversmith, who, as a side-line to his
trade, had set himself up as an alchemist. Into his hands, De
Rais entrusted a mark of silver, ordering it to be transformed

to gold. The would-be wizard took the silver and shut himself up in an empty tower to carry out his experiments. Three days passed, while De Rais waited impatiently in the Hôtel de la Suze. At last, however, his doubts were ended by the return of the silversmith. On the third day this latter reappeared clad in the long white robes of his adopted profession. Out of his solitary tower he emerged, his eyes bleared from work, and his tall, home-made magician's cap woefully awry. In thick-tongued accents he made his report. In a way, he muttered, he had succeeded. The silver had indeed lost its natural character. But, alas, it had turned not into gold, but into wine, and being very thirsty, the alchemist had drunk it all.

The futility of this ridiculous episode determined De Rais upon a course. In so serious and deep a quest, he saw at once the stupidity of relying upon the drunken antics of a local metal-worker. In order to succeed, he saw that he needed true artizans to work under his personal direction in the laboratory of the castle of Machecoul.

Sorcerers of all sorts were by no means scarce, while Brittany especially was overrun by these folk, the greater portion of whom were Italians. Italy had established a reputation for wizardry and, under the comparatively innocent garb of alchemy and spell-casting, there existed a host of exiles, murderers and thieves, who made a profession of death by poison or by stiletto.

Blanchet was despatched to search the country and to secure the services of the best practitioners in France. From this ruck, he made a careful selection and sent to Machecoul four men. There were three Italians: Antonio da Palermo, Cesare Rapporta and the Marquis de Ceva; and, one Jean Petit, a Picard. All were professionals of good standing replete with theories, with past experience and with unbounded hope of great success.

Their knowledge, they stated, was exact, and their skill far surpassing the blundering efforts of an amateur no matter how endowed with genius. Their art was difficult, this they admitted readily, yet though everything could not be understood at once, they would attempt to make their business as comprehensible as possible.

The purpose of their search being the transmutation of metals, cures, spells, the causing of death or abdominal pains to distant enemies, could be neglected; nor were the other branches of the art of sorcery—such as love philters, the Elixir of Life, or the ridding of fleas and demons, required. As to astrology, evocation and the foretelling of the future, these arts need only be practised as they happened to aid work at hand. The task of making gold was admittedly arduous, yet in the past it had been done, and it was entirely within the realm of possibility.

The beginning of their work was characteristically scientific. All miscellaneous, heterogeneous and isolated recipes were discarded as being irrelevant and useless. Instead it was decided to follow out logically one of the several well-established theories of the trade, examining its virtues and supplementing or correcting its lapses and errors. While each experimenter had his own ideas as to procedure, the whole business could be reduced to three or four basic principles which might be used either separately or commingled.

One theory was quite simple, yet in its working out lead to much diversification and refinements of method. All metals, according to this belief, were composed of two elements, mercury and sulphur. Were these combined in the correct proportion so that the hard yellow flavor of the sulphur should be sufficiently strong without destroying the white and soft qualities of the mercury, gold would be achieved. The first task, therefore, was to treat the fluid metal by a process which would solidify it (sulphur losing its yellow character by being melted). As, in medieval laboratories, there were no means of producing a temperature of −40 degrees centigrade, the attempt was made by the addition of various reagents, the exposure to certain powerful influences and the baking of the metal under the proper astrologic and chemical conditions.

This was but one theory, for the basic essence was not always admitted to be mercury. A deep and cosmic philosophy asserted that the metals lying in the bowels of the earth were generated there by the action of the stars. In the course of their development within the womb of Mother Earth, they were said to pass slowly from a base to a precious state. In order to reproduce this process, the baser metals had only to be treated either with the reagent that caused their change or (and this was more generally accepted) by the substance that had originally caused their generation. At any rate, the initial step of research was the determination of the nature of this substance which could be called the seed of the stars, the Philosopher's Stone, or more briefly, the Grand Elixir. It seemed unlikely that mercury as it appeared within the laboratory was the element desired, and at this point, a thousand schools of thought diverged.

The Grand Elixir was most variously described. Some said that it was quicksilver purified of the elements of fire, earth, air and water, with which (being a natural substance) it was most certainly defiled. Others stated it to be a powder, a vapor, or a liquid. It was, by different interpretations, considered to be transparent, or, sometimes, white, amethyst (this being a rather favorite alchemic color), or a substance blue as the sky or, again, more changeable than opal. Some philosophers, with almost uncanny prevision, had stated it to be an essence neither vaporous, solid nor yet of a liquid character but, rather, formless, without taste or color. Unlike the scientists of a later age, they knew little of its actual nature; for at that time the dynamo and the induction coil were absent from the laboratory.

In addition to its power over baser metals, the Grand Elixir was endowed with other qualities. By nature, it refined brute matter to a purer state. It had a strongly curative effect upon the human soul; and when properly applied, it was able to lift from the groaning backs of all humanity the tremendous burden of Original Sin. Besides these functions, the Grand

Elixir was useful in many minor ways. It was invaluable, for
instance, in the locating of hidden treasure, in restoring youth,
in curing coughs and colds, and in taking soup stains out of
rugs.

As the work commenced, Gilles de Rais spent much of his
time in the laboratory. Night and day he supervised the efforts
of his workmen, watching the flaring of the furnaces and bending with eager interest over the curious, bubbling crucibles.
Continually new combinations were attempted, and in the bowls
and oddly shaped retorts were formed strange and horrible
messes from which there issued acrid fumes and almost intolerable stenches.

With Antonio da Palermo, he bent, crouching, over a leaden
bowl in which reposed a waxy yet corrosive substance that
was at once greasy to the touch and burning to the human
flesh. It was a deadly agent first discovered and described by
the Great Albert. Over this, Da Palermo poured a fuming,
sharp and biting liquid isolated according to the laborious instruction of the famous Arnauld de Villeneuve. Fuming and
hissing, the liquid devoured the solid with almost explosive
force, while with mingled horror and delight the magician
watched the process. Sparks of the flying residue fell upon
the fire turning the flame a brilliant amethyst, the very color
that the Elixir had been described.

At last, the mixture in the bowl subsided, leaving a clear and
watery liquid in its place. Cautiously Da Palermo removed it
from the fire, letting it cool and sniffing it at intervals. It had
no odor. Into it a bit of copper was dropped, and it sank harm-
lessly to the bottom. Again this residue was boiled while the copper still remained untouched. Once more it was cooled and a
portion fed from a silver dish to a cur which was kept chained
in a corner for such purposes as this. The dog, weak with thirst,
lapped eagerly, then backed hurriedly away, wishing obviously
for the human power to spit. Otherwise he was unharmed. Thus
encouraged, De Rais touched the liquid with his finger which
emerged wet, but otherwise unaffected. Da Palermo now lifted

the bowl to his lips and savored it gingerly. It had a clear and bitter taste not greatly different from that of brackish sea water. No doubt the experiment was another failure, yet the flame had, under the influence of the newly made substance, changed color. The water in the bowl was boiled away and there remained a dirty whitish residue which was, save in its effect on flame, remarkably inert. Carefully Da Palermo collected it, placed it in a little box and labeled it "Amethyst Fire." Opening a shallow cupboard, he placed it among a row of other boxes, all labeled and described, for future reference.

§ 3

In the bargain which Gilles de Rais had signed with Jean of Brittany for the transfer of the castle of Champtocé, there had been inserted a clause of delay which was agreeable to both the parties. Duke Jean was in no hurry further to antagonize the King, while De Rais wished opportunity of covering up a portion of his life.

Secure as he thought himself to be from the malice of the world, he had a very human fear of being found out. The great Baron, magnificent even to his sins, was a glittering and attractive figure. The frenzied murderer, hiding his monstrous lusts within a secret tower, was a creature of another sort. Both were Gilles de Rais. One face, admired and respected, he paraded proudly to the world; the other, the hidden, dreaded, shameful one which he loved with a shrinking terror and hid in the caverns and culverts of his secret places, must be preserved from the destroying light of day.

As he circulated among the seething retorts and strange vapors of his laboratory, he knew that in the cistern of Champtocé there yet remained the remnants of his passion. Before the castle should pass for ever into foreign hands, he knew they had to be destroyed.

Since the signing of the contract, there had been little chance for any business of this kind. On hearing of the transfer, the heirs had set themselves to work, despite the vigorous denials by both contracting parties that any such transaction had ever taken place.

The most ardent of these was René de la Suze. Besides a natural family interest, a considerable portion of his income was derived from the rents of this disputed castle. Therefore, on hearing of the proposed transfer, he hurried to the Court of René of Anjou, then in active charge of the Angevin duchy, and asked his aid. This young man had no great liking for the Baron de Rais. There had occurred in the past pillaging and robbery upon the highways by the household of Champtocé that was not in accord with principles of law and order. His chief concern, however, was that by the sale of this castle, it would pass out of his control into that of the neighboring duchy of Brittany.

René of Anjou thereupon declared that, in virtue of its owner's violation of the royal interdict, the castle was forfeited to its overlord, which was to say, himself. So, having claimed the castle and, to his own satisfaction, closed the matter once and for all, the young Duke departed for a visit to his property in Bar.

No sooner had he gone, however, than Jean of Brittany took a hand, instructing his brother, Arthur de Richemont, who was home for a few weeks on vacation, to take the place by storm. This, De Richemont accomplished by sending a lieutenant and a handful of soldiers into Anjou. With professional ease, they performed their task and raised above the cone-capped towers, the ermine sprinkled banner of the Breton dukes.

By this move no one was pleased. René of Anjou was insulted; the royal interdict was violated in fact; the time clause in the contract between Jean of Brittany and Gilles de Rais was hopelessly broken; and René de la Suze was deprived of his income. To make amends, Duke Jean removed his troops, and René de la Suze now took possession. This was a slight improvement, as René of Anjou was tactfully eliminated. But a vital error had been committed. In his zeal of capture, René de la Suze had taken the place in the name of the King of France.

Charles VII, hearing that he had suddenly become possessed of a fine castle, looked up the law and discovered certain lapses upon the part of its former owner. De Rais had, at the time of his accession to his property, neglected to do homage to his monarch. In a letter to the baffled René de la Suze, the King now demanded the castle for himself.

Poor René was beaten. There being nothing further he could do, he turned to his brother and demanded terms. With him, Gilles de Rais consented to make an agreement. In return for resigning all interest in the estate, and for surrendering before a weak attacking force, René de la Suze should receive, in compensation, the estate of La Motte-Anchard. Outplayed by a greedier and more skilful world, René sighed, and agreed to terms.

With a fanfare of trumpets, the army of Gilles de Rais set forth from the portals of Machecoul, leaving behind the battery of alchemists busy before their crucibles. Not an army such as marched in victory across northern France almost a decade ago, but a theatrical troop of halberdiers and archers went out, clad in gilded mail and in embroidered cloaks.

With them rode their master and certain of his agents, who obviously were not intended for the storming of a fortified castle. Beside De Rais rode Henri Griart, the librarian, Hicquet de Bremont, Rossignol, Gilles de Sillé, Robin Romulart and Etienne Corrillaut, the last-named two being ex-members of the choir.

To lend a sort of sanction to the enterprise, Jean de Malestroit, Bishop of Nantes, accompanied them as an official guest and as an unaccredited ambassador from the Duke.

Across the frontier of Anjou they rode, in pretense of military zeal. Before them up the Loire, they espied shortly the towers of their goal, flying the arms of René de la Suze, and the banner of France. In silence they approached, not yet sure that the bargain would be kept. The bridge across the moat had been, to be sure, conveniently lowered, but before them, the great gates of the castle were closed securely and locked and bolted.

As they halted before the walls, a herald rode out a little way in front and blew a long blast upon his trumpet. From his pouch he drew a parchment and, reading it, intoned, apparently for the edification of a near-by peasant, florid demand for the surrender of the castle.

Upon the parapet over the entrance gateway, an answering herald now appeared. Another blast resounded, while this herald read a short and polite defiance. This done, he vanished from the walls and the baronial guard rode manfully against the heavy gates. Locked though they were, the intrepid warriors threw themselves against the bracing beams while half a dozen fumbled with the locks. A quarter-hour's work sufficed, then with much creaking the gates swung inward and the attackers entered unmolested into the sunshine of the courtyard.

Here they were welcomed by the retainers of the castle: stewards, gardeners and a score of lackeys. Of the defenders, there was left no trace; for with the first attack, they had withdrawn through the postern gate and were now encamped a short way down the river in the pleasant shade of the forest.

In celebration of this capture, and of the now imminent transfer of the castle to the Duke, a banquet was held in the handsome dining hall at which Jean de Malestroit was guest of honor.

"To the Lords of Champtocé!" proposed the Baron, raising his glass of wine. "However," he confided to the Bishop, "should my friends, the alchemists, succeed in their efforts, I may again be master of my home."

"Knowing the fondness of our Lord the Duke for this most pleasant place," replied the Bishop, "I fear I must, out of loyalty to him as well as out of general piety, append the words 'Heaven forbid.'"

"Surely there is no sin in alchemy," asked De Rais, "when it is practised in its purest state?"

The Bishop smiled. "Pure alchemy?" he said. "How odd it sounds. In my experience, that art does not abound in purity. Mammon was, unless I have forgotten, a fallen angel."

§ 4

Jean de Malestroit departed on the morrow for the city of Nantes to report to his friend the Duke, the complete success of the latest transference of Champtocé and the conclusion, at last, of its details of acquisition. It was the Duke's intention to take possession as soon as possible, and he waited only for official confirmation of its capture.

For a short distance, Gilles de Rais and his glittering bodyguard accompanied the good Bishop. But at a mile or so from the castle, after a formal farewell, the troops with their commander left him and returned. At the castle gate, the bodyguard was dismissed and sent to their camp without the walls, while De Rais alone entered the gateway on foot.

There remained to him but a short interval before the arrival of the Duke would put an end for ever to his ownership. Yet in this space of time he planned to waste no moments in vain regrets. The hours were precious, and work was to be done.

He crossed the courtyard to a small turret, and entering through a narrow doorway, he ascended to the ramparts. Along these he walked until he arrived at the top of the postern tower. Here he stood idly upon this flat circular roof looking out at intervals through the embrasures in the parapet at the pleasant countryside that surrounded him. Below him, at the foot of this tower, was the postern gate which opened on the river's bank. Against this, he saw with satisfaction a heavy wooden barge moored along the shore. It appeared to be loaded with hay and with coarse sacking, and it rode high out of the water. For a short time he waited upon this roof breathing the clear air and enjoying the sunshine. Then, with a half sigh, he entered a small door at one side and descended a worn spiral stairway to the chamber below. For it was here that in the past he had conducted his mysteries and held the sport of Kings.

It was a large bare room, square in shape, within the circle of the tower, fashioned of stone and completely unadorned with hangings or with decoration. At one end a fire was built, and before it upon the floor were two heaps of fuel—one being of dried wood, and the other of freshly cut branches. Near them there rested a pile of dirty sacking similar to that which he had seen upon the barge.

Henri Griart and De Sillé were talking in the center of the room. As De Rais opened the door and entered from the stairway, they broke off their conversation and approached him.

"We are ready to commence," said Griart. "The preparations are complete."

"Let us begin then," De Rais ordered, "for we have much to do. Let what is possible be accomplished here, though I am afraid that we must carry much to Machecoul."

"I wish that journey were already finished," said the librarian. "I do not look forward to the trip."

"Nor I," De Rais assured him. "A dreadful cargo passes from this place upon its final journey, and I, who have no fear of death, tremble to look upon the aspect of my sins."

"Consider the allegory," said De Sillé softly. "A barge load of ancient sins descends to the river of death. Who, Cousin Gilles, will take the helm?"

"Enough of this," cried De Rais harshly. "We have a task to perform, not an allegory to interpret."

"Yet it is said," went on the priest, "that Satan comes in person for his own and, more than that, supplies the escort."

"Be quiet, blast you! There are no demons here."

"Who knows?" replied the priest, and in a monotone he repeated the conventional phrases of an exorcism: "Avaunt, ye powers of darkness and of fallen splendor. Avaunt, ye creatures of evil who have by rebellion fallen from the grace of God into the nether pit. Avaunt, ye to your proper homes of wickedness. So I command ye in the name of God, the Father, the Son, and the Sublime Essence!"

De Rais glared at him angrily. "Be still!" he shouted, "and let us commence our work."

By the chimney, Hicquet de Bremont, Corrillaut and Robin Romulart were busy with the fire which blazed up from the fagots and caught hungrily at the layer of heavy logs that was spread above them. From their places, De Rais summoned Corrillaut and Romulart to his side, leaving De Bremont to tend the blaze and to create an all-consuming heat. As they came up, he explained their task.

Between the square walls of the room and the round ones of the circular tower which contained it, there were of necessity four semicircular spaces. Directly above the postern, a small door opened upon the spiral stairway that led both to this gate and to the roof above. Opposite this was built the fireplace now blazing with De Bremont's logs. To the right, was the small cell-like chamber where De Rais had slept during the nightmare of his orgies; while on the opposite side there was a similar chamber. This latter was empty even of a cot, while in the center of the floor there descended a great circular shaft perhaps six feet across, capped by a heavy lid of oak timbers.

Gilles de Rais, Corrillaut and Robin Romulart entered this chamber, and with straining muscles they raised the wooden lid and slid it back across the floor. In silence, Henri Griart brought from the other room a length of heavy rope, one end of which was passed over a beam which crossed the cell some distance below the actual roof. With this serving as a rough pulley, a loop was made in the other end, and a piece of board inserted. Into this loop Corrillaut thrust his legs until he was able to sit as in a swing. The coil itself was tightly held by De Rais, Romulart and Griart. As Corrillaut swung himself out over the black mouth of the shaft, the other three paid out the rope, hand over hand, and allowed him to descend into the well. Into the darkness they lowered him until the rope slackened and a muffled cry announced his safe arrival at the bottom.

The rope was now raised, and to it were fastened a lantern and a large basket which were, in turn, let down to the waiting Corrillaut. Romulart, given the task of managing the lift, now pulled again upon his rope while the other three waited beside the black top of the well.

Slowly he pulled, and slowly within the shaft the basket with its hideous cargo rose. As it reached the top, Griart by means of a crooked staff swung it out over the solid floor. Quickly and without hesitation, he picked it up and carried it to where, stripped to the waist, De Bremont was tending his fire. The latter lifted it and threw its contents upon the blaze. As it fell with a crash of sparks and an ensuing roar of flame, De Rais, suddenly struck with horror, tore away his eyes.

"Oh, God forgive me!" he cried in a loud voice. "May God have mercy on their souls!"

At noon the business was adjourned. De Sillé was dispatched to the donjon in search of food and wine; and on the hard floor of the stone chamber, the laborers consumed their meal. From the bottom of the well, Corrillaut appeared, a strange and terrifying figure. Dust and dirt clung to him in tatters, while his face was almost obscured behind his grime. Breathing the hot air of the incinerating chamber in avid gulps, he disentangled himself from the swing and lurched across the room toward the stair which led him upward to the roof.

Afterward the task was taken up again, while with approaching darkness the work increased in speed. De Sillé was forced to take his turn at the rope, while through the room, De Rais, become a slave driver, strode and shouted, urging them on to greater efforts. Yet as the baskets passed him, the Baron mourned these unfamiliar corpses, repenting with a vicarious zeal, and voicing a remorse that was a formula for the occasion. For him they had no longer any meaning. Praying for each, he beat a figurative breast in unbelieved contrition.

At last the final load was raised and deposited on the floor before De Bremont's fire. The latter stepped back now from the chimney.

"No more can be done to-night, my Lord," he said. "The burning must now cease so that the fire may exhaust itself, and be cool by morning."

De Rais nodded. "I, too, am exhausted," he said, "and

enough has been accomplished. Let us leave the final details of the task until the morrow."

The weary assistants left their work and disappeared in the direction of the donjon to wash and rest and quench their thirsts. Through the narrow door opposite the chimney, De Rais left the room and ascended again to the roof of the tower. Here he remained watching the sunset and regarding the peace of the river that flowed so close below. To the west, in which direction he planned to travel, there lay a heavy bank of clouds colored with flame and gold from the sinking sun beyond.

Bathed and clean, his hair and beard trimmed and newly tended, Gilles de Rais once more at Machecoul sat in the outer study of his own apartments. A flagon of wine rested beside him, and from it he drank at intervals. But the wine did not completely soothe him. Instead he grew restless and morose and thoughtful. He had, he considered, embarked upon a task which was not yet concluded; for in an empty dungeon were stacked, beside the wood that was to destroy them, the corpses he had brought from Champtocé.

What remained had been placed upon the waiting barge and carried to an empty landing-stage not far above the town of Nantes; for the river was too shallow to conceal them. Here they had been lifted out and hidden in a wain, and covered with a layer of straw.

From the Loire they turned southward along the rutted roads that led to Machecoul, traveling as far as possible by the country lanes and avoiding the occasional villages that lay along their route. For a good portion of their journey, they kept to the dark paths of the forests whose overhanging branches brushed against top and sides of the wagon as though with clutching fingers they tried to snatch away the coverings of hay and straw to uncover the deadly cargo that lay concealed.

The occasional peasants who saw the passing of the slow-moving cart, watched it without interest. For nothing in the garb or manner of its silent conductors gave any hint of their identity. Dirty and unkempt, the grim figure upon the driver's seat bore slight resemblance to the brilliant noble they might have seen on horseback surrounded by a gallant cavalcade.

Avoiding the village of sagging slate roofs and the avenue of ancient elms, the wain approached the castle from a path that wandered through to Falleron Wood and drew up at length, unnoticed, by the postern gate.

Again within the confines of Machecoul, De Rais was not at ease. For weeks he had been harassed by the urgency of this business of obliteration; so that now, although the serious portion of the work was done, he was haunted by the minor fragments that remained. To sleep, the final evidences of his sin must be destroyed—must vanish from his life.

Restlessly he arose and paced the room, sure of his decision yet uncertain of details. He had no wish for the aid of those who had worked at Champtocé. That phase had come to its conclusion. Yet a strong and private secrecy was needed. Further confidants became abhorrent. Casting about, he considered Roger de Bricqueville as an assistant. Together they could pursue the work and then forget; but his cousin had slipped a little from his confidence, and De Rais dismissed the thought. De Sillé would refuse, while Rossignol whom he could trust, was sick abed.

Suddenly his mind halted in its tracks, and there rose before his mental eye the picture of himself kneeling in the dew-spread morning outside his chapel, while from within there rang out the purifying tones of song. By his music, the singer had been saved; and but for that, his body should have lain beside the remnants of the others in the empty charnel-house.

On the impulse of a curious and perverted justice, he opened the door of his study and spoke in low tones to the man-at-arms who always stood within the passageway.

"Fetch Rossignol, though you must drag him from his bed," he commanded, "and fetch my cousin, Gilles de Sillé, also."

Pale with fever, Rossignol appeared, and followed by his master and the priest, he descended the cavernous passages that led to empty dungeons. As he walked, dulled by his sickness, De Rais explained what he must do.

In a deep chamber, whose low-arched ceiling rested upon the tops of massive piers, a fire had been lighted and now burned reluctantly, giving forth a stifling heat. From the chimney, a heavy smoke curled outward crawling along the soot-stained surface of the mantle and circling downward in little gusts. Before the fire the boy, already blackened by the smoke, coughed and trembled in the heat. Behind him, in the center of the room, his arms folded in determination across his chest, stood the Baron de Rais, frowning heavily and talking to the priest.

"How strange a thing is death," he said. "Each one of these I knew and loved. Each I have slain with different variance of sentiment, yet now in death they are all alike. Bright blue eyes have ceased to gleam. Curling hair is sere and threadlike. The pleasant flesh of youth has shrunk away, and in their hideous death they are identical."

"So are we all," said De Sillé, "once we have ceased to be."

"Our souls alone," mused the Baron, "remain unchanged. Freed from our living corpses, they, at least, like those of these poor creatures whom I loved, are free at last, and liberated in eternity."

"They tell us so," remarked the priest, "they who pretend to know."

De Rais looked at his cousin sharply. "Priest though you are," he said, "you even doubt our final hope. I wonder how you dare."

"Is it conceivable," said De Sillé contemptuously, "that if I did not disbelieve, I could dare to have a hand in *this?*" He tapped with idle finger a silver reliquary that hung about his neck. "Pray for my soul!" he added scornfully and left the dungeon.

By the fire, Rossignol had ceased his work, overcome by a fit of strangled coughing. Suddenly he ran from his place and knelt in piteous supplication before his master.

"Let me go, my Lord!" he cried. "Before my God, I can not

do this thing any more. I am sick to death, and the smoke is choking me. I can not breathe nor see."

De Rais glared at him in fury. "Get up!" he shouted. "The task must be completed."

"I am dying," moaned the boy. "The smoke is killing me."

"Thank your God," said De Rais harshly, "that you are not among the rest. Back to your task!"

Rossignol staggered to his feet and went to his fire. For a while he labored feebly, his fever working in a dull monotony of pain. As he raised a heavy log, he shuddered, burst into an agony of coughing, and fell forward upon his face.

De Rais crossed the room in angry strides. "Get up!" he shouted, but the boy lay still, inert upon the floor. In rage, the Baron kicked the fallen figure, but it did not move. Frightened, he knelt beside the boy and laid his hand upon the feebly beating heart, for Rossignol was yet alive.

His anger had left him. Gently he raised the boy in his arms and, leaving the dungeon, carried him across the castle to his own apartments.

Servants undressed the boy and laid him in the bed. To the room was summoned the castle doctor who came in haste and took control.

By the light of candles, De Rais remained beside the bed watching the fitful breathing, while the physician labored at his art. Hours passed in the dark chamber, and at last the black squares of the windows lightened to the murky gray of dawn. Sadly the doctor rose from the quiet figure.

"Our vigil, my Lord," he said, "is at an end. His heart has ceased to beat."

CHAPTER XIV

§ 1

SHORTLY after the death of Rossignol, there arrived at Machecoul a ducal emissary, well guarded by a company of heavily armed soldiers. With them they brought the final payment of the gold which Duke Jean had promised as the purchase price of Champtocé. The ducal messenger was fêted elaborately and with cautious haste sent back to Nantes, while the treasure was given to the hands of Roger de Bricqueville.

The treasurer received it and sought an audience with his lord.

"Sire," he said, "I have in my possession our last great sum of gold. When it is gone, we shall be forced to rely upon the meager forces of our revenue."

"I doubt if we shall starve, Roger," replied De Rais complacently. "Our estates are not destroyed, and even yet we could buy out more than half the nobles of the realm."

"Not at one time."

"Of course not. I mean that many barons are worse off than we."

"Surely," said the treasurer, "but few maintain the expenses that we bear. Our body-guard is not diminished. Our chapel yet boasts its bishop and its many clerics. The choir is reduced as you well know, while many other dignitaries have passed from our employ; yet, as a counteraction, we are now saddled with a corps of wizards who are an even greater drain upon our funds. I beg you, cousin, that we cut our staff to reasonable limits. Surely a dozen priests would be enough; two score of men-at-arms instead of two hundred; half as many pastry cooks; a quarter of our lackeys. For when this gold I have at hand is spent, we shall be poorer than we were."

"Your fears are groundless, Roger," said De Rais. "Our poverty is of small duration for we are on the verge of wealth, of treasure illimitable, and of a fortune such as we have never seen. A moment passes, and once more we raise our head. Gold is the power of the world, and gold awaits us. There shall be treasure rooms of gold overflowing into the courtyards; steaming crucibles of new made metal shall pour their wealth out from the laboratories, deluging us with the flow. For a moment only, must we wait, patiently, and in mock humility, while we gather up our strength. This month, this week, to-morrow, will witness our success; and then, before our wrath, the petty men who have robbed us of our castles shall feel our hand and tremble."

De Bricqueville bowed.

"Yet our alchemists are slow. I doubt if even Da Palermo expects to end his search this month."

"It shall be soon—before our gold is yet exhausted. That I promise you."

The treasurer looked worried. "My Lord," he said, "Flamel consumed a lifetime in this search, and he was greater than is Da Palermo. Perhaps our wizard will succeed; yet at the shortest, a decade seems a fair allotment."

De Rais sprang to his feet. "Satan's blood, Roger, I can not wait ten years! The fever of the unmade gold is in my veins. Should Da Palermo fail, yet other means exist. Cost what it may, I swear that gold shall be achieved."

"Then I advise," remarked the treasurer, "a close examination of the progress of the laboratories. A change in personnel might well be made."

Acting under the suggestion of Roger de Bricqueville, Gilles de Rais ascended to the laboratory and there found Da Palermo alone. It had grown quite dark; and save for three torches whose flaring light caused curious leaping shadows to dance upon the walls, the only other illumination was a dull fire of

charcoal over which the magician bent, stirring it with ritualistic movements by means of his short wand.

Upon a tripod, a pot rested above the hissing and bubbling,
while from its depths there rose a thick and yellow fume. The
magician, engrossed in his experiment, made no gesture of welcome. With his left hand he scattered into the fire a white powder, while at the same time waving his wand above the brazier
in curious curves, and tracing mystic patterns in the air. Then,
bending over the fire, he blew upon it softly, repeating to himself a conjuration. From the embers burst a brief flame of
brilliant green dancing upon the coals yet scarcely touching
them. It went out, and Da Palermo removed the pot from its
tripod placing it upon a stool beside him and stirring it vigorously.

De Rais approached the side of Da Palermo, and with him
peered down into the seething, ill-smelling liquid. A dirty froth
covered the top, and this Da Palermo skimmed carefully with
a copper ladle. Below there lay a clear brownish liquid which
he decanted, while upon the bottom of the pot reposed a muddy
sediment. Holding a torch over the pot, so that he could see
the interior more clearly, the magician scraped this substance
and examined it with microscopic precision. With the tip of his
knife he removed from it a tiny speck of yellow substance and
held it out, stuck to the polished blade, for De Rais to see. It
was a flake scarcely bigger than a pin-point.

"Gold," said the magician in an awed voice. "Minute, corrupt and scarcely discernible, but gold without a doubt!"

De Rais' eyes glittered in excitement. "Found!" he cried.
"Found at last, the secret for which I have so long awaited.
Have you the formula, my friend, so that the process may be
done again? Multiply it, Da Palermo, a thousandfold and
wealth unlimited is ours."

"You do not understand the difficulty," said Da Palermo. "I
will, therefore, explain. While I have made a tremendous step
toward my discovery, I have not yet achieved success. Look—
how small a fragment reposes on this blade; yet the making

cost perhaps a hundred crowns. Were the experiment increased a thousandfold, I might perhaps create a crown piece of the precious metal at many times that cost in elements. There is as yet a weakness in my procedure, and still I must continue with my labors."

"Continue then," commanded the Baron. "Spare no effort, for we are almost at our goal."

"No," said Da Palermo seriously. "There is an error in the very method. I beg, my Lord, the privilege of a confidential interview."

"Speak out, my friend, this is a favorable moment."

"I begin with embarrassment," said Da Palermo, "because I must, in justice to yourself, admit the limitations of myself, while also criticizing others. Let me commence, then, with the statement that the men selected for this search are badly chosen. Magic is, as you are well aware, a wide and highly specialized field in which a hundred vocations are included."

"This was in my mind," De Rais assured him, "when the hiring was done. Having no need for necromancers, astrologers, evocators, or sorcerers, I have chosen alchemists pure and simple."

"So I know," went on the alchemist, "yet it would, perhaps, have been more serviceable to have considered the aims desired rather than the means employed."

"You mean that in the search for gold, the other arts are sometimes useful?"

"Precisely. Alchemy, although a broad term including many fields, is often a classification of method, not of purpose. Many who search for gold by hidden means are hardly alchemists, while many more avail themselves of this name as a sort of cloak, though in reality they are dealers in spells, in philters, in medicine and the like. This statement applies, I regret to say, to the staff employed at Machecoul."

"You mean that I am duped by worthless mountebanks?" exclaimed De Rais.

"Not at all. Yet none of us are masters of the art for which we were employed. I, myself, am perhaps the most valuable of your staff; for my skill is well diversified. I am a competent general practitioner of my art. My specialty, however, is poisons. Among my books, I possess formulæ for many sorts of death. At my bidding, I can cause a man to fade away and die; another to fall suddenly as though smitten by a club. Trances that resemble death; death that is like a trance; exotic states wherein the victim imagines himself to fly bat-like through the air; a poison so delicate that it leaves no trace behind; these are my triumphs—yet, as you have seen to-day, I also can make gold."

"What of the others then?"

"They are all less than I. My countrymen are of little value. Rapporta also deals in poison. De Ceva attempts by mystification to hide the depths of his ignorance. As for Jean Petit, the Picard, he is at best a clever pharmacist."

De Rais considered this indictment. "Why then," he asked, "should I not pack them off?"

Da Palermo rubbed his hands softly. "That is my advice," he said.

"Come now, my good sorcerer," burst out the Baron, "since you are little better than the rest, what reason have I to retain *your* services? Why, after your confession, should I place you above these bungling thieves?"

"Two reasons," replied Da Palermo. "Firstly, I am of good standing in my profession, acquainted with the best practitioners in France, and able to detect a fraud; and secondly, I have just now made gold."

"Two excellent reasons," replied De Rais, "and in addition you are an honest man. You, at least, shall be retained."

"Thank you," said the magician simply.

§ 2

The conversation with Da Palermo, as well as the survey of the laboratory which Roger de Bricqueville had suggested, demonstrated to De Rais the futility of relying upon the success of white, or lawful magic. Undoubtedly, as he had seen himself, the metal could be achieved by the fortunate conjunction of mutually sympathetic elements, yet the hope of final triumph by this means was tenuous.

It was necessary, therefore, to go deeper into the hidden arts, and to attempt the employment of the supernatural. Although terrified by the thought of forces which he must unleash, De Rais was driven by the monstrous thought of failure to make this choice.

Gold was the necessity upon which depended his career and, though he was filled with a horror of trafficking with the terrible and unknown powers, gold, he had sworn, should be obtained.

Leaving Da Palermo in charge of the laboratory of Machecoul, immersed in his retorts and phials, watching with calculating eye noxious fumes and seething pots of alchemy, the Baron moved, accompanied by his retinue and confidants, to Tiffauges, the greatest and the darkest of his castles.

This irregular, trapezoidal fortress was well suited for the new undertaking on which he had embarked. If possible, it was grayer, sterner and more melancholy than even was Machecoul. Certainly it was large, while its very situation was barren and forbidding. Through the sparse valley surrounding it, the River Sèvre split its course, meeting at the base of a roughshaped promontory the murky waters of the Crume rivulet which drained the half-flooded marshes below the bare plateau. Upon this hill, within the circling of a deep connecting moat, the fortress itself was built.

Four flat towers reared their formidable bulks at the corners, while smaller cylindrical turrets broke the uneven surface of the walls. Within these outer ramparts, a triple cincture of wall and bastion cut across the central enclosure and guarded, with threefold security, the donjon and the high massive main structure that lay along the outer wall and contained, under its peaked roof, the living quarters of the castle. Herein were situated the ceremonial hall, the vast dining-room, the kitchens brightened by the fires on the hearths and by their reflections upon the rows of copper pots and kettles that were hung upon the blackened walls. In this part, too, were sculleries and well rooms, a huge storehouse under the long slate roof intended for the keeping of grain and arms. One found here other halls, bedchambers lighted by narrow windows, dark stairways and narrow passageways.

Opposite this, against the innermost of the inside system of defensive walls, there was another building long and low in shape intended as a barracks and a quarters for the servants. Beyond, lay a maze of courts and alleys, bare or overgrown with grass, while at the end of these there lay a great bare space of packed-down clay which served as a parade ground.

Above the Crume rivulet, close to the donjon, there rose a small round tower in which there were a number of deserted chambers. Mounting a circular stairway that followed the outline of this tower, one ascended past various disused apartments and came out at last at the topmost floor. Here was a round chamber that consumed the entire diameter of the turret and was roofed by a round dome of masonry. Just below the commencement of the dome, were two narrow windows shuttered by solid blinds of oak that could be closed to shut in any light or sound.

In the curve of the wall, a narrow door led to a branching passageway that led to different places within the fortifications. One arm led straight downward to the Crume itself; another followed the course of the wall to the audience chamber, near which there was a connection with another path that descended by a steep ramp to the dungeons and oubliettes below. The third and darkest of these tunnels led also downward until, reaching the cellars, it wound about, dipped underground and emerged suddenly behind the altar of the ancient crypt below the chapel.

He who held this room, therefore, was in command of the walls, the donjon and the prisons; while he was also in communication with the priests.

In this place, Gilles de Rais constructed his laboratory, and amid the curious trappings of mystery he commenced the work of conjuration. From Machecoul, he brought a certain Jean de la Rivière, a man adept by his own boast in the arts of evocation, yet by no means a very great sorcerer. A certain caution advised De Rais to begin with a minor creature; for he feared as yet the work he had undertaken, and wished to become a little familiar with its dangers before the greater man arrived.

Jean de la Rivière was installed, therefore, in the newly made laboratory where, by the light of torches and of high lamps, he moved about, barefoot and clad in druidical white, reciting and mumbling over the vapors and multicolored flames. Beside him De Rais, a tall cap of parchment upon his head, encouraged him in his attempt to control the services of Hell.

In the course of this quest, they set forth, one evening, by the postern gate and headed across the misty plain in the direction of a clump of scrub and brushwood. Of the party, there were four, each carrying certain of the articles necessary for successful conjuration. Griart and Jean de la Rivière led the way, followed by the Baron and De Sillé who talked together in subdued whispers.

"Though I have doubts concerning the abilities of our conductor," confided De Rais, "I tremble in my soul for what he may bring forth."

"Let the sorcerer worry over that," advised De Sillé. "We do no more than watch."

"Yet we, also, shall be exposed before the very force of Hell."

"Faith," said the priest, "is our amulet of safety."

"If there is forgiveness in the abasement of humility, if there is power in the utterance of prayer, I am secure. God knows that I have been absolved a thousand times of my offenses, and that my faith in Him is great. Nevertheless I go with hesitating steps. To-night we play with dangerous things. God understands the weakness of the flesh. Sins of the spirit are of another order."

They entered, now, the copse of gnarled and dripping branches, and seated themselves upon the damp moss. A torch thrust into the ground between them, lighted up the leaves and limbs that overhung them. From De Rais, Jean de la Rivière took a naked sword. Armed with this and with another torch, he left them and, pushing aside the foliage that blocked his way, he went out from the copse into the marsh beyond.

In silence the three waited, staring at one another and at the torch that flared between them. Outside, not far away, they heard the sorcerer intoning his commands, repeating over and over with slowly increasing insistence, a catalogue of mystic words. Occasionally, in the semi-darkness, the Baron crossed himself meditatively, while beneath the reassuring touch of his hand, he felt the carved surface of his little reliquary.

An hour, perhaps, they waited, straining their ears in the silence, or turning a little to see, beyond the enclosing branches, the flicker of the wizard's torch.

They became aware, at last, of another sound added to the dreary incantation. A noise of distant roaring became audible, increasing in volume as though it were approaching. It drew nearer, becoming more articulate and frightening. For the cry was that of a savage and ravenous beast. Louder it grew, snarling and bellowing, while from the unseen evocator there burst a cry of startled horror. Breathless, the three within the copse waited, while from the marsh the sounds grew in terrifying clamor. A struggle was in progress; for they could hear the shouting of Jean de la Rivière, the thumps of blows, and the heavy breathing of the combatants.

Suddenly the branches parted and, wild-eyed, the sorcerer burst among them. His coat was torn, his clothes muddied and his face was covered with blood. Panting and out of breath he dropped to the damp moss and lay there for a moment watched by the other three. Slowly he revived. "A beast of Hell!" he cried. "Look, I am torn and wounded by his talons."

"What sort of beast?" De Sillé demanded.

"Hideous and frightful," gasped the sorcerer, "as black as night, and in the body of a leopard."

§ 3

From Tiffauges messengers were sent, armed with gold, upon a secret mission. Gilles de Sillé went to Paris, secretly, and almost unseen upon the route. Hicquet de Bremont traveled to Lorraine upon the strength of confidential information. While Blanchet, the never-failing, betook himself to Italy, carrying a letter from Antonio da Palermo to Giovanni de Fontanella, who was the Duke of Florence.

At Tiffauges, Gilles de Rais waited, working and learning what he could of sorcery. Letters came at intervals from his envoys. Without the gates of Paris, De Sillé had discovered an ancient hermit living in a ruined tower and had captured him with gold. Already they were on the road.

De Bremont, too, had met his man, a wizard of the utmost skill, recently emerged from the mysterious depths of the Black Forest and speaking a curious jargon with a thickened tongue.

From Florence, Blanchet wrote of the hospitality of Italy and of a secret occult group that circled about a certain Niccolo dei Medeci.

In succession, bad news came from France. At the very gate of the barony of Rais, the Paris sorcerer had slipped and, laden with his gold and baggage, had fallen from the bridge into the Loire, and so was drowned. A few days later, De Bremont returned in haste and quite alone; for the learned German had also perished. Suddenly, within an hour's ride of Champtocé, this man had been stricken with a sudden fever, and died upon the road. As he lay in death, his body had turned black and hideous, while over it had danced a green-blue flame that had consumed it utterly.

From Italy, Blanchet sent word that he had met the famous Niccolo dei Medeci and, through him, come in contact with a bold and fearless man. "Father Prelati," he wrote, "fears neither God nor Satan, while his skill and erudition are the marvel of this city. He comes with me upon my journey to Tiffauges within two days and will undertake the work we have begun."

In July of 1438, Father Prelati appeared at Tiffauges, accompanying the returning Blanchet. To the expectant De Rais, well prepared for an eccentric mystagogue laden with crystals, charts and curious robes, this new sorcerer presented a rather upsetting picture. He was, in fact, a sleek, dark-haired young man whom one suspected of being competent in whatever business he was engaged. His manners were suave, and his polite conversation flowed with gracious ease. French, Latin and Italian were spoken with studious precision and facility, while his appearance was as courtly as was his speech. His long brown fingers were well manicured, his beard and hair precisely trimmed, and his black clothes bore an elegance and correctness that were extremely distinguished. As to his age, De Rais guessed that he was under thirty.

Into the household he insinuated himself deftly, exploring its capabilities and personalities. Of the laboratory he was filled with praise.

"In this chamber," he said to De Rais, "everything has been supplied, and it is here that we shall be regaled, you and I, with spectacles such as few mortals have ever witnessed. In this very room, I tell you, miracles shall be wrought and marvels of my art committed. I am happy in the discovery of this room, my Lord, and congratulate you upon its creation."

"I am impatient, Father Prelati, for the commencement of these wonders," said De Rais. "Let them begin at once."

"All in good time," replied the Italian coolly. "Before I start, I must be sure of certain things. To-morrow we will have a talk."

To-morrow did not, however, bring the talk. Instead, Prelati spent the day in visiting the dungeons, discovering the stairways in the walls and talking endlessly with every member of

the household who came across his path. For the sorcerer had
no wish to leave success to chance.

He had come to Tiffauges with a very definite purpose. In
the freedom of this isolated castle, supplied with wealth
and boundless opportunities, he hoped to succeed in certain
experiments that he had not dared perform in Florence. He
believed fully in the evil powers, and considered himself more
than a match for Satan, whom he wished to bind by a contract
of his own concocting. In the meantime, he was perfectly willing to make gold, to raise djinns, or to perform any of the tricks
that were necessary to please a curious master. Of these sub-
terfuges, he was a master. Sleight-of-hand, the use of mirrors
and hidden machinery, unseen accomplices, a certain luminous
paint, were all at his command to be employed with shameless
effrontery. The problem in which he was interested was one of
epoch-making importance in the realm of evocation. In his
extensive research, and in his experimentations, he had begun
to doubt that the mere employment of incantational formulæ
was sufficient completely to subjugate the Fiend. A bribe,
perhaps, was necessary.

In De Sillé he found a willing guide. Together they left the
laboratory and descended the intramural passageway to the
chapel crypt. De Sillé pointed out its antiquity and the narrow-
ness of its fenestration, and compared it to the chapel above.

Prelati took up the comparison in a broad and flowing style.
"In this," he said, "we have a double edifice. Above, light in
construction, illuminated by leaden-laced and tinted windows,
and embroidered by the fantasy of man, there is the house of
God. In form it is similar, yet it differs in each detail from this
substructure. For this is massive, subterranean, and lighted by
flaring tapers. The solid pillars resting upon the earth itself
branch out into the slender shafts above. The wide bright
nave of the Christian chapel rests directly upon the heavy
barrel-vaulted tunnel in which we stand. From the level of the
courtyard, one sees at first a chapel, well made and handsome,
raised a little above the earth. But from within, one recognizes

that it is in truth a massive building dug into the earth upon whose solid roof is raised an unimportant edifice of frail construction."

"That which is above . . ." murmured De Sillé to himself.

"Ah," remarked Prelati, "so you, also, dabble with the truth."

Content at last with his discoveries, Prelati, a few days after his visit to the crypt, sought out De Rais and entered into his promised conversation.

"I am ready," he said, "to commence upon my operations."

"You delight me, Prelati, and under your accomplished hand, I feel sure that gold shall not be long away."

"I trust not," said the sorcerer, "unless my hands are tied."

"That they shall not be," De Rais assured him. "I have placed the laboratory and all its resources at your command, even Jean de la Rivière shall do your bidding."

Prelati frowned. "I could well dispense with that white-haired rascal," he said. "I wish no fools around me."

"By his art, Father Prelati," declared De Rais in rebuke, "that magician raised from Hell a beast of marvelous proportions. I myself can bear him witness."

The Italian smiled suavely. "I perhaps misjudge the villain," he said. "Yet he did not, I feel sure, allow you to see the beast."

"Am I a fool, young man!" burst out De Rais. "Did I not hear him roar? In God's name, this leopard was a very beast of Hell and raised from the bowels of the earth not half a mile from where we stand."

"Let us then forget the episode of the leopard. What have you in your hand?" he asked suddenly.

Gilles de Rais opened an empty fist. Over it Prelati dropped a silken handkerchief and, peering under its lower edges, raised it a trifle. Amid a great struggling of the cloth he withdrew by the tail a wriggling lizard which he deposited gently upon the ground. With a flash, the reptile vanished.

"It might easily have been a leopard," said Prelati coolly, "had such a beast instead gone foolishly to sleep in the reach of my hand."

De Rais laughed. "Is that your sorcery, my friend?" he asked.

"That is the magic of lies," Prelati replied, "a not very difficult art, though a most impressive one. Nevertheless it is entirely as valuable for the achievement of gold, as is the sort of magic which brews ill-smelling soups in the hope of finding, amid the garden weeds and boiling castle rubbish, the key to wealth."

"Flamel made gold by natural means, as did Da Palermo, my own alchemist. I believe it to be entirely possible."

"I am not convinced," said Prelati. "Gold as well as lizards, may be materialized even in the pots of alchemists. Tell me, why did not Flamel rule the earth? Gold is all that is needed."

"If you are so convinced," said De Rais sharply, "I should like to know why you traveled all the way from Italy. Did you merely wish to convert me from my faith in sorcery?"

"You speak lightly of sorcery, my Lord," said the Italian. "Let me assure you that it is a very deep and a very terrible science. We deal with forces we scarcely understand. We stand eternally upon the brink of Hell, and occasionally we lean too far. The fools who prate of transmutation, who babble of the essence of the stars, and talk of reproducing the natural and gradual refinement of lead to gold, which once took place within the womb of earth, disgust me. You know their theory. But you have not forgotten another: 'God created the heavens and the earth'; and God played not with planetary movements. We seek gold. Gold is of supernatural origin, and to find it, only supernatural means avail."

"For that reason," said De Rais, "Blanchet found you in Florence and brought you to Tiffauges."

"Were I a saint, I might apply to God," said Prelati, "but I am not a saint; therefore, I must seek elsewhere."

"I await your evocations."

"I doubt them," said Prelati, "for I can not believe that any Lord, be he terrestrial, celestial or infernal, listens greatly to the whining of a beggar. This I tell you, my Lord. I shall not mumble feebly in the darkness, but I shall raise my voice shouting to the utmost of my strength. I am prepared to go to any lengths to achieve my purpose. I am no weary alchemist, and I do not plan to fail. Whatever the cost, whatever the risk or sacrifice, if I embark upon this task, I shall not hesitate until the power of Hell is opened to me, and Satan is my slave."

"I tremble for your soul."

Prelati raised his voice. "Our souls!" he cried. "We are together in this deed."

"You are alone, Prelati. I dare not face the Fiend."

"I tell you we are joined in this. Would Satan give me his wealth for you? By God, it would turn to ashes in your hands! Side by side, we meet the Prince of Darkness, or we meet him not at all."

"I have too great a fear of Hell," said De Rais. "Already too many sins are resting on my soul. I am no peasant lad dazzled by a pail of ducats, to give up life for such a trifle. Gold shall be mine. I swear it. But my soul shall be retained."

"Your soul is safe," Prelati reassured him. "Nor do I long for Hell. Satan shall appear before us—yes, before you also; but we shall be well hid. I tell you I am no country conjuror playing at my trade. I am skilled in every portion of my art. For these past ten years do you suppose I have neglected the circles and pentacles of protection? I swear that you shall be as secure in the presence of Albiron himself, as in the presence of a leprous peasant. But touch them not."

"And yet I am afraid. Suppose your pentacles should fail?"

"Then both of us are damned."

"You terrify me."

"You must face the risk."

"I fear," said De Rais, "the Evil One and all his works. I fear the grinning maw of Hell. I fear the powers that are unseen and terrible; and I fear, Prelati, for my soul."

"Then you refuse them all—gold, power, Satan, ambition and the services of Francisco Prelati."

"No" said De Rais slowly. "Gold I have sworn to have, and I dare not refuse my oath. I shall follow your commands."

§ 4

A day was set, selected by the wisdom of the astrologers, for nothing could be left to chance. The ninth day of the month had first been chosen, as nine, the number, embodies wisdom, mystery and safety. But later this was changed, as a specific reference forbade it. Of all the numbers in the list, nine alone was impossible for conjuration. Instead, they settled upon the eleventh, a day of evil reputation, yet one of power, which was selected by the counsel of the astrologers.

Brave in battle and in dangers of the earth, Gilles de Rais looked forward with a quaking inward terror; for the Pit with all its well-understood horrors lay before him, yawning its flaring jaws in hunger for a victim. Death lay before him as he trod the knife-like rim of Hell. A single waver in his mortal balance would send him to a death that was everlasting, terrible and beyond recall. Death of the body he scarcely feared, yet this was death of soul; and at the thought of this, he shuddered and was filled with a horrible and cold-sweated fear. There lay he knew, but the thin circle of Prelati's charms between De Rais, the living, and the irrevocable end he did not dare to face.

Minutely he followed the exact detail of preparation. Rigorously he fasted, bathed and anointed his hair and beard with oils. New garments, white and undyed, were washed with holy water. In the jeweled dusk of the chapel, he knelt, fasting and in humility; while over his suppliant form by his own authority, the full cohort of his priests repeated three times a lofty and sonorous mass and bestowed upon their kneeling lord the vast benevolence of God.

Thus passed the day of the eleventh; and while he waited deep in prayer and fasting, Prelati prepared himself for the ordeal. In the laboratory De Sillé was at work sprinkling the chamber and the instruments with dashes of holy water, and

A Medieval Conception of Hell

repeating powerful exorcisms. For the chain of protection must be complete.

At midnight, the chapel gate opened to admit Blanchet, walking silently and clad in chasuble of a metallic green. With lowered head, he approached the altar and there, in a heavy monotone, he prayed aloud. Through the shadows of the nave, De Rais came slowly toward the priest and knelt beneath the heavy wooden crucifix. Bending toward the penitent, and in whispered silence, Blanchet administered the sacrament.

Confessed, absolved, purified of soul and strong with the Body and the Blood of God, Gilles de Rais stepped from the altar, and with the priest, descended to the crypt below. Before the secret door he hesitated for a moment, weighing again his fears. Then pressing boldly against it, he saw it open before the darkness of the passageway.

He stepped in and closed the door behind him. Before him spread the yellow, feathered globe of candle-light that illuminated, within its reach, circles of brilliance upon the smooth walls and the worn footway. Beyond lay a thick fog of blackness through which he pushed his way, cutting it with his sphere of light. A corner brought the darkness closer, and as he touched the narrow sides, he felt the stonework cold and dripping with moisture. Following the course of the rampart, the tunnel turned again, rounding the angle of the donjon. Beside him, an arched doorway cut a black pattern in the oases of the candle-light. For here the passageway branched; and by this door, there was the path ascending to the banquet hall above.

Close beside it, barred by a heavy grille, another tunnel descended by a stairway to the labyrinth of dungeons and torture rooms below. A fleeting wish to leave his present path presented itself. Upward he knew there lay the pleasant lighting of the banquet hall. A fire blazed in the chimney and the cheer of food and wine awaited.

Passing the intersecting roads, he pushed his way onward, shielding his taper carefully lest its flickering glow should be extinguished. The level of the floor now rose before him, and he ascended a sort of ramp which circled upward in a large spiral. A third archway presented a final opportunity for escape. It too led downward but, escaping the prisons below the court-yard, it turned sharply and came out upon the quiet bank of the Sèvre beyond the castle wall. As he passed this door, his steps became slower with the steepness of the climb, and more reluctant as he neared his destination.

An oblong of yellow radiance marked the ending of his path, and in the doorway of the laboratory he halted to regain his breath. Before him lay the knowledge of an unknown power. Evil in its very essence, sublime and undiluted, was to be re-vealed. While he, the fearless Gilles de Rais, would lift a cor-ner of the leaden curtain of obscurity. The vanity of the moment reassured him, and in silence he entered the laboratory.

Draped in heavy black, its windows closed by the solid shut-ters, the room was lighted by a dozen tapers. The furnace in the chimney-place was dead and cold, but in the center of the room there burned a small brazier set upon a tripod. Beside it there stood two square stools such as were used to support the ends of coffins. Except for these and for a little table upon which rested a box of various articles, the room was stripped of furniture. Upon one stool reposed a sheaf of parchment in-scribed with magical wisdom written in the blood of goats, while upon the other there was a brandy bottle duly consecrated by the prayers of Gilles de Sillé.

By the brazier, Prelati was standing conversing with De Sillé and absently stirring the fire. A white robe, tightly belted about his waist, descended to the floor. Embroidered upon it was a large gold circle enclosing the secret seal and pentacle of Solomon. Upon his head a tall cap, in form resembling a mitre, rose above a crown of gold traced in silver with protec-tive designs. De Sillé, also, was in white, but his robe was un-decorated save for a tiny crucifix suspended about his neck.

As De Rais entered, the sorcerer indicated that he seat him-self upon the floor behind and a little to the right of the brazier.

De Sillé also sat upon the floor, while about them Prelati traced upon the ground a triangle whose apex was the brazier. Holy water, blood and powdered charcoal made up the substance of the paint, and as the evocator drew out his design, he muttered to himself a lengthy formula. About the triangle he circumscribed a circle, and beyond this two other slightly wider rings, leaving all four figures incomplete so that he could enter again into the inmost space.

At the four corners of the outer ring, four pentacles were drawn and closed completely, while within them the mystic names of *Agla, El, Iah* and *Adonay* were written. Returning through the incompleted rings, the evocator turned now to the segment at the east, between the triangle itself and the inner circle. In this space, he wrote with careful hand the word *Alpha* and deposited beside it a candlestick of brass in which there stood a taper, black and unlighted. In the opposite, or western, segment, he wrote *Omega* and set a similar candle down. Passing between the Baron and De Sillé, he leaned over the third space and drew, as the horns, two crosses in the Greek fashion, while between them he wrote the sacred initials of the Savior.

Passing once more through gaps he had left in his design, Prelati left the circles. Around the room he walked, intoning a valuable ritual and extinguishing one by one the torches that had lighted the room. Directly above the brazier burned a high lamp from which, reflected from its cap of parchment, descended a cone of light that fell upon the floor in a small circle whose edge was all within the triangle.

Reentering the figure, Prelati closed the triple wall with pentacles and stepped within the triangle. Carefully he lighted the two side candles and sealed that inner figure with another pentacle, which was the last of the defenses. The magic circle was complete.

From a ewer, the evocator raised a few drops of holy water, and with damp fingers touched it to his brow and breast. He stood, now, behind the glowing brazier, partly illuminated by the high lamp above him whose rays descended upon the floor in front of him. From the ewer, he sprinkled holy water to the east, then to the west and north and south and, finally, upon the four pentacles that were drawn outside the figure wherein he stood.

Save for the single lamp and for the two side candles, no other light existed but the glowing of the coals within the gratings of the brazier. Beyond, the room was hung in darkness.

From the coffin stool beside him, Prelati raised a small box of iron, taking from it a substance for the fumigation. With careful movements, he sprinkled it upon the coals before him, and there rose up a thick white smoke, filling the narrow cone of light and suffusing into the air a heavy, sweetish perfume. Waving his wand above the fire, Prelati began his conjuration.

"Oh, Creator of this fire and flame by Whom all things are made, I exorcise Thee that this fire shall be unable to do hurt to any here enclosed. Bless, O Lord, this fire and sanctify it in the name of the grand Adonay."

Upon the floor crouched the two witnesses of the evocation, fascinated and intent upon the careful ritual. Upon the fire Prelati poured some of the contents of the consecrated brandy and entered upon a long and repetitious incantation.

As it progressed, the first novelty of terror wore away, and Gilles de Rais experienced a sense of boredom and of cramped legs. The dull monotony got on his nerves until he wished to shout and order lights. The darkness became oppressive.

But gradually staring through the smoky cone of light into the glowing embers of the brazier, he became relaxed, devoid of sufficient energy to move. Above the coals he saw the magician's wand waving slowly back and forth, never varying in its movement; while heavily, the droning voice continued, lulling him into a leaden repose.

Distantly through the heavy atmosphere, he heard the ritualistic deliberation of the magician's words:

"Eyes of cancer, go into this potent flame and blaze in fumigation. Anise and camphor, enter in and fume. Gall of bull and powdered wormwood, go and blaze. Accept, O purifying flame, my offerings of conjuration. Calamis and saffron, go and blaze. Burn ye, coriander and wood of aloes. Ants' eggs, go. Henbane, burn with seeds of poppy. Enter cannabis, musthalperate and hellebore, fume and blaze. . . ."

Drowsily the Baron listened, intent upon divergent things. Within the chamber which had ceased to be beyond the outer pentacles, the air grew heavy; so thick it seemed that sounds were muffled by the cloak of incantation. The steadiness of the bright coals that had oppressed him, became a prison for his eyes from which he did not care to look away. The magic cone of light spread out, widening to incredible dimensions, to shrink again into a thread of brilliance. Beyond its outer rim there was no longer space. A pall hung there, impenetrable and far away.

Eased delight suffused him as though he sat without the edges of a golden plain, gazing upon red moons whose presence told the mysteries of life and death and put them in their proper spheres. Again the red moons shrank, becoming pin-points of an angry flame within the narrow brazier.

Words from the magician broke upon his ear, meaningless in import yet fitting with his mood.

". . . So I shall conjure ye, demons of the nether world; for your names and seals are known. Belial, slimy essence of corruption, lord of vice and pestilence, deity of Sidon, hear my words. Orias of lion shape, tailed with a serpent, commander of the force of time and space, demon of astrology, you shall arise. Beelzebuth, hideous of aspect, whose giant membrane wings crowd out the sky, master of the land of shadows, hear me. Scirlin and Barron, messengers of mean importance, heed the power of my strong demands. . . ."

Interminably the chanting voice continued, while behind the brazier, Prelati stood, rapt and motionless, moving his wand above the embers. To De Rais, the very element of duration had ceased to be. Beyond the circle of the evocation, nothing existed or would again exist. Here he had lived for ever, yet in the quickness of a heart-beat. He sat, isolated, alone and timeless, within the true expanse of space.

Somehow, his attention became riveted upon Prelati's wand so steady in its moving arc above the coals. In a little arc it swung, back and forth, beating a hideous pulse within his brain. Its movement was a thing of monstrous horror, and he stared upon it as though his eyes would burst under the strain. Through a mounting cloud of drugged and perfumed smoke, he saw it waving in its mad command upon eternity. As he watched, it slowed its pace and halted in mid-air. Slowly it moved again, dragging him in its course, and pointed, motionless and straight, into the outer darkness.

Suddenly the invocation ceased; and a pounding silence filled the cone of light. Through it burst the voice of the evocator, shouting hoarsely in a hideous command:

"Scirlin!" he cried with a voice that lashed the soul. "Beelzebuth! Lucifer! Demons, I command! Solymo! Astaroth! Madilon and Saroy, I command you!"

Dragged from a lovely dream, De Rais cried out within his soul, as though his cherished peace was ripped and torn by a hideous cruelty. In anguish, he listened to the repetitions. Seven times Prelati called the demons to appear. Then, with a great "Amen," he ceased and pointed swiftly with his wand beyond the curtain of the darkness.

Staring outward, De Rais saw nothing. The world was at an end beyond the wizard's wand. Yet in the blackness he sensed a presence that had come into the chamber. No form could be discerned without the circle, yet in the unseen distance, a figure was rising from the floor. Infinitely slowly, it mounted upward, gathering itself within the darkness, and spreading outward with a horrible precision. Against the solid pall of black, the figure assumed a sort of outline; showed a bulk yet blacker than its surroundings, growing more solid, until the Baron clearly sensed its presence. Formless, nameless and unseen, it grew in horrible enormity until its very features could almost be determined. Huge, bat-like wings spread out, encircling the shaft of light. Smaller grew the haven of the pentacles, compressed in their embrace. The creature was beyond comprehension, vast as was infinity, and evil with the sin of madness. Before the illimitable horror of this being, a paralyzing dread secured the Baron, and he crossed himself in panic.

Suddenly the figure of the evocator leaped. Whirling, he seized a box of fumigants and threw the contents on the fire. A sharp biting stench arose, and from the brazier issued clouds of acrid clarifying smoke. Sulphur and vinegar assailed the Baron's nostrils, while at the same time he heard Prelati shouting exorcisms in a paroxysm of fear. Slowly the figure of the monster wavered, faded and seemed to disappear.

A wave of terror seized De Rais, and again in possession of his strength, he sprang to his feet with frightened shouting. From the enclosing circle, he rushed headlong toward the door, his cousin, Gilles de Sillé, at his heels. As he traversed the room, the evocator gave a shriek. "Halt, my Lord, in God's own name!" he cried in a terrible voice. "Return to safety, or all of us are lost!"

But the door was gained. Thrusting it open with superhuman force, the Baron, followed by his .faithful priest and cousin, tumbled chattering into the darkened passageway.

From the chamber they had left, came sounds of a terrific conflict. Blows resounded, and cries of anguish from the unfortunate sorcerer penetrated the passage. For a while, they waited in the darkness paralyzed with fear, until the shouts and crashings died away. Then, with daggers drawn, the two opened the door and peered•in.

In the center of the room, the brazier smoked sullenly, and about it upon the floor lay the overturned stools, the table and a mass of scattered implements. Into the room they rushed and lighted the torches about the walls. By the full illumination, they saw Prelati, half without the magic circle, lying prostrate upon the ground.

His face and head were cut and bruised, and his magic robes were stained with blood. They turned him over on his back, and he stared upward, his face contorted in pain. "Something went wrong," he moaned. "My God, I nearly failed." Suddenly his eye rested upon the reliquary that hung about the Baron's neck. "That!" he sobbed, raising himself upon an elbow. "It was for that, that we have nearly perished!" His eyes closed, and he fell back unconscious upon the floor. Together they carried him to his chamber and put him into bed. Leaving him, they crossed the courtyard toward the keep. A dew lay lightly upon the ground so that their footprints could be seen. In a lingering uneasiness, De Rais looked back and counted them. Two sets there were, and both were human. In relief, he gulped a breath of air and entered the confines of the castle, hungry for the sanity of wine.

§ 5

For seven days Prelati remained in bed, recovering from his injuries and pondering upon the possible causes of his near disaster. To De Rais he half apologized for his outburst concerning the reliquary.

"I am sure," he said, "that there was something wrong. And it was only by the greatest of good fortune that we escaped alive. The Fiend was rapidly exceeding in strength my power of control, while the manifestation was not at all what I expected."

"My reliquary, no doubt, upset your calculations."

"I am not at all sure of that now. But certainly some mighty force opposed us. There may have been an adulteration of the ingredients of fumigation; a lack of spiritual willingness upon our parts; a slip, possibly, in the very method that I employed. I am baffled by the problem."

"But," objected the Baron, "you have raised the fiends before."

Prelati hesitated. "I must confess," he said, "that Beelzebuth, incomplete as was his evocation, is to date my greatest and most proud success. Barron, Scirlin, and others of lesser importance have obeyed my call and appeared before me as clearly as I now see you. Until the other night, however, the mighty lords of the infernal hierarchy have escaped my art. But now that I have made a beginning, I intend to continue toward eventual success. A difficulty is, that for the conjuration of the Fiend himself, there is no complete written instruction."

"Then how will you proceed?"

"We must go back," said Prelati. "I do not care for needless risk."

"At present," said the Baron, "I, too, have little stomach for another failure. The jaws of Hell were close enough to terrify my soul."

"Therefore, my Lord, I shall renew the conjuring of minor fiends in an attempt to learn from them the secret we desire."

As he lay in bed, Prelati was perturbed. During his experiments, he had achieved a certain proximity to the hellish powers, yet the pact which he desired appeared to be as far away as ever. Of one thing, however, he was certain. To command a force so strong and terrible as that of Satan, was a task of the utmost difficulty. He had sufficiently raised the curtain of obscurity that hid the nether world so that he realized the vastness of the infernal chaos as well as the fact that half-hearted or distrustful means were worse than useless.

As he had told De Rais, he intended now to catechize the lesser fiends, demanding, by the power of his spells, the knowledge which he lacked for a complete attempt upon the gates of Hell. He had, however, strong doubts that these beings would be of service. From De Sillé, he had received a new idea upon the cosmic complexion of the race of supernatural beings, and he set about, while on his sick bed, a thorough survey and cataloguing of his own.

There were, he knew, a vast legion of curious beings who lived upon the earth, or near enough the reach of man, to be well known by him. Elves, succubi, sprites and similar creatures were admittedly both earthly and supernatural, yet great differences existed in their natures.

Of these creatures, he had made, at one time in his career, a careful study, collecting the various descriptions and purging them from legend and from the poetry of bards. According to this view, the tribe of elves, fees, goblins, gnomes and similar beings were creatures of mature yet delicate form, dancing in robes of silver cobweb upon the hills and woodlands. Scientific observation had, however, thoroughly dispelled this myth. Competent observers, both peasants and otherwise, described them as a small hairy folk dwelling in caves and crevices. Apparently they were harmless, being neutral rather than being either good or evil. Surely they did not yield to evocation, nor yet to prayers. In the cosmic scheme, they were perhaps, soulless like the beasts, or similar in status to the unbaptized babes and to the pagan philosophers. At the risk of disagreeing with Saint Augustine, Prelati assumed that they were descendants of the pagan gods, stripped for all time of their important powers and hence unimportant for his purposes.

Familiar spirits, attending upon their masters in the guise of cats and toads, could also be discarded from his thoughts. These were corporeal yet changeable in shape—demons of some shackled order set to the definite task of attending to the witch or wizard to whom they had been given and who, in return for loyalty, must feed them from a damning and supernumerary breast. These also could be disregarded from his calculations.

Of the pure demoniac order, yet free from servitude and ranging apparently at will over the face of earth, another class must be considered. Vampires, banshees, incubi and succubi, werewolves and warning spirits were, it appeared, fiends at large, being semi-detached from the ranks of Lucifer and charged with spreading evil in the world. They could not be evoked by incantation, but could be laid by human or by churchly means. Of this order, were the demons that entered into men and swine, and vanished before an exorcism. Surely they were not great folk. It was known that many such—like vampires—depended upon corpses for their nourishment or locomotion; and one had even vanished before the menace of a legal process.

Barron and Scirlin, the minor fiends whom he evoked, were
of another category. For they, at least, were evocable; yet the
wizard wondered whether they were in fact of any more importance.

As soon as he recovered from his wounds, Prelati enclosed
himself within his laboratory and, following the ritual that he
had used in Florence, he summoned Barron to appear. This
fiend obligingly materialized, terrific in his scent of brimstone,
sonorous and cryptic in his answers, but of little value as to his
conversation. A careful questioning brought forth evasions, and
Prelati saw clearly that his only purpose was deception intended
to lead the unwary to the brink of Hell.

In order to progress, the sorcerer now understood that he
must turn from these futile creatures and approach the jaws of
Lucifer's domain by a bolder and more direct path. The king
is not beheld when stable-boys are bribed.

To make a bargain, what had he to offer? His own soul, already endangered, would scarcely be sufficient to a hopeful
demon; nor did Prelati wish to give it. At the back of his mind,
there had lurked, for some time, the thought of sacrifice as a
propitiation, and for this purpose he had originally considered
the soul of Gilles de Rais. Now, however, he half gave up the
thought. Like his own, that of the Baron was also insecure,
while its owner clung to its possession with a desperate grasp.
Though major sins might be committed, the Baron was not yet
ready to give up his hope, nor could he be completely damned
because of his own resolution. His frequent prayers and masses,
and his constant absolutions put an end to Prelati's hope in this
direction.

Disturbed in his mind, he had long talks with Gilles de Sillé
concerning the satanistic view-point. The priest was full of theories concerning the infernal world, and was thoroughly convinced upon the necessity of satanic adoration and the worship
of the Evil One. To Prelati, this seemed, perhaps, the true approach. At any rate, it certainly was worth attempting. The
sorcerer had reached the limit to his craft. One worshiped God

before one prayed for rain; and in the inversion, it seemed likely that a devil's mass might be the necessary prelude for an evocation. Yet the Baron, he was afraid, would not yet quite so boldly risk his soul. Vaguely he began to build a plan of action embodying his different theories.

Shortly after the conclusion of this experiment, Prelati received a request from De Rais to visit the Baron's chambers and to discuss there the progress of the work. He found the Baron in a discontented mood.

"I am disappointed, Prelati, that we have not further advanced," began the Baron. "On the occasion when the great Beelzebuth entered our laboratory, I felt a joy of exultation that we were near our goal. Yet since that time, our efforts have had rewards in magic serpents and in other idleness. What hinders you? Of money you have unlimited funds; of opportunity, twenty-four hours of the day are yours; of materials, cooperation, books, assistance—all are within your hand. My patience, Prelati, is at an end, and I must ask the question. Have you or have you not the power to summon Lucifer?"

"I have, my Lord."

"Then call him forth."

"Once, when I first arrived," said Prelati evenly, "I told you that sorcery was a deep and terrible profession. The Fiend does not play tricks for the curious to watch. Unwittingly you have yourself pointed to the reason for my hesitance. Lucifer possesses a shyness of a sort."

"So," laughed De Rais harshly; "then Satan, like a blushing bride, trembles before the advent of her bridegroom. Will my kisses sear the modesty of Hell?"

"Even as the bride," went on Prelati, "the evil forces have a touching modesty. They care not for the cross."

De Rais raised his hand to the reliquary that hung about his neck. "My salvation," he asserted, "is not dependent upon a sign. God in His infinite goodness, protects me within a pentacle of faith."

"The reliquary is a sign, my Lord, but it is a symbol, also, of our non-success. Satan is the master of deceit, yet you come to him with weapons in your belt, attempting to treat on equal terms with Hell while repeating inwardly a Pater Noster. And so, my Lord, the Fiend but laughs and plays with us as we attempt to play with him."

"In this matter," said De Rais, "I am in deadly earnest. Nor have I any wish to play the fool. Call up the evil powers, and even they shall be convinced. I shall retain my soul, Prelati, but I shall meet with Satan face to face."

"Yet to achieve your end, you will not budge an inch. I am not asking for your soul, my Lord. I merely ask adherence to my full commands."

"Under no circumstance," said De Rais, "will I consent to hazard my salvation. From that position you must now proceed; for I refuse to fail."

"Homage to the Fiend is needed," went on Prelati; "for he has made demands."

Clearly thought out and perfectly adapted to his own conclusions, the answer which the Baron sought had taken shape within Prelati's mind.

"I have done my utmost," he began, "to bring the forces we desire to the laboratory. So far I have succeeded; yet from this point onward, I am beyond my strength. No man unaided may do more than I, who have stretched the very limits of my art. One course alone remains. I am not using idle speech; for what I say, I know. Homage must be rendered, as I have said before, and must be attended by a sacrifice of blood."

"Blood is easily obtained, Prelati," said the Baron.

"Yet blood, such as I ask, is of another sort. Satan is no pagan deity to be glutted with the blood of beasts. He is the very essence of evil. Sins of the flesh and sins of spirit are his currency. True sacrifice, he then demands. A creature, human and living in the upper air, must die in homage to the Lord of Darkness. And with the sacrifice must go a soul."

De Rais shuddered. "A sin against the Holy Ghost," he muttered. "My God, how vast a sacrilege!"

"A soul demanded, my master. Such sacrifice, and such alone, is worthy of that Power. Devotion, my Lord, means more than incense and mystic phrases, and you must make your choice. Terrible though this expedient may be, it is our only course. Dare you to face the homage due to Hell, or will you shrink at its enormity? As emissary of the dreaded Fiend, I read his ultimatum. Thus, as his temporary agent, I cry forth his hideous demands. In the name of Lucifer, of Satan and of the Hellish hosts, I make my claim upon the life, the blood, the heart and entrails for my invocation. I ask a human soul to be delivered, in humility, to Hell."

"I hear, and yet I fear to understand."

"Consider briefly, and let me know your mind. A soul demanded to depart in sin. Not yours, nor mine, but one that lives outside our lives. A soul of purity, untarnished and undamned."

Before the prospect which confronted him, Gilles de Rais fell into silence. He became retrospective, looking back upon his path. Step by step, he saw the way that he had come. Sorcery had encroached upon him with a steadiness that appalled him. Easily had he slipped from harmless alchemy into the very presence of the Fiend when he crouched within a slender diagram that was, itself, beyond the sanction of the Church.

Great as he knew his crimes to be, the bounty of his God enclosed them all, for in his heart as well as in his feudal duties, the Baron had remained a loyal vassal. Though he had consented to a traffic with the Enemy, he had not left the ramparts of the Church. Yet now he stood upon the brink of crime so dreadful that he shuddered at its very possibility. Murder in all its hideous ferocity he knew to be a sin against mankind, but he had dealth with life and death, and did not fear them. By his sword, Blackburn had vanished from the earth; by his command, the company at Rainfort had ceased to be; and in his curious passion, the innocents had fled to God.

Their deaths had been to him a witness of his human power. And now within his grasp there lay another strength vast, inhuman and infinitely more terrible. A godlike power had been offered, one which he feared to use.

Gods shuffling their wearied armies across a broken field, beckoned to the vanity of man, and Gilles de Rais, not caring from which camp had come the call, nor searching much its nature, accepted, with startled fear, the invitation he could not resist.

"A soul," he said slowly, "is needed by the Fiend. I, Gilles de Rais, am not afraid to give. My choice is made, Prelati. Satan shall answer my command, and to the jaws of Hell an infant's soul shall be consigned."

§ 6

The crypt of the chapel of St. Vincent was chosen by Prelati as the place in which the worship and the ceremony of infernal sacrifice should be performed. To aid him in the many details, and to assist him also in the planning of the ritual of demonolatry, he called in Gilles de Sillé. The latter was most helpful; for from his past experiences with the satanists, he was able to supply a vast amount of practical direction. A certain secrecy, they felt, must be observed, and for this reason Machecoul instead of Tiffauges was selected.

Orders were sent there for the place to be vacated by the servants of the castle; and attended by a minimum of confidential and trusted men, the company of celebrants set forth.

Besides De Rais and his two counselors, there traveled also Blanchet, Henri Griart, and Etienne Corrillaut—making six in all. Roger de Bricqueville was left behind. While he was outwardly a loyal and trusted adherent, a story had reached (some time before) the knowing ears of Gilles de Sillé, and had been stored away for such a time as this.

For some time past, the treasurer had rather obviously withdrawn himself from the career of Gilles de Rais, nor had he ever taken any part in the mysteries of the tower chamber. Indeed, he had been most careful that he be absolved from any blame of sorcery, of witchcraft, or of other crimes. Yet he well knew all that passed within the walls. For a greater reason than this, however, De Sillé thoroughly distrusted him.

Emerging long ago from the charnel-house of Machecoul during the final burning of the bones from Champtocé, the little priest had seen a figure lurking in the darkness of the passageway. Pretending to be oblivious, he had passed from sight but had instituted a shrewd and well-bribed investigation. The lurking figure had indeed been Roger de Bricqueville, but, more damning than this fact, had been the presence of two women with him. Without a doubt all three had witnessed, through some aperture, the scene wherein young Rossignol had met his death.

Since the affair of the charnel-house, Robin Romulart had also died; so that no more than these six could be mustered for the present expedition. Hicquet de Bremont had been sounded out, but while professing the greatest loyalty and discretion, he had declined to lend his presence.

Arrived at Machecoul, they commenced at once their preparations. To De Rais himself, they gave the task of the decoration of the crypt; while under the guidance of De Sillé, Prelati drew up the plans of the ceremony. Blanchet undertook the minor tasks; collecting incense, causing costumes and vessels appropriate for the work to be obtained, and the like.

For days he rode about the countryside; visiting cloth merchants in search of heavy hangings; employing sewing women for the well-designed embroideries; interviewing satanists and booksellers; visiting a baker in a half-deserted hamlet; and bringing a cabinet-maker blindfolded to Machecoul.

He stopped, returning from one of these expeditions, at the end of the long avenue of elms, almost against the castle walls, where stood a cottage, ancient and tumbledown, squatting in a swamp of filth. From its chimney rose a heavy cloud of smoke that circled downward upon the sagging roof. The door, rotten and repaired a hundred times, was half open, and through it came a stale and ugly smell. Lowering his head, he entered in and found himself within a dirty and disordered room. Save for the doorway, no other aperture admitted light or air; so that the atmosphere was damp and foul.

Toward him across the muddy floor, came a woman of a most forbidding aspect. As disordered as the room, her sparse gray hair matted upon her head, Perrine Martin approached with heavy strides. Beneath the bundle of rags which encased her, she was a strong and large-boned woman whose knotty hands gave evidence of physical power. Her eyes, small and curiously yellow, looked at him unblinkingly through narrow pupils.

"Ha, friend Priest," she said suddenly, "what news?"

"I have a commission for you, Perrine," he said. "Two favors are needed for my Lord de Rais, and both you can supply."

The witch regarded him balefully. "Gold in advance," she said, "and any brew my Lord commands."

Blanchet laughed. "We have no need of brews," he said. "Firstly, a meeting has been called which seven may attend; and secondly, a sacrifice is asked."

The woman nodded. "Seven shall come," she said, "and we shall bring the goat."

A piece of gold fell from his hand into the clutching fingers of the witch. Quickly she bit it, and as the priest went out she slammed the door upon his back.

Once more outside, Blanchet shuddered. "Now for a bath," he muttered to himself; "already I begin to itch."

Impatiently De Rais awaited, while the work of preparation went on, idly curious of what was intended, yet without a burning interest. His fever for the magic arts was waning, as had before it waned his desperate thirst for gold. Without thinking, he began to want a change, to leave the wizards to their own devices and to embark upon some new experience. Once more he felt unsatisfied and oppressed by a secret need of outlet.

Something had choked his energy and destroyed his wish for life. Vainly he fussed about the castle, inspecting draperies and garments. Stupidly and dull-eyed, he read magic books concerning evocation and the fiends of Hell, caring little for their contents. The interval between his conversation with Prelati and the ceremony promised in the crypt had been too long, and the suspense was gone.

Yet when the time arrived, he was refilled with eagerness. Together the six companions were fed a mighty banquet in the late afternoon, whereat they gorged themselves with food, flooding their bodies with a flow of wine. With the conclusion of the meal, they rose and separated, to rejoin later in the crypt.

This place had undergone a complete alteration. Nothing of the bareness now remained. The floor between the rows of piers was covered with soft carpets, upon which were spread a hundred cushions of different shapes and colors. Along the sides of the nave, sewn together and passing around the piers so as to shut off the narrow aisles, hung long curtains of black and scarlet silk, bespangled with stars and broken crosses. Across the apex, beneath the arch at the commencement of the half-dome, there was suspended a heavy tapestry which Blanchet had borrowed from a wealthy sorcerer. Upon a ground of dull green, there rose a life-size figure of Prince Lucifer with blazing eyes and greedy dripping jaws.

Alone, De Rais entered the infernal chapel and walked across the thick soft carpets to a low stool or hassock surrounded with a plenitude of pillows. Here he sat, reclining easily against the wall of curtains. He had not long to wait, for there entered now the troop of worshipers. They came, suddenly rushing into the place, reeling and shouting in hilarious profanity. Quickly they subsided among the cushions, but they kept up their conversations. To his surprise, De Rais counted ten, but who they were he could not tell for each was garbed in a torn and fusty gown beneath which projected common heavy boots. Upon their heads, concealing face and neck, were fastened hideous grinning masks; some purely bestial, some intended to represent the sins of man, and some (more horrible still) were masks of demons. All were black and all were hideous. He alone had shown his face. Sprawling among the pillows, they talked noisily with muffled voices and occasional shouts of laughter.

The harsh cry of a horn resounded raucously; and from behind the tapestry, there entered two figures. First came Prelati, majestic in a chasuble of ruby red upon which was embroidered the hideous form of Beelzebuth in apotheosis. Behind him, there came a smaller figure masked and horned, upon whose breast, in flaming scarlet, appeared the figure of a broken crucifix.

The pair approached the altar and halted there. This latter was a curiously made thing which, until that moment, De Rais had scarcely noticed. Resting upon four red Priapic legs, its top was covered with a heavy, dull black cloth upon which rested six candlesticks of iron, three at either end. In these were thrust six candles, black and flaming as though made of pitch. In the center, were two fragments of a crucifix, while above it, suspended by a heavy rope, there hung a colossal and distorted goat of wood nailed upon a broken cross. Before the altar a mass of black tapers sputtered and smoked upward toward a darkened ceiling.

From an obscenely carved lectern, Prelati raised a sort of missal and began the ceremony. The book he held within his hands was curiously sinister. Bound in goat's skin whose shaggy hair yet adhered, there was written in characters of red upon its black and yellow pages, a world of blasphemies and curses. From his lips, Prelati called down maledictions upon the Heavenly Hosts, shouting defiance and words of hatred and contempt upon the Trinity of God and upon His sacraments.

From behind the altar, Prelati raised a bowl of dirty pewter, filled with consecrated wine. With a battered brush, he flung it out, sprinkling toward the worshipers.

"Let His blood then lie upon our heads," he cried, "and on the heads of our descendants."

A raucous laugh burst from the worshipers and subsided to a muttered silence. Reading from the book, Prelati intoned an invocation and a praising of the fiends of Hell.

From the beginning of the ceremony, De Rais had sat in silence, trembling at the extent of the sacrilege. Idly, he counted over the participants, and discovered their number to be an even dozen—an unusual number.

"Count yourself," a voice whispered in his ear. Turning sharply, he beheld one of the masked figures lying upon his back beside him. The voice he recognized as that of Blanchet. "Twelve celebrants about the person of the Fiend," the voice went on. "In everything, the Demon is the ape of God."

Dropping the invocation, Prelati took up now a strange, inverse and general confession which asked forgiveness of the hellish hosts for virtues committed upon the earth. Into this confession, the participants joined, their voices shouting suddenly or repeating in a monotone the phrases that were read. In the black chapel, the din grew louder. Curses and blasphemies were shouted wildly. Cries of passion and of hatred burst from the recumbent forms.

Suddenly the noise subsided. Prelati had reached the end of the confession. For a while he mumbled garbled phrases of the mass, repeating certain portions backward, distorting others to a horrible significance, and dedicating certain fragments to the gods of Hell.

From behind Prelati, the horned figure of the pseudo-fiend came out and sat cross-legged upon the altar.

A corner of the tapestry was now pushed aside, and there entered a company of boys in scarlet shoes and silver robes, who circulated among the worshipers. In their hands, they bore trays of silver upon which rested chalices of wine and spirits, while beside the liquids there were piles of cakes. As the trays approached, the sprawling celebrants partook greedily, gulping the wine and devouring a number of the wafers as though to satisfy a lust.

Upon the altar, the squatting figure was swinging back and

forth a censer from which poured out dense clouds of sorcerous incense. At intervals, Prelati drew a cross upon the ground by a movement of the toe of his left slipper. Coming to an end, he ceased his mumbling, and once more the harsh metallic horn rang out.

Suddenly those upon the floor rose up and carrying the remains of their wafers with them, they crowded to the altar. Turning his back upon it, Prelati raised up from the ground a gold ciborium. From it he removed a wafer cut to a triangular pattern and dyed with blood. With infinite disgust he spit upon it and dropping it to the floor, he ground it to a dust beneath his heel. Before the mask of the one upon the altar, the others held up their hosts and, like the priest, they too then threw them to the floor, trampling hastily upon them.

From the pewter ewer, Prelati sprinkled the worshipers, spilling a portion of the wine upon the ground while making frequent crosses with his foot. Dismissed from the altar, the celebrants returned to their places among the cushions, while once more the silver-robed boys passed wine and cordials.

A stillness suddenly had fallen. The boys had gone, and the priest had stopped his voice. From a darkened space some distance from the altar, a figure rose. In its hand it bore a bundle of rough cloths. Slowly, with careful steps, this masked one approached the altar and laid the bundle in the arms of the cross-legged pseudo-god. He, in turn, placed it carefully upon the altar-cloth and, descending from his perch, took up his place behind Prelati.

The latter held forth his hand for silence, and commenced upon a horrible and ritualistic prayer.

"Our master of infernal power, who has his abode in Hell, terrible and frightening is your name. Your kingdom is among us and your will is our allegiance. Protect us in sin. Encourage us in the abominations of our deeds. Glorify us in evil. Teach us, O Lucifer, to hate and villify our Creator. For thine is the power of Hell.

"Lord of all evil, homage and sacrifice we bestow upon you.

Hatred we give you; contempt and blasphemy are on our souls. Sacrifice we have brought you; for you are a cruel and unjust god. Spurn it not, O master of the world of sin, for it is of a precious value; more potent than the blood of beasts is this, our sacrifice that lies beneath my hand. Accept, O Lucifer, our gift."

With a quick gesture, the masked figure tore the covering from the bundle on the altar-cloth. There lay, trussed and gagged, the body of a human infant.

"Prepare, O victim, for the sacrifice. Child of man, who has escaped baptism," Prelati shouted, "I dedicate your soul to Hell!"

De Rais had started to his feet, staring with fascinated horror upon the diabolic figure whose clutching fingers grasped the handle of a shining knife. With a drunken lunge he leaped forward and fell across a heap of cushions.

Blanchet raised him up. "The sacrifice is done, my Lord," he said.

Into the crypt there came the serving boys dragging long trestles and cloths to cover them. Tables were set up raised but slightly from the ground, and were laden down with food and wine. Reclining on the cushions and the carpets, the celebrants began their meal, while from the darkened aisles behind the black and scarlet hangings an orchestra commenced a loud and vibrant playing.

Near the altar, De Rais had joined Prelati and the little figure of the fiend. The latter had slipped off his evil mask; had become again De Sillé, priest of the diocese of St. Malo, and cousin to his lord. In great excitement, De Rais was whispering to the two. For in the final act of sacrifice, his interest had suddenly awakened from a sleep.

The ancient passion was once more revived, strengthened by its interlude of dormancy. Unleashed by the scene he had just witnessed, the thirst for blood became an overwhelming force, and in the vivid recollection of the crime, it shrieked for victims with insatiable demand.

The Black Mass ended all attempt at evocation. Even Prelati could see that they had lost their interest to De Rais; and he was wise enough to withdraw from the Baron's presence. Leaving the castle, the evocator took a cottage in the village of Machecoul.

Upon De Rais had settled down his lust. Murder became again a drug, demanding ever greater doses and ever greater pains. Singly, sometimes together, a host of victims passed for ever through the greatest of the mysteries, so that their lord could glut his passion in a sea of blood.

Upon the instrument of death, De Rais performed strange rhapsodies, fingering with avid touch the human keys, and playing out his melodies. The crashing chords of heartless violence were followed by a soft refrain of silent death. There were the swift arpeggios of silver daggers drawn across the unsuspecting throats; and in the base, there rose a horrible and disemboweled shouting.

CHAPTER XV

§ 1

Coming out one night into the midnight coolness of the ramparts, Gilles de Rais found himself completely alone. Below him, stretched and rambled the black outlines of the fortress enclosing the still gardens and walls, the separated buildings and the uneven, spidery tracing of the chapel of St. Vincent. Beyond the confines, he could see the plain, dotted with wisps of crawling fog, the avenue of ancient elms which led to the dark mass of the sleeping village and the deep obscurity of the Falleron forest. Behind him, he had left the sins of earth cooped in the heavy odors of the murder chamber.

It was curious how suddenly one emerged. The very threshold he had crossed between the room which he had left and the cool rooftops where he stood, had been a frontier of tremendous difference. Satan ruled within. Whether with immeasurable and hideous authority he had mocked, lured on and rushed upon his evocator to retreat again in sulphurous mirth unmet and unattained, or whether, by a subtler presence, he had surveyed with absent calm the steady damning of a lustful soul, his province was the same. Laden with the dregs of hope, and burdened with a nausea of sin, De Rais had left this realm and entered the clear night of God.

The stillness, the quiet of the river and the castle were His without admixture. Walking along the parapet, De Rais became His guest, treading carefully upon a borrowed land. In the purity of midnight, De Rais experienced a remote though powerful disgust, and as an antidote his very skin drank in the fragrance of the air. There was no lust on earth, he felt, that could not be transmuted here; and at a corner of the wall he knelt and prayed.

Fervent, devotional and passionately adoring, his prayer marked out the end of his emotional charge. He was again replete with the fulfilment of his lust. Trembling and in mortal fear, he withdrew his soul from the proximity of Hell.

As he prayed, the figure of De Sillé, moving quietly as though he were a shadow, appeared behind him.

"This is the time," he said, "for you to make your choice. Two Powers have spread out their claims, and both demand an answer. One we have called our Creator—yet within our flesh were built its lusts, its passions and its obscenities. One we have called our destroyer, the enemy of Him who made us. Which, Cousin Gilles, is which?"

De Rais stood silently against the parapet.

"Both have been honored," said the priest, "and both demand their dues. I bring to-night a message from the coven. In the forest yonder, they will hold their festival to celebrate the god that they think true. Examine in your heart your own belief. The Church and Other Faith await."

Staring at him, De Rais spoke slowly. "To-night," he said, "and for ever more, my soul is in the hands of God. He is my salvation and my hope, and I renounce my sins. To-morrow we shall leave for Nantes."

De Sillé turned away. "Your choice is made," he said. "Good night."

§ 2

De Rais had fled from Machecoul as, so long before, he had also fled from Champtocé and as he wished, at intervals, to flee from certain portions of his life. Nantes supplied the necessary change, and in the sumptuous Hôtel de la Suze, he busily prepared a spectacle. Once more, a drama was to be presented, intended for the benefit of his soul, the glory of his God, and to call forth again the cheering populace whose applause was necessary to his damaged vanity.

Weeks of delight were spent in preparation. Weeks they were demanding the constant labor of generalship, artistic selection and creative skill within a field in which he knew himself to be a master. He experienced again the half-forgotten pleasure of the feel of fine brocade slipping carefully through appraising fingers, of the mental exercise required in the designing of the triple-storied stage, of selecting from his hotel the fittings accessory to the settings and the stage, and of the rush of purchasing and hiring, and the countermanding of orders.

At the sides of the stage, he had two balconies built, and so arranged them that the place which Jean de Malestroit, the Bishop of the city, should occupy would be no more important than the place (directly opposite) which was reserved for De Rais' unrecognized, though highly gorgeous prelate, the so-called "Bishop" of Machecoul. This was a harmless, though annoying insult to the true Bishop, and one that the Baron greatly relished.

Another detail amused him. Blanchet, the incomparable, had procured from the local jail two men to serve as heralds. Almost identical in appearance, they were enormous creatures blessed with a hideousness of shapeless features that amounted almost to deformity. In compensation, they were possessed of magnificent bass voices so deep they seemed not to speak, but merely to vibrate slowly. They were two of a set of triplets, and had been held in prison awaiting the possibility of a trial for looting and for fratricide; the latter crime having to do with the disappearance of their brother who, as a merry prank, had been dropped by these into a cistern. There, it was assumed that he had perished, as no one had ever bothered to fish so great a rascal out.

So, when the proper day arrived, the two survivors, dressed in new livery of the House of Rais, were dispatched to proclaim with their bass voices to the citizens of Nantes the advent of the spectacle for which the square had been so long torn up.

Crowds had already gathered in the city, for a holiday had been declared; while peasants from the countryside and near-by

villages had also come to town. Through the narrow streets that
were overhung with crooked stone-and-timber houses, the heralds, accompanied by half a dozen halberdiers, pushed their
way. Before a wine-shop they halted, and blew with squeaky
effort on their trumpets. About them milled an interested
crowd, as much excited as though they had known nothing of
the preparations. Monks, peasants, blowsy shop women, and
gaudy prostitutes, brought from out of town for the event,
crowded close upon them, while at the edges of the gathering,
a few petty officials, clerks and minor knights listened with rapt
attention.

"We, noble and powerful Baron, Gilles de Rais," began the
gargantuan heralds as though reciting a difficult and ill-learned
lesson, "Marshal of France, Lord of Champtocé,"—which was
no longer true,—"of Tiffauges, of Machecoul, of St. Etienne de
la Mer Morte,"—which was then in litigation,—"of Pornic, of
Vuë and of other places, do by these presents make known,"—
in unison they took fresh breaths of prodigious gustiness—
"that by the express permission of the high and powerful lord,
Jean de Malestroit, by the grace of God and appointment from
the Holy Father,"—here they seemed to wander from their text,
—"Bishop of Nantes,"—another breath vaster than the first
was necessary,—"there will be given this day of the present
month, at two o'clock in the afternoon, in the square of Notre
Dame, a presentation of a Mystery concerning the life of our
Lord and Savior, Jesus Christ, and of Madam the Holy Virgin,
His Mother"—a last and final breath.

In reply, the crowd shouted its enthusiasm for the noble and
powerful Baron and for the high and powerful Lord Bishop.
Whereupon the heralds, flushed with triumph, resumed their
ambulations.

Long before two o'clock the square was filled, save for a long
straight aisle kept open by parading men-at-arms. At the end
of this was seen the stage flanked by two wooden towers (or
balconies) face to face. That on the left-hand side was hung
with curtains of blue velvet suspended on rings of brass from a

rod above, so that they could be drawn with ease and so shut out those who were within from the vulgar stares of the populace, or from any scene or phase of the life of Our Lord and Savior which displeased them. This box, decorated in gold with the arms of the city and with the arms of Jean de Malestroit, its Bishop, was reserved for the political and ecclesiastical dignitaries of Nantes, together with their guests, and for the visiting nobility. From it, a covered way of taut silk awning led across the square, connecting with the house of a certain magistrate. Having assembled there, the dignitaries had no need to push their way through the dense and evil smelling mob to reach their places in the balcony.

The second of the twin towers was appropriated to the use of Gilles de Rais and of his followers. In place of blue, this balcony was hung in red; and there descended heavy curtains of a rich and brilliant velvet. In place of borderings of plain gold, white velvet marked the edges, upon which decoration a thinner edge of gold was sewn, from which descended a profusion of golden tassels. Like the other balcony, two coats of arms appeared. At the top there was the escutcheon of the House of Rais; a cross of black upon a field of gold; and below it, the arms of Machecoul; three chevrons on a silver shield. About the upper one there ran the lily border, the right to bear which was bestowed by Charles VII upon the occasion of his coronation.

In the May sunshine, the crowd awaited, watching the blue box gradually fill; and at the advent of each dignitary whom they knew, a welcoming cheer rose up. The other balcony was still deserted, and while waiting the populace sank into a state of apathetic coma. At length a fresh confusion and straining of necks betokened the approach of those for whom it was reserved.

Slowly De Rais was coming from the Hôtel de la Suze. Ahead marched his body-guard in gilded mail and inlaid helmets, progressing down the narrow aisle, two by two toward the stage and balconies. Slightly behind them, in cream-colored silk,

Gilles de Rais walked at the head of a procession. Over his shoulders hung a cloak of crimson velvet, embroidered with figures in gold and edged with ermine. His boots were black. By his side, an aide held out a casque inverted in his hands. It was filled to the brim with golden coins, and into this De Rais continually dipped his hand and, withdrawing it, scattered over the heads of his halberdiers handfuls of the largesse it contained. Behind him, scarcely less magnificent than he, came the train of his college in their scarlets and greens—the brocaded, gilded and embroidered prelates of his chapel. As they passed, one noted at the end two figures faintly out of place.

Together, talking softly, walked a short and plainly clad priest, smiling as though he were amused, while at his elbow marched a tall Italian in flowing robe and tall-crowned cap. As they passed, the watchers in the crowd nudged one another significantly. "The sorcerers," they whispered with delighted awe.

Across the square they filed with slow magnificence, and reached the scarlet curtained box. With great solemnity the "Bishop" of Machecoul sat down directly opposite the less gorgeous figure of the Bishop of Nantes in the opposing box. De Rais arranged himself in front, rising slightly to recognize the thunderous burst of cheers.

With due and tedious formalities, the drama began; and on the stage the players embarked upon the Mystery which had to do largely with the life of Our Lord and Savior and of Madam, the Holy Virgin, His Mother.

§ 3

The Mystery was a huge success, for it had brought a holiday unburdened by expense or the necessity of long or frequent masses. It was, as well, an occasion for the pleasant congregation of town and country folk, and gave an opportunity for many reunions, in the May sunshine, of old acquaintances.

The wondering admiration of the populace was not confined to the drama itself, but included all that touched upon the life of Gilles de Rais. He became a sort of local hero, a very Cæsar Augustus of the Nantais. He was remembered as a boy, riding in triumph beside the Duke himself, filled with the pride of youthful victories. Already at sixteen years, a glorious future had been predicted, and now, as he passed through the city imperiously erect upon his charger, while his body-guard fought off the pressing of the crowds, old gossips with pleasant pride in their astuteness, recalled the prophecies of glory that had indeed come true. De Rais became a legend, and to his name innumerable deeds of valor and of prodigy were linked. No other noble in the whole of France compared in his magnificence to this Baron of their native duchy.

In deafening enthusiasm, the Nantais clogged his path, cheering his haughty immobility as he rode among them, scattering from the inverted helmet on his pommel those golden coins he valued, by repute, so lightly.

Glancing occasionally sidewise from his saddle, in involuntary recognition of the adulation he received, the Baron circulated through the city, visiting the many churches and praying with inspiring zeal before the shrines of the galaxy of saints. To the religious enterprises of the Lord Bishop, he bestowed large sums and became conspicuous for a thousand acts of duty and devotion to the Greatest Feudal.

Yet while the Baron pursued his pious ambulations, a certain woman of the town had sought an audience with the Bishop of the city, and into his ears poured out a rambling and confused complaint.

The widow of Eonnet Kerguen lived in St. Croix, a suburb just outside the walls of Nantes. From here she came almost daily to the city to buy or sell, to attend mass, or to drink a glass of wine with her dear friend, the saddler's wife. On these excursions she often brought along her small son, Jean, who also had friends (of his own age) in Nantes. Now Jean, asserted Madame Kerguen, was a good boy at heart despite certain apparently incurable habits of lying, of minor stealing and of dirty hands. He was also apt to fill his mother's house with toads and beetles and stray curs which he collected in the market-place. Petty errors as these were, the good Bishop must understand that she, his mother, had more than once had recourse to the broom handle; and here Madame Kerguen burst most unaccountably into tears.

The Bishop was annoyed. While it was, of course, his sacred duty to listen to the troubles of his flock, to counsel them about their spiritual ills and to lead them to repentance, he felt that even the awful crimes of little Jean were properly within the province of the parish priest. Yet realizing the depth of feeling that had caused this embarrassed peasant to brave his episcopal isolation, he listened with resigned complacency and prodded her gently with his staff.

She would not, however, be hurried, but pursued her incoherent course with inept ill-spoken words. Some short time before, while she had visited the saddler's wife and was deep in conversation and her glass of wine, little Jean had escaped her eagle eye and slipped away as, the Bishop was given to understand, children are apt to do. Again the tears came forth.

"Dear, dear," murmured the Bishop from the depths of his compassion. And had he not returned?

But little Jean had soon come back, swollen with food and clutching a gold piece in his fist. As to his absence, he was strangely reticent, even under the unburdening influence of the broomstick. A kind man, he said, had fed him sweet cakes and given him his penny. It was the penny that had aroused his mother's curiosity.

In the market-place, however, secrecy was less well maintained, and there she had learned other facts. The Bishop delicately covered up a yawn, for the woman seemed interminable. When the question she would ask should finally arise, he was already decided on his reply. She must rest her conscience, he would say, and keep the gold piece; for gold was as common as copper with the rich.

On the day of the escape of little Jean, a number of ill-bred children had gone, as they often did, to the rear entrance of the Hôtel de la Suze from which alms were always given out at certain hours. There they had been met by a servant who invited them within. In the kitchens they were entertained and fed with cakes and wine and here, to their delight, they were visited by the Marshal himself, who had spoken to them all and bestowed upon each one a piece of gold.

The source of Madame Kerguen's information was a girl of eleven years named Jeannette, who had been of this party. Her story was exact in detail, especially to a wondrous description of the elegance of the palace which she had glimpsed through a half-opened door. On certain other counts, she was more vague. She could not swear, for instance, that all the children had emerged. Jean had, of course; for he had returned to his mother, but others might have lingered. One thing Jeannette recalled most clearly. As she was leaving, some one had said— whether to Jean or not, she did not know: "You have had no meat. Come back again."

Here the widow suddenly came upon her point. Little Jean had disappeared again. For a whole week, he had been absent from his mother's house, nor had any one in St. Croix or in Nantes itself seen any trace of his blue smock or dirty face. There was not even so much as a theft to account for his complete and most suspicious vanishing.

With patience, surprise and finally despair, his mother had awaited his return. In great anxiety she had pushed her search, even consulting at a vast expense the wisdom of a young astrologer. But nothing gave her any hope. At last she had paid a visit to the Hôtel de la Suze itself, and a curious answer greeted her.

"We know nothing of him," a steward told her. "There are so many boys who come."

Not one to rush easily to conclusions, Madame Kerguen was startled by the bruskness of the servant's attitude. At once her mind began to work, and, digging diligently into the market gossip, she built up with a speed that greatly surprised herself a disconcerting and by no means inconsiderable case.

Among the dozens of children employed in the household of De Rais were many from the town of Nantes. They served as pages, choristers, attendants and miniature men-at-arms. Nor were they always in the Baron's suite. Paul, the young son of Jean Hubert, had gone in service to Princay and had returned, clad in a red suit and quite puffed up with pride. Disdainfully he refused to leave the Baron for his parents, nor would he return to school. But Paul, like little Jean, had seemed to disappear. No letters came from Princay, nor had any one seen him for two whole years.

The small son of Regnard Douette had also been hired as a servant, but since his entry into the Hôtel de la Suze, he had not been seen again. Jean Jeuvet had hung about the kitchens of this palace until his mother in exasperation boxed his ears. He too had disappeared. A child named Aysée, ten years old, had been sent to beg, but he had not returned. Corlin Aporill, twenty years old, but very small and white-faced, bearing a birthmark on one ear, was gone. Guillaume, the child of Johanna Delit of the parish of St. Denys, Nantes, had gone to visit the Hôtel de la Suze and not returned.

Under the investigation of the widow, other disappearances came to light; and in each case, suspicion led to the handsome portals of the palace of My Lord de Rais. Eonet le Dagaye had lost a child of ten. Peter Couppene had been bereft of two. A son of Johannes Maguet had vanished in the same way.

Something, averred the widow, had happened to these children that was not natural. Perhaps the noble Baron had bewitched them, or possibly they had fallen to the hands of his magician without his knowledge. At any rate, it was, she saw most clearly, her duty to tell the Bishop of her findings and to beg him on her knees to end the scandal. As she grew excited, the Bishop rose, and promising to investigate at once, he suavely showed her out.

When she had gone, he sat back in his chair and pondered. The story of the widow was no idle tale. The exactitude of names and circumstance absolved her of invention. Nor was the disappearance of so many children to be put down to coincidence. He knew, of course, of De Rais' efforts at the magic arts, and being a well-read man, the idea of sacrifice at once occurred to him. Immediately he dismissed the thought, for though such things were written of, they could not actually take place. Nevertheless, investigation was in order.

At present, Gilles de Rais was high in favor of the Duke, yet against him the Bishop held two grudges. Firstly, the prelate had never forgotten the insolent affair of St. James de Beuvron, at the conclusion of which De Richemont and this same young noble had dragged him to a moldy Chinon jail. And secondly, Jean de Malestroit was still annoyed that in place of honor fully equal to his own, had sat during the recent Mystery in the public square the unofficial "Bishop" of Machecoul, who was a creature of De Rais. In case, he thought, my friend the Duke should change his mind about this Baron, it would be well to have more knowledge of what has happened to little Jean.

§ 4

The curse of restlessness, which ever robbed the Baron of the peace of satisfaction, descended upon him. Nantes, teeming with admiring crowds, and dragging him from his introspections into the fury of external life, had been the antidote to that ailment from which he always suffered. Yet since the episode of war, each interlude of mundane struggle had been of a duration shorter than the last.

Adulation palled, and he was quickly surfeited with the bustle of the crowded city. Peace became desirable, and he looked forward to the quiet of the ancient walls above the Sèvre. Another change was needed, and preparations were quickly made for the return to Tiffauges.

The brief epoch of Nantes was at an end, poisoned in his memory, as Champtocé was also poisoned. To Rainfort, where the company of traitors had met their death, De Rais looked back in horror, dreading the thought of ever visiting the place.

Machecoul and Nantes were added to this list of dwellings that were made ugly by participation in his lusts.

Without a conscious thought, almost against his will, he had at Nantes turned again from God into the devious ways of sin. In a burst of drunken passion, he had cried out for the blood he had forsworn. And while his mind was fingering the thought, his cry was answered as, though thirsty, he had cried for wine.

Though he had fled his crimes, Griart and Corrillaut and Blanchet had not believed his flight, knowing that he would hopelessly return. Being devoted, the plans for this relapse had been well made. La Meffraie, the witch, had come to Nantes, and in the kitchen of the Hôtel de la Suze, children were entertained with gifts of wine and sweetcakes.

Returned to Tiffauges, Gilles de Rais began a thoroughly aimless and unplanned existence. The magic of Prelati was let drop, no further experiments or evocations taking place. The murder lust had also died, and he remained, as a result, inert. For a period, perhaps the first in his career, his very energy had lapsed or, more correctly stated, had turned completely to his mental life.

He found himself unable to concentrate for long upon any given interest. A thousand pastimes were taken up and dropped before they were begun. Prelati and De Sillé, unable to follow the rapid changes of his mood, withdrew from his life to await a new stability of purpose.

De Raïs himself scarcely noticed their defection; for he was busy staring upon a crowd of horrors which threatened to engulf him. The God to whom he turned at midnight on the roofs of Machecoul had failed to bear him up at Nantes. On closer scrutiny, the Baron beheld at His side, the inverse deity his cousin had described. Flanked by the grinning coven of the Other Faith, the Lord Creator became a frightening figure. Behind, there rose two crosses melting into one. Upon the first the Savior, Jesus Christ, reposed; and on the other, a similar, yet distorted form cried out reproaches to his God.

From this group, the Baron turned away his eyes, searching

in emptiness for truth. Into the blankness of his gaze, there crept the children of his sins, bleeding and innocent and dead, pointing with stumps of arms upon De Rais, the sinner, who was damned by their extinction.

In morbid curiosity before this threatening throng, he turned away to face the symbol of his fall, the Fiend himself. Terrified by the grinning fangs of Hell, De Rais recoiled and faced once more the Majesty of God.

This was his ever-changing vision that troubled and upset his soul, nor could he find a single point from which to plot his course. They moved too easily and merged into each other. A remembered fragment of his life had given him once an ultimate stability. But this, too, was now blurred, distorted by the phrase of death: "Die, Jeanne, Idolatress, Heretic, Apostate!"

Into his life of tortured thoughts, there came two visitors, corporeal and of the world. Both were self-invited and, though arriving at Tiffauges within the balance of the year 1439, they were totally unconnected with each other, or with his life and struggles. Yet in his worried state, each one appeared to be of more than casual significance.

The first of these was a woman of curious history. Called by the name of Jeanne, married to a certain Robert des Armoises, and mother of two children, this matron had been recognized by Jean and Pierre du Lys, the ennobled brothers of the maid. From Italy, she had appeared, three years before, and had added to her stories of Italian wars the strange account that she was Jeanne Darc, rescued by an angel from the pyre of Rouen. Successfully she had lived at Metz, recognized by many who had known the maid. Even had she gone to Orléans unchallenged, and eaten there a banquet, while in the churches masses were yet sung in memory of the soul of Jeanne.

The difficulty she had anticipated at Tiffauges did not appear. Almost without delay, the audience which she sought was granted, and she found herself, still clad in armor, before the Baron.

Ruins of the Château of Champtocé

Sunk deep in a chair before a small fire, he scarcely raised his eyes to greet her, nor did he ask her many questions.

"I am Jeanne, the Maid," she had announced on entering his presence, "escaped, by the Grace of God, the flames of Rouen, and now alive and well."

"Sit down," he said.

But she preferred to stand. As she talked of her career, piling detail of her life upon detail, the Baron scarcely seemed to hear. Motionless he sat before her, staring at the carpet. To her, his eyes seemed dull and passionless. He looked a worn and wearied man, troubled and lined with care. In his black hair she saw a thread or so of gray, but he was young in years. She wondered whether he were not enjoying some joke on her behalf, and she became uneasy. But the dull eyes were never raised, nor did his lean hands ever stop their ceaseless drumming. He was oblivious to her presence, as though he were asleep. Even the birthmark behind her ear failed to interest him. And yet he did not sleep. A question from the Baron startled her.

"Do you come from God?" he asked.

"I come indeed from God," she told him; "you should know that as well as I."

A strange smile wandered across his lips and vanished into apathy. "Your voices," he asked tonelessly, "are they also from God?"

"They are the voices of my saints—as they have always been. Saint Catherine, Saint Margaret and Saint Michael; none others."

"Tell me," he said suddenly, sitting upright and staring off beyond her, "you hear them yet—these voices? They speak to you freely and with blessed ease?"

Pleased to have interested him at last, she made a slight concession. "They come more rarely now," she said, "for the great need is past. They give me counsel none the less, and I am guided by their wishes."

"And did they counsel you to come to me?"

"Why else should I be here?"

To her surprise his eyes grew bright, fired by a sudden flash of eagerness. "Tell me," he ordered, "what did they say of me?"

Madame des Armoises paused. This was, she knew, her opportunity; yet having escaped the cross-examination she expected, she felt embarrassed before the staring figure. A strange story of this noble crossed her mind, and staring down his gaze, she shivered faintly. From a dreaming or a dying man, he had become alert and seemed to blaze with an intensity she could not understand. Life had come back into his eyes that did not see her, and before their depths she faltered. An effort of her mind recalled her courage.

"My Lord de Rais," she said, "my council have sent me to your kindness as long ago they sent me to Robert de Baudcourt, the Governor of Vaucouleurs."

De Rais half smiled, and she thought relief was written his face. "What do you wish to say to me?" he asked. "I li with humility."

"I wish to go to my King," she said, "as once befo wished. Give me, I beg of you, provisions and some mer arms to be my body-guard."

"Nothing else?" he asked.

The false virgin contracted her brows in thought. "A f horse," she said, "and new armor to replace my own."

A curious laugh burst from the seated Baron. "Go," shouted in a mocking voice. "Men and armor, a valiant ho..e and gold are at your service. As do your saints command; thus Gilles de Rais obeys."

Madame des Armoises left the room in haste. She wished no further converse with this man. Once more he sat, inert, crouched within his chair. His eyes were closed, but on his cruel lips she saw again a smile. "Mad," she whispered to herself. "He is more mad than I."

Under a guard of men, she left Tiffauges bound for the Court of Charles. But Gilles de Rais did not attend her leaving.

§ 5

By the time the second visitor arrived, Gilles de Rais had recovered from his fit of brooding. Once more he had resumed an interest in the affairs of life, and in his mind he had begun to play with the idea of renewing his attempts at sorcery.

Almost imperceptibly, he lent his presence to the research upon which Prelati was engaged, visiting the laboratory as one outside its range rather than taking actual part. The sacrifices did not again take place, but about the magic circle, weird and unholy manifestations swooned and muttered, while the magician talked incessantly of gold.

It was wise, now, to talk again of this neglected need; for the Baron was once more impoverished. His expenses had been slowly lessened by his treasurer, but at one blow, the Mystery at Nantes had eaten up a huge amount.

Prelati hoped that, through the urge of gold, he could in time resume his work where, with the service of Black Mass, he had been forced to stop. But an event, completely unforeseen by all, gave further interruption to his work.

This interruption was the visit, in December, of Louis, eldest offspring of King Charles, and Dauphin of France. This prince, having become a little troublesome in Paris, (from where his father now was able to rule) had been sent out upon a mission to put down banditry wherever he should find it. The course of his systematic ramblings had brought him into Poitou and at last to the borders of the barony of Rais. From here he sent a royal herald announcing his arrival, and close upon the heels of his messenger, the Prince himself appeared before the towers of Tiffauges.

Warned in sufficient time, the Lord of Rais prepared a reception of tremendous pomp. Marvels of entertainment were produced with skilful ease. The royal quarters were hung with new and handsome tapestries. Coverlets and feather-beds of softest silk and swan's-down were obtained, while on the polished floors were spread down rugs of fur and of Oriental make.

Warm scented water was kept for ever fresh within the golden
ewers, while even quarters for the Prince's servants were prepared with elegance.

In the forest, beaters labored, driving herds of game within a
close distance of the castle. Actors and minstrels were summoned hastily from Nantes, and special cooks were hired.

On the day appointed for arrival, the Lord of Tiffauges rode
out in person to greet the Prince, and at his heels there followed
his body-guard of two hundred, glittering and polished to a
marvelous extent.

In appearance young Louis resembled his father, yet at sixteen the Dauphin was more assured than ever Charles had been.
The eyes of this young man were sharper and more determined.
Where Charles, when fronted with his insufficiency, had appeared baffled and afraid, Louis became resentful to a tinge of
craftiness. Charles had been self-mistrustful, but his son possessed an absolute assurance of his wits. Though I appear to
disadvantage now, he seemed to say, I know what I am about
and in the end shall win.

The period of festivity wore on, marked with elaborate feasts
and hunting parties. Wine and dainties flowed, and ceremony
was observed. One thing young Louis noticed with some surprise. Save for an occasional dancer, no women graced the
castle of Tiffauges. There were no female servants, no guests,
nor even pretty wenches passing silently along the corridors. In
curiosity, he asked his host about his wife and daughter.

"They are not here, my Lord," replied De Rais. "They may
be at Pouzauges. To find out more definitely, I must consult
my treasurer."

A later occasion allowed the Dauphin to broach the subject
of his mission to his host.

"You are no doubt aware," he said, "of the purpose of my
visit."

De Rais expressed a polite ignorance and listened carefully
to the prepared speech upon the evils and the prevalence of
lawlessness. "A worthy cause to strive for," he said. "The day

of pillaging, now that our King sits securely upon his throne, should surely end. There are no longer wars for an excuse."

"Yet much disloyalty remains," went on the Prince. "Too many nobles have dared to disobey the King, and he is planning punishments for these."

"Loyalty is a noble virtue," said the Baron, "and one that, in this distracted age, is too often forgotten."

"Which brings me to my point," the Dauphin said calmly. "I learn from my father and his ministers that there are one or two complaints against your conduct on this score."

"No doubt," remarked De Rais. "Complaints are easy."

"On more than one occasion," went on the Prince, "travelers passing below your castle walls have been attacked in grossest violation of the laws of France. Pillaging from Champtocé and other places has taken place upon the highways."

A flash of anger crossed De Rais at the insolence of this sharp-faced boy. "What if there has?" he cried. "Am I responsible for the robbers that infest my woods? Ask this question of His Majesty The King, and ask him also if he dares to send a force of men against me."

"Is that defiance?" asked the Dauphin.

De Rais' anger vanished before the calmness of the question. Somehow he felt a lack of true solemnity in the words.

"As to that," he said easily, "the ministers of Paris must decide."

Louis smiled at his answer. For a boy, his smile was strangely ominous. "Other charges have been made by those at Paris," he went on. "Let me state the grievance of the King. Against the royal wishes, you took by force the castle of Champtocé, held in his name by René de la Suze."

"That quarrel passes from my head to that of the Duke of Brittany, who has possession of the castle."

"Nevertheless you owe an unpaid fine for that offense."

"Have I refused to pay?"

"Another fine, connected with the disobedience of your marriage, is also due. You have failed in feudal homage to your

King upon occasion of your grandfather's death. A royal interdict was broken by the sale of your lands. This action is rebellious. And more serious than any of these, is the direct disobedience that caused you to defy a royal order commanding you to lead an army into the duchy of Savoy. These are serious crimes against the authority of the throne, and so they are considered by the royal council. In spirit and in fact they approach most dangerously to treason."

"I trust," said De Rais, "that you have not come for the purpose of upbraiding me. I am not terrified by threats of arms; nor, let me warn you, is my temper a very long one. Watch your tongue, young man, for though you are a prince, I am Gilles de Rais, and should not hesitate to clap you in a dungeon. It would be an easy way," he added, "to gain forgiveness for my crimes."

The young Prince eyed him, unterrified. "Of all this," he said, "I am come merely as a herald. I quote the council of the King who sent me on this errand."

De Rais rose. "Let us keep the discussion," he said, "until to-morrow. While we have talked, it has grown late."

"To-morrow," said the Dauphin with a great intensity, "we will resume our talk. For I have other and yet graver things to say."

He too rose and, bowing formally, left the room. When he had gone, De Rais resumed his seat. He was amused by the boldness of this fragile-appearing, dyspeptic Prince. Louis, he knew, was not a fool, and he read easily that more lay in the conversation than a mention of minor and half-forgotten offenses. The boy had something on his mind that was outside a social visit and was, De Rais was fairly sure, quite unconnected with his talk of banditry.

Suddenly something started in the Baron's brain. Was it possible that they had stumbled on his secret? Unconsciously he had suffered, since the arrival of the Dauphin, under a strain of secrecy. Harmless and innocent as had the visit been to all appearance, he had been slightly worried none the less. For there were in his castle the laboratory, the sorcerers and the evidences of his evocations. Worse than that, had Louis cared to search, he might have found the damning souvenirs of death. Easily had the Baron lulled these fears, denying them articulation and thrusting them back behind his outward thoughts of hospitality.

But now they burst in full upon him. "Yet graver things," had said the Prince. What others could they be? A wave of terror crossed De Rais. He saw his sin discovered and exposed before the world. Perhaps already murder was written on his countenance. With a cry he sprang from his chair and fled in frantic haste toward the laboratory. Griart met him in the hallway, flying like a maniac, all self-control abandoned by a driving fear.

"We must destroy the laboratory," shouted De Rais. "We are discovered, and everything must go to-night. Search for Corrillaut to help."

He ran on, while Griart, white with terror, ran off in search of Corrillaut. Still running, De Rais approached the laboratory, leaping up the circular stairway, panting with his burst of speed. Into the room he sprang, to find Prelati engaged upon his work.

"Clear the chamber!" he shouted. "Strip it to its walls. Burn the implements. Wall up the cistern. Everything must be destroyed and not a fragment must remain!"

With avid hands he tore at the black hangings, ripping them from the walls and heaping them upon the fire in the hearth. Startled, Prelati joined him, unknowing of the cause of this destruction, yet fearing also. The door again flew open admitting Griart and Corrillaut who, without asking for an explanation, joined the orgy. Vials of fumigants, charts, buckets of charcoal, great parchments upon whose surfaces were written the careful pentacles, the robes and caps of cabalistic decoration, all were thrown upon the flames. Closets were cleared, ewers of the blood of doves were emptied, the very brazier followed in the rush of cleansing.

In the fireplace the flames roared upward in the chimney, consuming with haste the accouterments of sorcery and illuminating the bared stone walls with a dancing flood of light. Into the night they toiled. Pails of water mixed with lime were poured upon the floor and swept into the cistern. From corners and chests about the room old fragments of research were unearthed and cast to join the mass upon the fire.

A dozen books, written in the curious script of magic, were rescued by Prelati. These were the sole survivors of the holocaust. Everything else the room contained, incriminating, suspicious or purely innocent, was hopelessly destroyed.

By dawn, the work was done. Save for the locked door that guarded the entrance to the cistern, no trace remained of laboratory, sacrifice or incantation.

Relieved and wearied from their labors, the three retired from the room with satisfaction. The obliteration was complete.

Secure and tired, the Baron faced the young Prince in the privacy of his library. Slowly and in a cautious fashion the "graver things" were brought to light. Carefully the Dauphin laid down his plan. There was, he said, mismanagement in Paris. What else could one expect from a ruler who was swayed by petticoats, and the nobles were oppressed. Their ancient rights were suddenly in danger, and more than one of them was ready for revolt. Gradually as he approached his point, the Prince discovered in his listener an unaccountable apathy. Gone completely was the flash of anger which had encouraged him the day before. The rebellious fire which he had anticipated had vanished overnight.

As he plead with fiery intensity for his cause, the Prince became more baffled by the strange reaction of the Baron.

In a massive calm, De Rais remained inert before the earnestness of his guest, watching the boy with vague and dreaming eyes. What mattered it to him whether there were yet struggles in the land of France? Idly he visualized the prospect of a civil war between the forces of the feeble Charles and of his corrupt councilors against a youthful and brilliant Prince, abetted by the bravest nobles of the land. This was "the graver thing" that Louis held before his eyes.

At this moment, unstirred by loyal anger or by the enthusiasm of revolt, De Rais was able to regard again the antics of the world. The ideals, the passions and the hopes that had stirred him in his youth were being laid again before him, and they had ceased to have a meaning.

"You have come," he said, "to a strange place for aid."

Louis stopped abashed. "You disapprove my plans?" he asked quickly.

"I neither favor nor oppose them," said De Rais. "I am no longer interested in France. Once I was moved as you are moved; but all my ambition and my love of war is stilled. I am, perhaps, a corpse upon the battle-field, mute and unhearing. I care for nothing now unless it be the soul of Gilles de Rais. Yes," he exclaimed, "I care for that with all the passion of my being. It is my last possession!"

Finding Prelati in the ruined laboratory, De Rais told him of the interview.

"This fiery Prince," he said, "has given me a nasty scare. Through him I have destroyed much of your work, yet I am grateful to him. He has shown me, unwittingly, an unseen facet to my nature; which is that I fear very little after all. Why should we live in dread, my friend, of life? Death is the only terror; but when that day arrives, I shall be ready. Perhaps I am foredoomed. But if I am, there is little I can do to influence the gods. Their judgments are already made; and our fates were most likely decided before we reached the outer air. To the devil, then, with cautious hidings, and with our sins behind locked doors. Let us live boldly and banish fear; for before we die there are many things to know. Let us now discover them."

With the departure of the puzzled Dauphin, another epoch in the life of Gilles de Rais was concluded. With bag and baggage, body-guard and traveling organs, he left the fortress of Tiffauges in France and crossed the Breton borders to Machecoul.

CHAPTER XVI

§ 1

In a vague cloud, a terror spread throughout the country of the lower Loire. That part of Brittany near the town of Nantes, some of western Maine, and the north corner of the duchy of Poitou were affected, as though a huge and evil circle had been drawn enclosing them. Within this ring, men went carefully at night bearing charms and crosses, and repeating fragments of the Gospels. Within their cottages, the women crouched against their smoking fires, fingering their rosaries with nervous hands and watching with fearful surveillance their children while they slept. A howling dog, lonely upon the moors among his sheep, brought icy shudders to the parents who, lying in uneasy sleep within the hovels, heard his melancholy. Demons were abroad. Spirits or vampires, screeching through the night, swooped dangerously down upon the sheepfolds and the lonely cross-roads.

None knew the origin of this new affliction, save that in it the witches had no hand. Their art was of old knowledge. Spells and pestilences were familiar enemies. One knew, perhaps, a word or so of magic; one had, upon occasion, bought charms or poisons from these folk, while homely village youths had frequently obtained philters to aid them in their wooing. Barns had often blazed suddenly at night by virtue of the witches' ministrations; but before this greater and more evil thing, the sorcerers had lost their strength, and in their failure, the fear of the unknown increased.

A curse was on the land. Some said that Satan had unleashed his fiends and sent them abroad, flapping their hideous wings

310

and seeking hungrily for blood. Without a warning, and without a cause, the evil suddenly would strike. No farmer busy with his fields had felt its hand. No housewife vanished from her duties. But here to-day, across a hundred farms the next, at hand again outside a near-by village, and far away in Nantes, a child would vanish silently without a trace.

Left (as was usual) upon a hillside to guard his father's sheep, a boy had not returned at nightfall. Another, lingering along the roadside on his way from school, had vanished from the earth. Near Machecoul, a peasant had delayed in pleasant company at the tavern, and in his absence his wife had gone to fetch the cow for milking. In their cottage, the children were busy with a game. Somehow, a child of nine had disappeared. Tiring of the play, he might have wandered out upon the roadside; but no one saw him leave, and he had not been missed.

Back and forth across the country flew the stories, relayed from mouth to mouth with trembling haste. Strange rumors grew, descriptive of the fear. Some children playing, had noticed little Robert before he had been snatched away. By a hedgerow he was seen talking to a man; but the children had paid little heed. Others, too, had seen this man at different times, and he could be described. Perhaps it was a man in a long cloak, perhaps a woman. Under inspired questioning, the figure at length grew clearer. Always he was reported muffled, and covered up from head to feet. Only his eyes were ever seen. Beneath his robe, a hump appeared, caused without question by the furling of his wings. Green-eyed and terrible, he limped as though he balanced upon a pair of stilts or hoofs; and as he talked he fumbled beneath his garment. At times he wore a beak and not a nose. Upon a lonely moor, a frightened peasant had heard the hoof-beats of a dozen riders; and as they passed, carrying with them, as he later learned, a solitary infant, he saw them riding at a furious gallop, cloaks flying out behind. Before his eyes, they mounted to the air and disappeared across the moon.

Through the web of rumor and of superstition, the terror had emerged with a living force. It had been hard to believe at first save with the shuddering credence one gave to tales of ogres, fiends and wizardry. Children died easily when food was scarce; nor were their vanishings uncommon. The land was disorganized and overrun with evil men. One found children sometimes, needlessly murdered by these roving bands and left quite dead along the roadsides. Some were stolen by gipsies and by traveling pedlers, and many others ran away.

Yet the fate of these whose vanishings were now discussed, was of a different order. There had entered recently a fiendish regularity, almost a method in the symmetry of disappearance. None knew where these infants went, nor were their bodies ever found.

From Nantes had come the first accounts, retold with shuddering horror and with fascinated half-belief. They had been stories of remote events—like tales of supernatural evil—frightening, yet distant in their application. But all at once they were confirmed. Within a mile, the blow had fallen and some one of a close experience was stricken with bereavement.

Spreading and pervading all the country, this dread maintained a nucleus or center. At first this had been Nantes, but as the legend grew and prospered, taking at last coherent force, a little village of dark sagging roofs built against the forest's wall, became identified with the plague. Without quite knowing why, the peasants spoke its name in whispers, or if they could, they spoke it not at all.

Thus, in the vicinity of St. Jean d'Angely, a group of tired weather-beaten peasants were seated at an inn. A cold mist had risen from the sea, chilling the world outside and depositing itself in a feathery web upon the wool of huddled sheep. Within the dark-beamed tavern, the guests delayed over their mugs of beer, stretching their legs before the fire in pleasant stupid talk and putting off the moment when they must cross the exterior dampness that lay between their comfort and their homes.

Some one had driven a team into the muddy courtyard and was engaged in stabling his beasts. From his drowse, the landlord listened to the shouts and tramping of the horses with peaceful resignation. No doubt the man would spend the night, which would necessitate for him the tired duties of hospitality. The landlord stirred restlessly at the idea, rebelling at the thought of effort. In the bar, he heard his wife moving busily about and welcoming the stranger. Perhaps, he thought hopefully, the man was on his way to bed. A silence fell upon the group as the bar door opened and the man came in.

With a sigh the landlord rose and motioned the newcomer to a chair. The latter was a pleasant-looking fellow, less ragged than the rest, but obviously of peasant origin, a villager beyond a doubt.

The silence grew in depth while the stranger took up his cup of wine. The familiar peasants became embarrassed and ill at ease. They did not know this man and felt constrained because of him. They were simple folk. The stranger also showed embarrassment, and to relieve it an ancient farmer broke the pause. By a great effort he leaned forward and asked the newcomer his name. The others, tongue-tied, approved the friendly gesture and felt profoundly grateful to their spokesman.

The stranger set down his glass and stretched his legs. "My name is Regnard," he said, "and I am from the village of Machecoul. A cobbler," he added gravely.

Again the silence fell, heavier by the many thoughts that no one dared to say. Not moving in their chairs, the countrymen turned away their eyes in order not to see this man. Slowly, the talk began again in forced whisperings, wherein the crops, the fog and local things were mentioned with a show of interest.

To their amazement, the spokesman again leaned forward, while the others watched and strained their ears. "An evil place, Machecoul," the spokesman said, as though the name were a reproach. Then angrily he muttered, "They eat our children there." And lapsed into rebuking silence.

The stranger made no reply, but stared into the fire. For even he could not explain the reputation which his village had acquired.

§ 2

The departure of the Dauphin had served to cut for ever the ties that bound De Rais to earth. As Louis rode away, puzzled by the apathy of his fantastic host, he left behind a sense of vast relief. During his visit, he had typified to the Baron the world that was scheming and troublesome, yet thoroughly intent upon its own affairs, and not concerned beyond.

Once gone, a reaction from the apprehension he had caused set in. The fear, the frenzy in the laboratory, the terror that the end of life was near, vanished completely from the Baron.

"My life has already been lived," he said to Griart. "It is too late to worry over consequences. When the mortal end arrives, I shall be ready; for, though I am not old, I fear that I am growing weary even of myself."

To De Sillé he amplified this sentiment in an attempt to justify himself. "Let us complete the strivings of our life," he said. "If there are evils which I have not seen, I have no longer fear to look. To God I commend my soul with deep humility and prayer, and to His mercy I must trust the hope of my salvation. No more can any mortal do. But until the day of judgment shall arrive, I cease to fear."

This was the sentiment that ruled within the household of Machecoul. The bars of hesitance were lowered once for all, and amid his vigils before the image of the Virgin, accompanied by his ever-swelling cries for mercy and compassion, the madness of the Baron's passion burst upon him.

For the first time in his life, he poured the entire energy of his being into the achievement of his sins. No other interest deflected him, nor was he hindered by the slightest scruple. His appetite for death had grown; to supply his needs, he organized a campaign of procuration.

The witch, Perrine Martin, who dwelt close by the castle walls, was taken into service. Going and coming upon her unwatched journeys, she brought with her great numbers of the children whom she lured with cakes and promised gifts.

Griart, Corrillaut and Gilles de Sillé also aided in the search. Many youths were hired for the service of the castle, of its master or of its other inhabitants. Children were purchased from their parents, as Rossignol had been obtained, and children came to beg.

To supplement this large supply and to enter more personally into all the phases of activity, there came into existence at this time a series of hunting parties in which De Rais took part. Muffled in heavy cloaks, their faces half-concealed, they would go forth at sunset from the castle gates. Corrillaut, De Sillé, Griart or Eustache Blanchet were the companions whom the Baron chose. Sometimes they went together as a group of five; at other times a single intimate accompanied him.

As a rule, the towns and villages were avoided. Instead, they rode in silent gallop through the empty fields and forest, always in a fresh direction. From the windings of some forest path, they would emerge upon the darkness of a barren moor. Halting, they scanned the hills that lay around them. Not far away, a speck of fire burned upon a hillside, and across its face the hunters could see the moving outlines of the sheep. Stealthily they would approach, drawing rein not far away to watch with eager eyes the movement of the flock. Sometimes they saw a peasant hunched before the blaze, and turning, they galloped onward, searching for the sudden and the unsuspecting victim.

At other times, success was their reward. Among the beasts they would espy a child asleep, tired from playing shepherd. Spurring suddenly, the dark-clad riders would charge among the flock, scattering the animals in all directions. Startled from his dreams, the boy would spring up with a cry. With lightning speed, the hunters would dismount and seize him, holding him tightly lest he shout, and tying up his arms and legs. Then, as quickly, he was lifted up and thrown sack-like across a waiting saddle, while the men remounted and covered up their burden with the volume of a cloak. In silence they rode once more, cloaks held before their faces, galloping at furious pace for the seclusion of their castle.

The stealth lent fascination to the chase that Gilles de Rais pursued. The motion of the horses through the gathering dusk, the occasional disappointments of the expedition, the speed with which the game was snared, aroused him to a new enthusiasm. But greater was the meaning of the capture which lent a tang not found when stags or rabbits were the quarry.

Often, returning empty-handed from the chase, the horsemen braved the alleys of a village to pause unnoticed by a cottage door and snatch the infant that played, unguarded on the sill.

§ 3

During the winter and early spring of 1440, the stories of the terror that had spread among the peasants, found their way to Nantes. From the mouths of the bereaved, and from the voices of a thousand frightened parents, the parish priests received the public rumor. Unlike the ears of individuals which receive information only to let it pass out through the mouth, the ever-listening ear of the Church heard with more circumspection, retaining the things it heard to be stored away for future reference, or to be kept as an addition to the universal wisdom.

In time, therefore, the clamor of the peasants found its way into the episcopal palace and was received discreetly by the Bishop. Like all good churchmen, Jean de Malestroit knew fully the inventiveness of popular imagination; but, being wise, he also knew its limits. Man in the mass was an embellisher of tales, but to the Bishop's knowledge, he had not the wit to make them up. A basis of truth, the Prelate was convinced, lay at the bottom of this variated hysteria.

The similarity in the reports was as arresting as the differences. From widely separated points of land, there came identical details. The heavy cloaks and mounted figures riding at night across the land, became too frequent in the telling to be disregarded. The folded wings, the horns and other satanic manifestations, bore a great resemblance to one another; but with a proper skepticism, the Bishop paid no heed to these.

The traditional aspect of the Fiend was quite familiar to his flock, and in an occasional vivid flash, some peasant practically revealed that his detailed acquaintance was closer to the witches' god than to the acted devil of the mountebanks.

Of other closeness in the accounts, the Bishop was more careful. Certain aspects recalled to him the story of Madame Kerguen, and of the loss of little Jean. First, there came the general fear of Machecoul, where children were devoured. This village was the very center of the storm, and in its streets there had been many vanishings.

Through his priests and agents, Jean de Malestroit instituted a systematic searching for all data that was credible and pertinent. Every one connected with the disappearances was questioned upon the most remote details. The Bishop himself arranged the form of interrogation without submitting to the questioners themselves his own beliefs.

The results of this procedure brought several facts to light, the most important of which was an odd recurrence of certain persons who were seen upon the days when children vanished, either just before or shortly after the event, close to the actual scene. There were, perhaps, a dozen of these repeated names, and they were noticed in too many isolated villages to have gone there by chance. Beyond a doubt they were connected with the evil.

By his secret means of information, the Bishop had them traced. Several were natives of the town of Nantes and were now absent from their homes. Relatives stated that they traveled, but did not know the cause. One whose name or description appeared most frequently upon the lists was a woman of an evil name, who was supposed to be a witch. Her home was at Machecoul. But of the rest there certainly could be no question of identity. One was the Lord of Rais himself. The others were his servants.

The evidence was not enough for legal form. Though it convinced the Bishop of the author of the crimes, he hesitated to take a further step alone. Gilles de Rais was far too strong to be attacked without a powerful reason and a strong authority.

De Rais himself, however, gave, in the spring, a cause sufficient for the Bishop to take action. A lull had fallen on his passion, and he was seized with restlessness. There happened at this time to enter into the involved negotiations that were being carried on, a difficulty that could be taken as an affront. Across the Baron's troubled brain there came a flash of warlike ardor.

The small estate of St. Etienne de la Mer Morte, not far from Machecoul, had been sold to Geffroi le Feron, the Treasurer of the Duke of Brittany. Largely at De Rais' request, there had remained due a certain unpaid balance. As long as this continued, the Baron saw a chance of repurchasing the place with savings or with the products of his alchemists. But in the course of time Le Feron became impatient and, without much ceremony, he appeared at St. Etienne and took possession, leaving his brother, Jean, in permanent command.

The news of this arrived at Machecoul as the fury of a long debauch was at an end, and swept before it with a purifying rage the fetid madness of the charnel-house.

Trumpets sounded in the courtyards, and the quiet castle burst into a fever of preparation. Men in armor clanked about the walls and rattled down the stairways. The body-guard was fitted with new shields. From the stables the horses were inspected and tried out in their gaits, while bits of broken armor were hastily repaired.

Ready for war, the private army of De Rais rode out across the lowered drawbridge and down the avenue of elms. For once, they were attended by no followers. The priests and monks were left behind; no choir-boys attended on their donkeys, nor was there much of luxury about the troop. The atmosphere was martial and severe; and the attitude defiant toward the world, whether represented by Geffroi le Feron or by the strict commands of ducal authority against the use of private force.

Arrived at St. Etienne, they broke their marching order and, with a circular charge, surrounded the estate. As they drew in, compressing the circle they enclosed, De Rais deserted them. Angrily he spurred his horse across the flat green lawn toward the chapel whence the droning of recited mass emerged.

Angered by the smugness of his enemy, Gilles de Rais threw wide the chapel doors. By the altar Jean le Feron looked up from his devotions. Rushing down the nave, the Baron reached the choir, and seizing the startled priest, he shook him by the neck.

"Out of the church, ribald," he shouted, "before I spill your blood upon the altar-cloth!"

Not waiting for an answer, he turned about and, dragging the outraged priest behind him, strode furiously up the aisle and out into the open. Le Feron's men had fled with wisdom and discretion, and in the castle the luckless priest was cast into a dungeon. Save for the feast to celebrate the capture, the victory was accomplished.

Serious matters were involved in this attack, and Jean de Malestroit lost no time in pleading them before the Duke. Officially, the latter was the friend and protector of De Rais. Against the wrath of France he had defied his King in giving commands that the royal interdict against the Baron should not be read within the borders of his duchy. Semi-officially, he had lent his aid for the recapture of Champtocé when it had been seized by René de la Suze. Money had been loaned when the Baron was hard pressed, mortgages were freely given and useless lands were purchased. Thus said the Bishop. Yet in reply of gratitude, this faithless noble had broken out in bold revolt against the strictest of the feudal laws.

The scandalous affair was made more heinous by the fact that Jean le Feron was a tonsured clerk and lived in the protection of the Church; while worse than this, the Bishop pointed out, he had been dragged by force out of the sanctuary of a chapel and from the very hands of God. And this offense was of a basic seriousness.

All this was urged in public. Privately, the Bishop continued his harangue, enlarging upon the stories which the Duke had already heard, of De Rais' searching for gold. No doubt he somewhat exaggerated the possibilities, but even the merest thought of a sudden and illimitable wealth descending on his vassal, disturbed the Duke profoundly.

He visualized the prospect of alchemic triumph. Once rich again, he knew that nothing could prevent the Baron from repudiating all past contracts, under the legal theory that they were in opposition to the royal interdict. With lavish bribes, the King could be won over, or even financed in a new invasion of the duchy. In that case he, the Duke, would be in an unfortunate position, and face to face with at least the loss of Champtocé, for which he had worked so hard.

In proper anger, therefore, the Duke dispatched to Machecoul two high officials to demand apology and satisfaction. With remnants of his rage, the Baron heard their insolence, and despite their curses, threats and promises of retribution, he had them dragged away and locked in the dungeons below the walls. In Nantes, the Duke retorted, by declaring him outside the law, and ordering a force of men to go against him. Machecoul prepared for siege.

A curious thing now took place which changed the course of these events. Arthur de Richemont was again in Nantes, and to his care his brother entrusted the subduing of De Rais. Somehow, this bitter warrior had never forgotten the young commander who had ridden by his side before St. James de Beuvron. Perhaps he suspected Jean de Malestroit of instigating the affair; and he bore no love for the Bishop. Patriotism and friendship, at any rate, he considered to be great virtues—despite the fact that in his world, he was alone in this belief.

Instead of proceeding in force against De Rais, therefore, Arthur de Richemont entered Machecoul as an honored guest. The fit of war had died within the Baron's heart, and they met easily, in friendship and with cheer. Old battles were relived, and there took place much talk of politics and France and old acquaintances.

When he left, De Richemont brought away the ducal officers and a complete and humble apology. The matter of St. Etienne was finished.

The Duke was satisfied and his honor was restored; but in the episcopal palace, Jean de Malestroit fumed with rage. He had been beaten in his scheming by his ancient foe, De Richemont. The overt act through which he wished to press his case against De Rais had fallen through, nor had he received any recompense for the outraging of the sanctity of the Church.

Disgruntled, angry and thoroughly resolved, the Lord Bishop of Nantes set out upon a private tour throughout his diocese for the purpose of investigating, sifting and codifying sufficient of the ever-growing mass of public clamor, to form a case against the Baron, which would be strong enough to command the ears of all the world.

§ 4

In the early summer of 1440, Jean de Malestroit commenced his secret investigation. In person he visited the parishes whence had come the rumors of complaint, leaving behind in Nantes a commission to which he relayed reports. In each town from which he thought he could obtain sufficient information he lingered, working with the parish priest, gathering together and having written down a mass of peasant incoherence.

It was not the custom of the courts to rely upon the fragile hope of direct testimony. Bribes and threats could change the memory of witnesses, while legal depositions could not with ease be sworn away. The Bishop labored, therefore, with a huge amount of transcribed nonsense, which was often invented by the teller, or was clearly irrelevant to the case at hand. The sorting and codifying of these despositions so that the truth could be revealed, he left to the labor of his commission, while he himself traveled through the Nantais country questioning the peasants and listening to their solemn oaths.

While Jean de Malestroit was thus engaged, the warmth of summer drew De Rais to Nantes. Tiring of evocations and of the gloomy fortress of Machecoul, he seized upon the excuse that the Hôtel de la Suze was to be sold. Thither he moved, set up his household, and commenced an urban life of pomp and open luxury.

The Bishop, he was told, was out of town—away on some mission of his own—but he had left behind officials of his staff thoroughly competent to attend to matters of the contract. De Rais was satisfied, and let the matter drop. He had no interest in the sale, and for a time he lived an easy careless life, such as was expected of a wealthy noble. The magic arts were dropped, nor did Prelati leave his cottage at Machecoul; yet despite the full publicity of De Rais' existence, a dozen infants disappeared from view.

From Nantes, the Baron moved to Vannes in search of the Duke, who owed, at this time, another payment on his purchases. Being in the position of an urgent creditor (for the life at Nantes had been expensive) as well as for other reasons, De Rais did not become a ducal guest; but put up at the Lemoine Inn, renting for his use the entire building.

Scarcely had he quitted Nantes, than Jean de Malestroit returned, filled with success and well pleased with his labors. In his presence, the commission met and rendered their report. There was no longer any doubt about their findings.

On the evening of the thirtieth of July, André Buschet, a servant of De Rais, knocked softly at the door of a large chamber in the Lemoine Inn, which served as a sort of common-room for the baronial court. The door opened, and Buschet entered. Sailcloth was stretched upon the floor, while in one corner was piled a heap of furniture. A table, upon which stood a number of bottles of wine, together with cold meats and cakes, was in the center, and about it were seated the Baron and his friends. In comfortable chairs there rested De Sillé, Corrillaut and Henri Griart, goblets of wine beside them or in their hands, while De Rais lay half-reclined upon a cushioned couch. Beside him, partly hidden by his silk-clad form, a long curved dagger and a coil of rope were seen.

By the hand, Buschet was grasping a boy whom, by good fortune, he had discovered loitering behind the stables. Unresisting, the child was led across the room to the Baron, who now sat up upon his couch. De Rais brushed back the matted hair from the boy's forehead and looked into his eyes.

"A pretty one indeed, friend Buschet," he said absently, "although if you had had him cleaned, he would have been more pleasing to the nose."

From his purse, he drew out a piece of gold and threw it to the servant. Buschet accepted it and went out, closing the door behind him. From within the other bolts were shot, and in the passageway the servant looked again upon his piece of gold. A remembrance of the hidden dagger crossed his mind, and he shivered involuntarily. Quickly he left the hostelry and hurried off to spend his wages in relieving sin. It was on this day that a paper which declared that Gilles de Rais, Lord of Machecoul and of Tiffauges, was a being of public infamy, was placed on record in the archives of the See of Nantes. And while this declaration passed its first night in the churchly files, three muffled figures crouched in the town of Vannes over the open top of a public cesspool. For Corrillaut had lowered the body of a murdered boy into its evil depths.

From Vannes the household of the Baron moved to Josselin, the former property of the Clissons, and stayed here briefly in enjoyment of its charm and quiet. A visit was now paid to Tiffauges where they remained until the middle of August. Something of the activities of the Bishop here reached the cavalcade, causing a certain uneasiness among the followers. Buschet was the first to leave. Unnoticed, he slipped off to spend his fortune in the fleshpots of the world.

Bourgneuf-en-Rais, now separated from the barony, and being a property of the Duke, was their next halting-place, and in this town De Rais took up his quarters at the Monastery of the Grey Friars.

In his repentant moods, he had made many oaths to one day join an order of this sort. Here, in the midst of monks, he found a curious pleasure in the austerity of their lives.

Of this he talked on St. Bartholomew's Eve while walking with the Abbot down a long grape arbor in the monastic grounds.

"You have told me," said De Rais, "that you, too, have lived an active life."

"I was a soldier," said the Abbot, "but that was long ago."

"How is it possible for you to be contented here," the Baron asked, "where the only stimulation is the murmuring of prayers and the companionship of tired monks?"

"At first I was uneasy," the Abbot admitted, "but I have learned to rest. God is a wonderful and peaceful friend."

"I envy you your faith, my friend. In my true heart, I long for rest and peace."

"The brotherhood awaits with open arms."

"But could you give me peace?"

"That is a matter of the soul," the Abbot said. "Completion."

"Completion is the state I seek," observed De Rais. "In my existence I have tried to learn all things of life—and yet a few escape. When I have discovered these, shall I find rest?"

"No," said the Abbot. "One can not slumber in the market-place. And for that reason, the churches and the monasteries were built."

From the direction of the chapel, Griart was approaching. The Abbot bowed, concluding the conversation, and walked away, his head bent in meditation. The librarian halted beside his master.

"Blanchet has arranged a banquet at the inn," he said. "This monastic bread is wearying to the palate. They are afraid of salt—these celibates."

The banquet was well prepared. For the night, the inn was cleared of other guests, and the doors were bolted shut. The room above the kitchen, usually employed for sleeping quarters, was cleared of bedding, while down the center there was placed a table covered with a white cloth and with a multitude of goblets. About this board, the guests were seated, while from below there rose the appetizing smells of cookery.

Beside De Rais, Guillaume Rodige, the landlord, bobbed his head in deferential and embarrassed pleasure. With lavish resourcefulness, the banquet had been planned with a brilliance that outdid, he said, the greatest of his expectations. Never had he concocted such a meal, and he hoped his noble guests would be content.

Blanchet, who had helped him with the menu, raised his glass. "To the prosperity of our host," he proposed. "May hunger never fall across his door."

Rodige bobbed his head and muttered a reply.

"Silence, villain!" shouted De Rais. "I have another toast to drink. Eternal peace!" he cried. "Let us, then, drink to God!"

The landlord crossed himself and hurried from the room. These folk were great indeed, and bolder than he liked.

The feast proceeded with success. Food was devoured with a relish and wine was drunk by gallons. Toward its conclusion, Corrillaut rose and slipped away to the accompaniment of vulgar jests. He reappeared, however, to introduce, with clumsy comedy, a startled peasant boy.

"This Bernard (bow, scoundrel!), surnamed Le Camus from a certain peasant who was the husband of his mother, has come from Brest, where he was whelped, to learn good French in Bourgneuf-en-Rais."

"A futile errand," commented Blanchet, "for here they speak a horrible and corrupt tongue."

"Nevertheless, it is his wish," asserted Corrillaut.

De Rais cut him short. "Be still," he shouted, "and tell the boy that in this room there lies a golden key wherewith he may unlock the secret of all hidden knowledge. Let us rise, my friends, for the initiation of young Camus into the mysteries."

Clumsily they drew back from the board and got up from their chairs. De Sillé seized the boy and dragged him toward a corner of the room, while close upon him crowded in the other guests.

In that room of feasting, above the kitchen of Rodige's inn, died Bernard le Camus of the town of Brest, the final victim of the Baron's passion.

§ 5

With the death of Bernard, surnamed Le Camus, the Breton tour came to an end, and from Bourgneuf-en-Rais the cavalcade returned to the castle of Machecoul. De Rais was again exhausted of his passion, and bored with his career.

As always at the termination of his debauches, he suffered from a deep depression of spirit which robbed his life of any zest. The ever-recurrent cycle had been concluded, leaving before him a period of inert apathy before he could take up some newer phase. In this mood, he felt that there was now no course remaining which he had not already tried. Sorcery had lost its interest for him. And, although Prelati in his rented cottage delved yet deeper into his secret studies, the Baron had abandoned any hope of his success. He had no further caring for the trappings of domestic elegance. The theater bored him, while his collections, once complete, were scattered now beyond repair. For a moment, he considered the joining of the quiet monks in their lifeless contemplations, but a certain understanding of his own career forbade.

Static and tedious as now was his own existence, he knew too well that this was but a temporary lull. After an interval, his energy would return again, pointed in a fresh and interesting direction; and in the meantime he must wait.

He saw himself caught in an eternal purgatory of repetition. Commencing with this desperate discontent, with which he was just now afflicted, he had so many times burst forth into some outlet of activity. The wars, the mystery at Nantes, the great display of Orléans, and the magic efforts of Prelati had, in the past, been his release. Again he felt the need of some new effort, built of huge proportions, to serve him as a rescue. Yet once this was achieved (this he knew also), his sins and lusts were fated to return, leaving him with their passing despairing and inert.

Over Machecoul, a new uneasiness appeared, causing a defection in the household. Buschet had left the train at Vannes. Roger de Bricqueville, the treasurer, had not returned from Bourgneuf-en-Rais. A courier dispatched from Machecoul returned with the story that the treasurer had left the monastery there upon a journey, saying that he was going to Savoy. No other word arrived.

In the village, Prelati and Blanchet in their joint household seemed to come less frequently to the castle. They were at work, they said, upon a difficult and dangerous experiment which took up all their time.

It was impossible that the Baron was unaware of the unpleasant rumors that came continually from Nantes. Rumors at the advent of which old servants, agents and dignitaries of the chapel would pack their goods and journey forth along the roads to France or to the south. The Baron's first annoyance at these leavings vanished before a sort of perverse pleasure as he watched his friends and lackeys slip away. Perhaps there now began his new adventure.

Gilles de Sillé, solemn and very churchly, sought an interview.

"Cousin de Rais," he said, "let us make a new excursion. Machecoul is at an end."

De Rais regarded him for a moment with some curiosity. "So I have gathered," he said. "Proceed."

"Whether you know it or not," went on the priest, "we are accused before the courts of Nantes of certain crimes. The charge is serious, my friend; so grave indeed that we must face not only the Duke of Brittany, but the strength of France, and, more than that, the Church itself. My knowledge is exact and unimpeachable."

"You think the Duke will dare to march against me? Then

let him come. I long ago have ceased to feel any fear."

"Even Machecoul can not defend your safety. The forces that are aligned against us are too strong, while secretly your body-guard is leaving your employ. My Lord, I beg of you to flee."

"To hide in hedgerows among a foreign people," replied De Rais. "To wander homeless from court to court unwanted and disgraced; to walk throughout the world an outcast with a price upon my head as a second Olivier de Clisson. No, Cousin de Sillé, that is no end for Gilles de Rais. I shall not quit Machecoul."

"If you refuse, then I shall go alone. I have a fondness for my neck."

"Where should I go," went on De Rais without conviction, "where I could be myself and not a wretched exile? That is a problem which even you, my friend, will find some trouble in answering."

"Once," said De Sillé, "I pointed out a choice you had to make. This is the moment of your choosing. The Church at last has turned against you, but the Other Faith awaits. Their network of protection spreads across the world, and in their ranks you will be saved."

"What is the price, De Sillé?"

"Mere worship at the shrine of sin. Already you are half-enrolled."

"I am no more than a spectator. Participation I deny."

"That is absurd," the priest replied. "Of good and evil, no one is immune. Yours has been a life of sin, and yet you hesitate before the outward recognition of yourself. Join us before the worship of the goat, and you are saved from death."

"Safety of the body," mused De Rais. "What else?"

"Power."

"Such as Prelati wields among his crucibles. A very minor strength."

"And glory of the soul."

"A strange and hideous glorification, cousin," said De Rais. "I cast it from me."

"Why?" asked the priest. "Already you are damned."

"God in His infinite mercy will have compassion," said the Baron. "In that great fact I place my hope. If, at this moment, I must choose my course, I shall retain my soul."

"What foolish hope you have," De Sillé sighed, "still to imagine you are saved!"

"I believe it," cried De Rais, "from the very bottom of my soul. O God, to Whom I pray, Father, Son and Holy Essence, in You I yet believe despite my crimes and wickedness. In You I trust, with a trembling and an overwhelming faith!"

"You are mad," said De Sillé, and went away.

With the departure of the priest, a sense of calm descended on De Rais. One by one, the body-guard took their leave unwatched, and with their going, the gold at hand grew less. Occasionally, the Baron visited the shrines in prayer; but the soft dimness of the chapel failed to arouse his piety. Once, out of curiosity, he visited the crypt below, once draped in the curtains of the sinful mass. But it, too, left him curiously unmoved.

Somehow, his resignation spread about him. Prelati returned more often from his laboratory, nor did Henri Griart nor Corrillaut have any wish to leave. Evil though I am, the Baron thought, I still have friends. I wonder why they do not go?

On the thirteenth of September, there arrived from Nantes a company of men-at-arms under two captains, Robert Guillaumet and Jean l'Abbé. To their surprise, the drawbridge of Machecoul was down, and at their approach the gates were opened from within. Half suspecting an attack, they rode without molestation through the arch beneath the towered gateway and halted in the courtyard.

Here they dismounted and were met by lackeys of the House of Rais. With quiet ceremony the servants led the captains across the flagging to the keep. Here they entered and, passing along a darkened corridor, were ushered in silence into a handsome room where, dressed in a suit of purple velvet, De Rais was sitting by a window.

At their approach he rose and greeted them. "I have already guessed your mission," he said. Then with a smile, he recognized the captain. "Often I have wished," he said, "to go to God, and here is Captain l'Abbé to lead the way. Let me accept your guidance."

L'Abbé bowed and handed him a parchment. "It is a writ for your arrest, my Lord," he said, "issued by the courts of Nantes. In the presence of these men, I give it to your hand."

De Rais held it to the window and read a portion. Then, stepping back, he raised his head.

"Nothing, my friends, within the range of human strength," he said with great solemnity, "can balk the will of God from being done. Let us go at once to Nantes."

CHAPTER XVII

§ 1

THE trial of Gilles de Rais became with his changing moods a drama, spectacle and tragedy. Under the black-beamed ceiling of the audience chamber within the ducal palace—the very room in which twenty years before the Baron had made his initial public appearance—it was conducted through a maze of culminating sensations.

As was usual, two trials, one ecclesiastical and the other civil, were prescribed, the former taking precedence both in temporal order and in importance. Over it presided Jean de Malestroit, Bishop of the Diocese of Nantes, and the Bishops of St. Brieuc and of St. Lô. Beside them, representing the civil code, sat Pierre l'Hopital, President of the High Court of Brittany; and one Jean Blouyn, of the order of Preaching Friars, who was Vice-Inquisitor for the district. Guillaume Chapeillon, who had assisted Jean de Malestroit in the collection of the evidence against the Baron, assumed charge of the prosecution.

Throughout the preliminary hearings, De Rais remained aloof and untroubled, boasting occasionally of his innocence, and hearing mass within his own most comfortable apartments which were above the audience chamber. So far, the indictment contained only charges of heresy and sacrilege, which accusations were based, he knew, upon slim or unimportant evidence. To him, it seemed that the trial became a gesture of authority and a matter to be compromised upon the payment of a heavy fine. Nevertheless, the confinement and the fact that he was denied the consolation of the sacrament, got on his nerves.

On October eighth the trial began in earnest, and Gilles de

331

Rais was brought before the court a prisoner. After the legal formulæ of commencement, the prosecutor read a summary of the charges and demanded a plea of guilty or of innocence. Holding himself erect, De Rais surveyed the chamber. Of the statements in the arraignment, he admitted only two: that he had been baptized and that he had repudiated the Fiend and all his works. The rest, he said, was false. In place of a proper plea, he appealed that he be taken to a higher court, one more worthy to try a person of a so-exalted rank.

Indignantly, the prosecutor upheld his charges, offering to take his personal oath that they were true, and demanding that the Baron either plead or else support his own denial by oath. This Gilles de Rais refused to do. He had no wish to add false witness to his sins.

The appeal was not allowed, and the court was then adjourned so that the jurists, who had fasted since the day before in order to insure the needed clarity of mind, might eat their dinners.

The second important session took place on the morning of the thirteenth and continued, with appropriate intermissions, for three days. The ecclesiastical court had been reconstituted so that it was empowered to conduct the trial and to impose the sentence.

In elaborate costume, wearing the ermine which was a privilege of only the greatest of the Breton nobles, and decorated with a great array of military and feudal orders, De Rais appeared before the bench of judging and advisory prelates. Below the platform, crowded the angry and impatient peasants; parents of the slain, and friends of the bereaved. Their cries and imprecations filled the room with turmoil and gave a splendid setting to De Rais' attack.

"Simoniacs and ribalds!" he shouted to the judges. "Rather that I should be hanged by the neck than that I should have traffic with such folk as you!"

Turning to Pierre l'Hopital, he asked indignantly how such a man could listen to the charges that had been read. "I am," he

concluded, "a Christian and a Catholic, as I have ever been."
Once more the court required that he plead and once more
De Rais refused.

Now finally completed, the full indictment of forty-nine articles was read by Guillaume Chapeillon, the prosecutor. Therein
appeared a general statement of the Baron's crimes, and the
crimes of Gilles de Sillé, Corrillaut, Roger de Bricqueville,
Hicquet de Bremont, Henri Griart, Rossignol, Robin Romulart
and André Buschet. As the articles continued, they grew more
precise, mentioning the names and dates of the assassinations
and bringing up specific charges of the sins which had been
done. One hundred and forty murders were definitely specified,
although the number was supposed to be between two hundred
and eight hundred. Children had been killed and disemboweled;
their slaughtered, immolated bodies had been burned or offered
to Satan amid a scene of hideous debauch and odious abomina-
tion. Conjuration, invocation of the infernal powers and subservience to the Fiend of Hell were charged.

Over his accusation, Chapeillon declaimed with fervid elo-
quence, while from the body of the chamber there rose the cries
of lamentation, the howls of anguish and the hysteria of the attendant crowd.

From time to time, the prosecutor suffered interruptions from
the tumult of the crowd and from the anger of De Rais, who
shouted out denials and uttered scathing comments on his
judges.

Article Number Forty-nine contained the ultimate summa-
tion, and with a sweep of oratory, Chapeillon read it out; that
Gilles de Rais was a heretic, an apostate, an offender against the
majesty of God and against the priesthood of the Church; and
that he was culpable of crimes so horrible that they could be
read in open court only if rendered in the Latin tongue.

Once more De Rais was called upon to plead. As the chamber
waited in expectant silence, the Baron burst forth into a tem-
pest of abuse, demanding again that he be tried by a superior
tribunal.

Amid his loud denials, the court declared him contumacious and, though he strove to shout them down, the judges pronounced upon him a solemn excommunication.

The two-day wait alone in his apartment above the audience chamber, unblessed by the comforts of religion, had upon the Baron a sobering effect. For the first time since his arrest, he became aware of the seriousness of his position. In this interval, also, his anger against the law for infringing upon his life grew less.

At any rate, upon his next appearance, De Rais presented a new and totally different aspect. Soberly clad, with downcast eyes—the very picture of a noble penitent—he entered slowly and bowed before the jurists. In a low and humble voice, he recognized the court, admitting that he had committed crimes within its jurisdiction. In tears and with a broken voice, he begged forgiveness for his previous harsh words. Once more, the prosecutor read the long indictment, calmly this time, translating and explaining as he read. To the first fourteen articles which dealt with the legality of the proceedings, De Rais made no objections, but he denied all charges of sorcery or of dealings with the Fiend. Then formally, and of his own volition, he plead "not guilty."

While he was taking oath, his left hand between those of Jean de Malestroit and of the Vice-Inquisitor, Chapeillon brought in as witnesses for the prosecution Prelati, Griart, Blanchet, La Meffraie and several others. Stunned by their appearance, De Rais refused to cross-examine them and they were led away. Falling upon his knees, the Baron begged that the ban of excommunication be lifted from his soul. To this, De Malestroit agreed and spoke to him with words of comfort and encouragement.

There ensued a period of legal routine. On successive days, the written depositions of the bereaved parents, the signed confession of Prelati and the evidence of sacrilege attendant upon the dragging of the unfortunate Jean le Feron from the sanctuary of the chapel of St. Etienne de la Mer Morte were read and entered in the record. De Rais admitted sacrilege, and made no denials of the abductions. Upon the subject of the magic arts he kept a severe silence. As the evidence was largely circumstantial, a confession from the prisoner was practically essential, and to this end the prosecutor asked for power to resort to torture. In the face of De Rais' stubbornness and the almost conclusive nature of the case against him, this request was granted.

At this, De Rais gave way to fear. Falling once more upon his knees, he offered to make a full confession to the Bishop of St. Brieuc, provided that he be heard in a room far removed from the torture chamber.

This confession was made in the presence of the designated Bishop and of Pierre l'Hopital, and was taken down in writing by a notary. At its conclusion, Prelati, who had already given evidence, appeared, and between the Baron and his sorcerer took place a scene of affection and of farewell. "Trust in God," counseled De Rais, "and we shall meet again in Paradise."

The final session of the trial brought forth a scene as remarkable as any which had occurred within the thirty-six years of Gilles de Rais' career. On this day the trial came to its end, conducted to a spectacular conclusion by De Rais himself who, in a new rôle, played the leading part.

Before a densely packed assembly, he now appeared to repeat and to make official the full confession of his crimes. His costume was this day of black brocade and over it he wore a hood of velvet, also black. Haggard and worn from an all-night vigil, his voice was reverential and subdued. As he had been a man of mighty sins, he now became, in his own eyes and for his audience, a mighty penitent. Word by word came his confession, read to the court and amplified by frequent interruptions and additions. In awed stillness, the audience chamber became a gigantic confessional; for in that room De Rais addressed his God.

Once as he paused, the frozen silence of the court was shattered by a woman's scream; and in the hush that followed, Jean

de Malestroit arose. Crossing the room, the Bishop raised a
veil, and with this cloth he covered up the tortured features of
the wooden crucifix upon the wall.

The Baron came at length to his conclusion. Laying the
written parchment upon the judges' tribune, he raised his face
toward the dark ceiling. "O God, my Creator and my well beloved Redeemer," he cried, "I ask Your pardon and Your
mercy."

To the surprise of all assembled, he now stepped forward
and, the focus of a thousand eyes, addressed the crowd, exhorting them as parents to raise their children in the sight of God,
in reverence of the Church and free from idleness or luxury. It
was these sins, he said, the evil direction and the freedom of his
youth which had caused him to offend against the holy Mother
Church. "Yet by this declaration," he went on, "by the shame
which shows upon my face, I hope to obtain more readily the
grace of God and the remission of my sins. Oh, parents, friends
of those innocents whom I have put to death, as Christians and
as followers of Jesus Christ, I pray you on my knees to give me
the succor of your pious supplications."

With these words he ceased, and in a heavy and impressive
silence the crowded court knelt down and prayed. Slowly, one
by one, the peasants, the parents of the maimed and slaughtered
children, rose and filed out, sorrowing, into the evening dusk.

The sentence which was pronounced upon him was in two
parts, yet each was in its substance similar. Another day was
needed for the reading of the verdict, and on the morrow the
jurists and the spectators again assembled. By the edict of the
court, De Rais was stated to be shamefully guilty of heresy, of
apostacy and of the invocations of demons; of crimes committed with infants, of sacrilege and of the violation of the
immunity of the Church. For these offenses he was excom-
municated and made subject to whatever penalties the law
prescribed.

Falling upon his knees in a flood of tears and anguish, he
begged that the decree of excommunication be removed. In

view of his repentance and contrition, this ban was lifted and
he was readmitted to the Church and granted absolution.

The civil trial was merely an abridgment of the ecclesiastical
proceedings with which it had been in session simultaneously.
Despite a sort of insanity plea stating that the Baron had been
invaded in force by several well-armed and desperate fiends and
was, therefore, unaccountable for his acts, the verdict was
unanimous. Death was prescribed; to take place by hanging
and by the use of fire. The date of execution was set to be the
following noon.

Griart and Corrillaut, meanwhile, had also been tried and had
received the same conviction. In view of this, the Baron made a
special plea: that as they had sinned together, they might suffer
for their crimes in unison. "I am the cause of their fall," he
said, "and at the moment of their passing, I wish to hold them
up and speak to them of their salvation. For should they die
and I remain alive, they might imagine that I have been spared
and so fall to despair."

§ 2

Upon an island in the Loire were raised three gibbets in a
plain; and under these three pyres were arranged. Upon the
twenty-sixth of October, a great procession started for this
place. Praying for the soul of the murderer of their children,
the peasants and townsfolk wound their way to the river, accompanied by chanting monks and by a company of priests. In
the dense and weeping crowd appeared a number of the nobles
of the duchy, among them Jean of Brittany. From the Carmelite Church where Gilles de Rais was to be buried, they issued,
singing penitential psalms.

Absolved and purified, the Baron came out of his prison upon
his final journey. Filled with a great humility, he walked with
Corrillaut and Henri Griart through the narrow overhanging
streets of Nantes, his head bent forward and his eyes unseeing

of whereon he trod. Filled with a mystic resignation, he paused
before the Hôtel de la Suze and spoke in words of consolation
to his fellow prisoners.

"There is no sin," he said, "so great that God in His paternal
goodness will not forgive it; for He is ever readier to give His
pardon than we, the sinners, are to ask. Let us thank Him that
we are dying possessed of our consciousness and that we are not
struck down unprepared. Death is a little thing and once we are
released, we shall see God in Paradise."

To this sentiment, his fellow criminals agreed, and to the
sympathetic crowd De Rais addressed himself, beseeching their
forgiveness.

Once more the procession took up its way and came at length
to the field of execution. Under the eyes of the attendant thousands who lined the banks of the Loire in mournful silence, the
Baron, holding within his golden reliquary a tiny portion of the
True Cross, mounted upon the scaffold. Making a brief and
touching plea that he should be remembered in their prayers, he
turned away from the massed numbers of his final audience.
About his neck was placed the rope, while Corrillaut and Griart
shouted him a last encouragement. Below the pyre was ignited,
and Gilles de Rais, commending his soul to Saint Michael and
Saint James, stepped from the platform and, suspended by the
neck, quickly died.

About the hanging form, reluctant flames curled up, and accompanied by a very host of tears and lamentations the soul of
Gilles de Rais rose, well heralded to Heaven. No doubt the
ceremony of his entry there was quite in keeping with his life on
earth.

For three days there was fasting in the city, while fervent
supplications for his soul rang out from many churches.

Henri Griart and Corrillaut met their deaths with fortitude
and resignation, comforted by the words and the example of
their master.

To the others of the company of intimates, different fates

CCXXXII.

Seal of Gilles de Rais

Château of Machecoul To-day

were given. Francisco Prelati, who had also suffered trial, was
sentenced to imprisonment for life, clemency being owed him
for his full and valuable confession. Being a magician in more
than several ways, he soon escaped and, taking a convincing
alias, became official alchemist to René, the son of Queen Yolande. Justice, however, achieved at last its due and he was
hanged in 1456 for holding prisoner a treasurer of France.

Roger de Bricqueville, possessed already of a good start, remained for sixteen years in hiding. In the year that Prelati met
his death, the treasurer of Gilles de Rais received full pardon
for his crimes.

Gilles de Sillé, protected beyond a doubt by the concealing
cloak of his much trusted Other Faith, vanished completely
from the eyes of France. Rossignol and Robin Romulart were
dead. The others fled.

Liberated from the control of her husband, Catherine de
Rais, who had been Catherine de Thouars, suddenly asserted
herself. Under her direction, the protest of the heirs was once
more revived and was submitted to the King. It was claimed
now that Gilles de Rais was mad, and that whatever contracts
he had made were void. At first it failed, but later it received
support, and the estates were partly restored.

Upon the strength of her petition, Catherine married herself
at once to Jean de Vendôme, and to their son descended the
fortress of Tiffauges. All of the property which remained of the
estates of Rais, of Craon and of Laval was sold and all the
servants, monks and men-at-arms were forced to seek a new
employment; for in her renewed life, Dame Catherine wished
to keep no memory of him who from her youth had been her
husband.

For her daughter, Catherine also found a husband. Marie de
Rais married Prégent de Coétivy, one of the great ones of the
duchy; and on his death, to save her property from the en-
croachments of her relatives, she became the wife of that proud
noble, André de Laval, who had fought with her father in the
wars and was now Admiral of France.

Before the flames consumed the corpse of Gilles de Rais, he was cut down and carried by a company of women back to the Carmelite Church in Nantes where he was given Christian burial. The ashes of Griart and of Corrillaut were scattered to the winds.

A curious evidence of filial affection came from Marie, his only child. Upon the site of execution, she built a calvary in honor to his memory. Strangely, also, this monument became a place of pilgrimage, and to it came to pray a crowd of mothers and of barren women. Perhaps, in sympathy for their afflictions, he interceded for them with the Hosts.

THE END

INDEX

INDEX

Ingram Content Group UK Ltd.
Milton Keynes UK
UKHW010703130723
425033UK00003B/22

9 781446 505137